FUSION OF THE WORLDS

Ali Godji of Garie.

FUSION
OF THE
WORLDS
AN ETHNOGRAPHY OF
POSSESSION AMONG THE
SONGHAY OF NIGER

Paul Stoller

THE UNIVERSITY OF CHICAGO PRESS

CHICAGO AND LONDON

The University of Chicago Press, Chicago 60637
The University of Chicago Press, Ltd., London
© 1989 by The University of Chicago
All rights reserved. Published 1989
Paperback edition 1997
Printed in the United States of America

01 00 99 98 97   5432

ISBN 0-226-77544-5 (cloth)
ISBN 0-226-77545-3 (paperback)

Library of Congress Cataloging-in-Publication Data

Stoller, Paul.
   Fusion of the worlds : an ethnography of possession among the
Songhay of Niger / Paul Stoller.
        p.   cm.
   Sequel to: In sorcery's shadow.
   Bibliography: p.
   Includes index.
   1. Songhai (African people)   2. Spirit possession—Niger.
I. Title.
DT547.45.S65S75 1989
966'.2600496—dc 19   88-29205
                                                        CIP

For Sidney and Goldie Stoller
and
Adamu Jenitongo (1882–1988)

CONTENTS

One doesn't study the spirits, one follows them.

—Adamu Jenitongo, zima of Tillaberi, Niger

One thinks that one is tracing the outline of the thing's nature over and over again, and one is merely tracing round the frame through which we look at it.

—Wittgenstein

PROLOGUE

In 1970 Adamu Jenitongo, a Songhay *zima* (possession priest), invited me to a possession ceremony in Tillaberi, Niger. The cry of the monochord violin (*godji*) reverberated in my ears. Men and women danced to the beat of the gourd drum (*gasi*). Spirits violently seized the bodies of their mediums, throwing them to the sandy dance ground. Although I understood none of its elements, the power of the ceremony overwhelmed me. I continued to attend possession ceremonies regularly from September 1970 until I left Niger in June of 1971.

In 1976–77 I renewed my contact with Adamu Jenitongo and other zimas among the Songhay. Late in 1977 Mounmouni Koda, an old *sorko* (praise-singer to the spirits), initiated me as a *sorko benya* (lit., "the sorko's slave"). My initiation transformed me from a passive observer of Songhay possession to an active participant. My instructor taught me spirit praise-poetry, introduced me to spirit plants, and made me handle spirit objects and spirit costumes—"to get to know them." He introduced me to spirit mediums not as a man writing a book, but as a sorko benya. That introduction and my fluency in Songhay thrust me into the heart of possession. When I attended ceremonies late in 1977, I knew something about the lives and passions of troupe members. I learned firsthand about the destructive dissension in many Songhay possession troupes.

In Songhay the typical possession troupe is a loosely organized group of people who are directly tied to the spirit world. The typical troupe consists of priests, spirit mediums, praise-singers, and musicians. The priests are men and women who diagnose illnesses caused by spirits and who organize possession ceremonies. The spirit mediums are women and men whose bodies are "taken" by spirits during possession ceremonies. The spirits use the medium's body to communicate to the community. Like Mounmouni Koda, my initiator, the praise-singers are all sorkos. Some of these men are principally praise-singers; others, like Mounmouni Koda and his son Djibo Mounmouni, combine praise-singing with the practice of sorcery. The musicians are generally men who apprentice themselves to master violinists and drummers. The troupe stages ceremonies periodically throughout the year, but the moment of greatest possession activity is the hot season (April–June), the period preceding the rains and the planting season.

By virtue of my initiation as a sorko benya, I became a member of the Tillaberi possession troupe in 1979. Adamu Jenitongo insisted on my "backstage" participation. That year I dressed the possessed male mediums in their spirit costumes. My participation as a sorko benya in possession ceremonies gave me a rare glimpse of the dynamics of the troupe. I learned how ceremonies are organized, sacrificial animals procured, and people paid for their services. I could judge for myself the personal, social, and cultural commitments of spirit mediums, priests, praise-singers, and musicians.

In 1981 and 1982–83 I resided with Adamu Jenitongo in Tillaberi. In 1981 I participated in several public ceremonies, including a rain dance. I also participated in several individual ceremonies. Adamu Jenitongo staged these to treat people suffering from spirit-related illnesses. In some cases Adamu Jenitongo beckoned the spirits to treat Moslem clerics; in others he called to the spirits to heal his mediums. I also lived with Adamu Jenitongo during the 1982–83 cool-dry season (November–February), during which he taught me about spirit plants and trees. We made sacrifices. We chanted incantations. We danced together. I memorized spirit praise-poetry, the meaning of which we discussed.

In 1984 I returned to drought and famine in Niger. In times of crisis, possession troupes intensify their activities. During a two-week period in July of 1984, the Tillaberi troupe staged ten possession ceremonies. That year, the drought decimated Tillaberi. Many people died.

My long and intense participation in the Tillaberi troupe has plunged me deeply into the human dimension of possession. To grasp significantly possession in Songhay we need to explore what Maurice Merleau-Ponty called the texture of inner space, in which "quality, light, color, and depth . . . are there before us only because they awaken an echo in our body and because our body welcomes them."[1] Probing the inner space of Songhay possession carries us inexorably into an ethnographic dimension that considers the lives, problems, and thoughts of possession priests, spirit mediums, praise-singers, and musicians. To apprehend the inner space of Songhay possession, one needs to sense the pain of pre-possession sickness, to appreciate the financial burdens of initia-

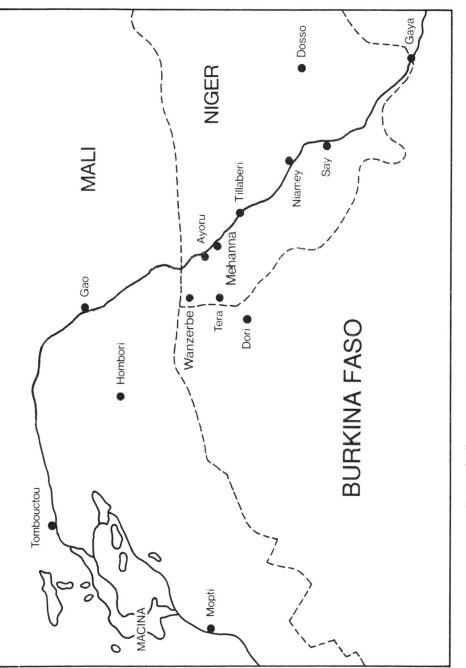

Principal villages in Songhay country. (All photographs by the author)

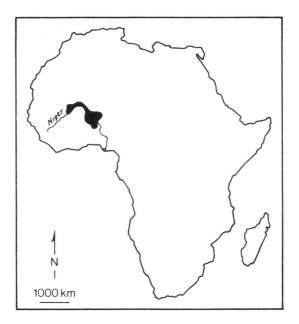

Songhay country.

tion, to realize the dangers of walking the zima's, sorko's, or musician's path, to comprehend the human costs of dissension in Songhay.

This book complements *In Sorcery's Shadow,* a book I wrote with Cheryl Olkes about my apprenticeship to Songhay sorcerers. Like *In Sorcery's Shadow, Fusion of the Worlds* is based on long and intensive field missions among the Songhay of Niger in 1976–77, 1979–80, 1981, 1982–83, 1984, 1985–86, and 1987. My longstanding membership in the troupe enabled me to witness both the wonders of possession—the breathtaking pageantry, the streams of colors, the ribald laughter, the horrifically funny deities—as well as the underside of the possession troupe—the relentless jealousy, the abject wickedness, the interminable spite, the murderous arrogance of its members.

In Sorcery's Shadow is a memoir, a narrative about the very private "world of eternal war" in which sorcerers protect themselves from and attack others with their "deadly words," magic arrows, and topical poisons. The world of possession, by contrast, is quite public, having the aura of carnival with its bright costumes, energetic dancing, pulsating music, kaleidoscopic action, and frenetic energy. Despite these contrasts the Songhay worlds of sorcery and possession are inexorably linked—by the spirits. Many of the sorcerer's powers are derived through his or her association with the spirits. And in some cases, like that of Adamu Jenitongo, sorcerers combine their private ministrations with the public work of the possession troupe priest.

The sharp contrasts between the Songhay worlds of sorcery and possession demand different kinds of books. The sorcerer's private world demanded a private textual strategy—a memoir that borrowed many literary techniques used in fiction, including the ongoing presence of the author-as-character. The public world of Songhay possession, a veritable montage of imagery, calls for a mixing of genres. In contrast to *In Sorcery's Shadow,* I am minimally visible in *Fusion of the Worlds.*

Fusion of the Worlds is therefore not the story of my association with a possession troupe; it is rather the multifaceted story of one possession troupe in Songhay—that of Tillaberi, Niger. After chapter 1 in which I briefly introduce the reader to possession and to the history, structure, and sensuality of the Songhay world, I describe, in part I, the organization of the Tillaberi troupe. Here I attempt to bring into relief the textures of the lives of the individual Songhay in Tillaberi—possession priests, spirit mediums, praise-singers, and musicians. These individual portraits are complemented by a more generalized exposition which informs the reader of the ethnographic background of possession in Songhay.

In part II I re-create major possession ceremonies staged by people with whom the reader is already acquainted—a fusion of the personal and the public, the individual and the social. I also discuss the relations among possession, symbolism, ecology, history, and politics.

In part III I probe possession in contemporary Niger, focusing on the relationship among possession, Islam, and drought. Here the reader confronts the full cultural significance and social ramifications of "dissension" in Songhay.

The epilogue focuses on the multivalent significance of the "fusion of the worlds," a seam in Songhay cultural space that merges natural and preternatural phenomena and conjoins modern and traditional experience. In the epilogue the presentation of two ceremonies, witnessed in 1987, demonstrates how Songhay use possession to make sense of their multifaceted experience-in-the-world.

As in *In Sorcery's Shadow,* a key feature of this book is the direct speech of characters. Longer narratives like those of Sorko Djibo Mounmouni were tape-recorded and translated by me. Other narratives in the book are either based on interviews or were reconstructed from my field notes. Generally, x would occur and I would record in my notebook the occurrence, including dialogue. There is no foolproof method for reconstructing subjective experience. Tape-recorded conversation is better than reconstructed conversation. But even tape-recorded conversation suffers from the "exuberances and deficiencies," to use A. L. Becker's apt phrase, of the transcriber and the translator.

ACKNOWLEDGMENTS

This book is the result of the collective efforts of many people, nor could I have traveled to Niger without the support of many foundations and institutions. Fieldwork in 1976–77 was financed through generous grants from the Fulbright-Hays Doctoral Dissertation Program (G00-76-03659) and from the Wenner-Gren Foundation for Anthropological Research (grant no. 3175). Research in Niger in 1979–80 was made possible through a NATO Postdoctoral Fellowship in Science. My work in Songhay in 1981 and in 1982–83 was made possible through grants from the American Philosophical Society and West Chester University. Grants from West Chester University and the Wenner-Gren Foundation made possible field studies in 1984. Faculty development grants from West Chester University funded fieldwork in Niger in 1985–86 and in 1987. My anthropological mentors at the University of Texas, Annette B. Weiner and Joel Sherzer, taught me the most important lesson of intellectual pursuit: how to ask questions. My ethnographic mentor at the Musée de l'Homme, Jean Rouch, taught me the most important lesson of anthropological fieldwork: how to let others speak for themselves. In Niger I must acknowledge the late Seyni Kountché, president of Niger, who granted me numerous authorizations to conduct ethnographic research in Niger. At the Institute de Recherches en Sciences Humaines I have received warm encouragement from Djouldé Laya, Djibo Hamani, and Arouna Sidikou—past directors, and Boubé Gado, the present director. After months in the bush Jean-François Berger, Tom and Barbara Hale, Jim and Heidi Lowenthal, Tom Price, the Djibo family, and Kathleen Heffron invited me into their homes and treated me with graciousness and kindness. The following people have read and made helpful comments on various versions of the manuscript: Paul Riesman, Ivan Karp, Jean-Pierre Olivier de Sardin, Jean Rouch, Jean-Marie Gibbal, Dan Rose, John Chernoff, Tom Hale, Michael Jackson, Barbara Tedlock, Dennis Tedlock, John Stewart, and Billie Jean Isbell. Their critical comments have aided substantially the process of revision.

Cheryl Olkes, who observed scores of Songhay possession ceremonies in 1976–77 and in 1984, has been a participant in this project from the beginning. It is through her considerable and talented efforts that the text is coherent, readable, and faithful to the social realities of Tillaberi.

Without the wise counsel of the late Adamu Jenitongo, my "baba," I would have nothing to say about Songhay possession. He was a remarkable man; I was privileged to know him.

PERSONAE

From the Social World

Adamu Jenitongo	a powerful sorcerer and principal ritual priest in Tillaberi who died in 1988
Kedibo Jenitongo	sister of Adamu Jenitongo
Moru Adamu	son of Adamu Jenitongo; a drummer in the Tillaberi possession troupe
Moussa Adamu	son of Adamu Jenitongo; a tailor
Jenitongo Seyni	father of Adamu Jenitongo
Hadjo	wife of Adamu Jenitongo; Moussa Adamu's mother
Jemma	wife of Adamu Jenitongo; Moru Adamu's mother
Daouda Godji	principal monochord violinist of the Tillaberi possession troupe
Amina	Daouda Godji's first wife; died in 1984
Alzouma	Daouda Godji's second wife
Mamadou Godji	a monochord violinist in Tillaberi
Halidou Gasi	the nephew of Adamu Jenitongo and a drummer in the Tillaberi possession troupe
Djibo Mounmouni	a sorko living in Mehanna and Narmarigungu
Zakaribaba	an herbalist and sorko who is Djibo Mounmouni's brother
Koda Mounmouni	the father of Djibo Mounmouni and Zakaribaba; died in Mehanna in 1980
Djingarey Sodje	a sorko who was a soldier stationed in Tillaberi
Djimba	a sorko who died in 1982
Issifu Zima	a possession priest in Tillaberi
Moussa Zima	a possession priest in Tillakaina, a small village two kilometers north of Tillaberi

Gusabu	the "chief" of the Tillaberi spirit mediums
Mariama	a spirit medium in Tillaberi
Rabi	a spirit medium in Tillaberi
Hampsa	a spirit medium in Mehanna
Karimoun	a spirit medium in Tillaberi
Halima	a recent initiate into the Tillaberi troupe
Mounkaila	a recent initiate into the Tillaberi troupe
Fati	a spirit medium in the Tillaberi troupe who initiates novice mediums
Fodie	a spirit medium in the Tillaberi troupe who initiates novice mediums
Soumana Yacouba	a French army veteran and spirit medium in Tillaberi
Fatouma Seyni	a spirit medium and diviner in Mehanna
Issaka Boulhassane	a descendant of Askia Mohammed Touré; he lives in Mehanna
Boreima Boulhassane	Morkio Boulhassane's brother; he lives in Tillaberi
Jean Rouch	an ethnographer and longtime student of the Songhay
Paul Stoller	an ethnographer and longtime student of the Songhay

From the Spirit World

The Tooru (nobles of the spirit world; deities of nature)

Harakoy Dikko	deity of the Niger River and mother of Tooru spirits
Cirey	deity of lightning and son of Harakoy
Dongo	deity of thunder and adopted son of Harakoy
Moussa Nyori	deity of clouds and wind and son of Harakoy
Hausakoy	deity of smithing and son of Harakoy
Mahamane Surgu	deity of war and son of Harakoy
Faran Baru Koda	youngest child of Harakoy

Sadyara   the snake who controls groundwater; Harakoy's companion in her village under the Niger River

The Genji Kwari (the White Spirits; Muslim deities)

Serci   the chief of the spirit world who resolves disputes

Alpha Duwokoy   the "cleric" who vomits ink and performs miracles for mortals

Dungunda   Serci's first wife

Garo-garo   Serci's second wife

The Genji Bi (the Black Spirits; deities of the soil)

Moss'ize   guardian of the soil; a Tooru captive

Zatow   guardian of the soil; a Tooru captive

Maalu   guardian of the soil who is welcomed to Tillaberi during Halima's initiation

Baganbeize   guardian of the soil and farming; a Tooru captive

The Hargay (Spirits of the Cold; deities of death and infertility)

Nya Beri   mother of the Cold Spirits who lives in cemeteries; a clairvoyant

Fasio   daughter of Nya Beri

Jendi ceeri   lit. "neck breaker," daughter of Nya Beri

Toway   "the twin," daughter of Nya Beri

Dundo   daughter of Nya Beri

Nyalia   "the beautiful woman"; daughter of Nya Beri

Kong'ize   "the slave daughter"; daughter of Nya Beri

Hadjo   daughter of Nya Beri

Mumay Wanzerbe   a prostitute; daughter of Nya Beri

Hamsu Belley   a prostitute; daughter of Nya Beri

The Hausa Genji (deities of sickness and death)

Adam Hausa   deity of blindness

Baba Sora   harbinger of good will

Fulan Benya   deity of paralysis

PERSONAE

The Hauka (spirits of colonization; spirits of force)

Istanbula	the "chief" of the Hauka
Lt. Marseille	the French lieutenant
Commandant Gomno	the governor-captain
Ceferi	the nonbeliever
Fadimata	a powerful girl
Zeneral Malia	the general of the Red Sea
Lokotoro	the French doctor
Commandant Bashiru	Captain Bashiru
Capral Gardi	corporal of the guard
Funfun'ize	the incessant talker who steals from other Hauka

Others

Nisile Bote	fisherman and father of Faran Make Bote
Maka	a river genie
Faran Maka Bote	fisherman and the ancestor of the sorko
Zinkibaru	a river genie who battled Faran Maka for control of the Niger River
Zirbin Sangay Moyo	a mythic crocodile that ate Niger River fishermen
Atakurma	the "elves" of the Songhay bush

Zakaribaba Sorko speaking to Serci.

1

LOOKING FOR SERCI

Clack! A sharp sound shattered the hot, dry air above Tillaberi. Another clack, followed by a roll and another clack-roll-clack, pulsed through the stagnant air. The sounds seemed to burst from the dune that overlooked the secondary school of the town of a thousand people, mostly Songhay-speaking, in the Republic of Niger.

The echoing staccato broke the sweaty boredom of a hot afternoon in the hottest town in one of the hottest countries in the world and, like a large hand, guided hearers up the dune to Adamu Jenitongo's compound to witness a possession ceremony.

The compound's three-foot millet stalk fence enclosed Adamu Jenitongo's dwellings: four straw huts that looked like beehives. At the compound's threshold, the high-pitched whine of the monochord violin greeted me. Inside, I saw the three drummers seated under a canopy behind gourd drums. Although the canopy shielded them from the blistering Niger sun, sweat streamed down their faces. Their sleeveless tunics clung to their bodies; patches of salt had dried white on the surface of their black cotton garments. They continued their rolling beat. Seated behind them on a stool was the violinist, dressed in a red shirt that covered his knees. Despite the intensity of the heat and the noise of the crowd, his face remained expressionless as he made his instrument "cry."

A few people milled around the canopy as I entered the compound, but no one began to dance. The clack-roll-clack of the drums ruffled the hot Sahelian air, drawing more people to the compound of Adamu Jenitongo, the zima or possession priest of Tillaberi.

When the sun marked midafternoon and the shadows stretched from the canopy toward Adamu Jenitongo's grass huts at the eastern end of his circular living space, streams of men and women flowed into the compound. Many of the woman wore bright Dutch Wax print outfits—bright red flowers, deep green squares contrasting with beige, brown, and powder-blue backgrounds. Many of the men wore white, blue, and yellow damask boubous—spacious robes covering matching loose shirts and baggy drawstring

1

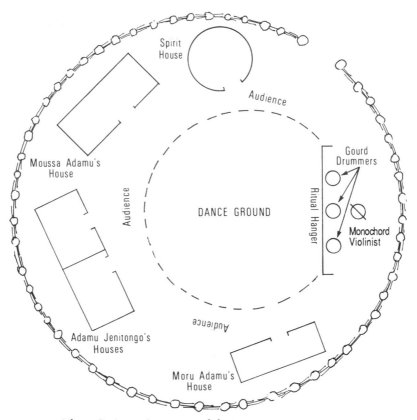

Adamu Jenitongo's compound during possession ceremony.

trousers. Vendors with trays of goods balanced on their heads were right behind the spectators. They sold cigarettes, hard candy, and chewing gum to the growing audience.

The music's tempo picked up; the buzz of the audience intensified. A number of young children danced in front of the musicians, but they were unnoticed by the swelling crowd and the possession troupe's major personalities. Adamu Jenitongo, the zima, remained far from the crowd, and the spirit mediums had not yet left the spirit hut—the conical grass dwelling in the easternmost space of the compound.

More people joined the audience. The relentless cries, clacks, and rolls of the music compelled three old women to dance; the crowd cheered. They sauntered onto the dance ground, grinning at one another. The loose flesh of their furrowed faces flapped as they danced.

Three movements distinguished their dancing. At the outset when the beat was slow, they danced in a circle. Moving counter-clockwise to the slow beat, they kept their arms at their sides. When they stepped forward they pressed their right feet into the sand three times. Eventually, the dancers broke their circle to form a line at the edge of the dance ground in preparation for the second dance movement. The musicians quickened the tempo, and each woman danced forward toward the source of sound—the ritual canopy. They came closer and closer. The tempo raced toward its climax. Just in front of the canopy, the dancers furiously kicked sand. The musicians slowed the tempo, signaling the third dance movement. The dancers remained just in front of the canopy, moving only their heads and arms to the music. They turned their heads to the left while sliding their right hands along their right thighs. Then they slid their left hands along their left thighs, shaking their heads to the right. The musicians played and the dancers shook their heads from left to right, left to right. Beads of glistening sweat sprayed into the air.

One gifted dancer, an older woman with a face puckered by the sun, delighted the crowd with her graceful pirouettes followed by her clumsy bumps and grinds. Her performance so inspired a member of the audience that he broached the dance ground and gave her a five hundred franc note (about $2). The dancer took the money, held it high above her head, ran over to the canopy, and gave the note to one of the drummers, who put it into a common kitty. Even so early in the afternoon, the excitement of the music had generated a healthy pot.

The music swept the old possession priest onto the dance ground. Prompted by the dancing of his colleagues, Adamu Jeni-tongo, a slight, short man whose ebony skin stretched across his face like sun-weathered leather, matched the musicians' frenetic pace. He glided toward the canopy, his sharp eyes transfixed on the violinist. Someone gave him a cane. He held it above his head and danced furiously. Concerned that the dancing could strain his old heart, his sister, Kedibo, whisked him from the dance ground. Despite its brevity, the old zima's vigorous performance elicited generous contributions to the kitty.

Soon after Adamu Jenitongo's turn, one of the old women danc-

A woman doing the *gani*.

ers shooed the children from the dance area. Now the dancing was limited to those men and women who were part of the Tillaberi possession troupe. The musicians played the music of the White Spirits, the deities who resolve social disputes and offer advice to people who are about to change their lives. The leader of the mediums, Gusabu, strolled into the dance area accompanied by two of her "sisters." They circled counterclockwise.

The musicians struck up the theme of one particular White Spirit, Serci, "the chief". A praise-singer chanted:

> Dungunda's husband. Garo Garo's husband.
> Zaaje. White salt. Master of evil.
> You have put us
> Within your own covering of clouds.
> Mercy and Grace.
> Only God is greater than he.
> He is in your hands.
> He gave the angels their generosity.
> You are the master of Kangey.
> You brought the birth of language.
> You brought about victory.

The drummers chanted the praise-poem repeatedly as they and the violinist held the audience in thrall with a syncopated profusion of clacks and rolls cut by the wail of the violin. The three mediums approached the musicians. Gusabu, a large woman with a fleshy face and watery eyes, took a further step toward the musicians. She swayed to the sounds in front of her, behind her. The praise-singer burst through the crowd, a torrent of poems pouring from his mouth. As Gusabu swayed, the sorko chanted praise-songs to the White Spirits and the Tooru (spirits controlling the natural forces of the universe—water, clouds, lightning, thunder). He juxtaposed his praise with the insult, "nya ngoko" (fuck your mother). "If the spirit does not respond to praise-poetry," the sorko told me, "it will come to earth to demand retribution for my insults."

The musicians gradually quickened the tempo. Gusabu bobbed more rapidly now and shook her head back and forth, back and forth. Sensing that the spirit Serci was hovering just above the dance ground, the violinist upped the tempo even more. Gusabu twisted her body and pumped her arms; she perspired profusely. The sorko shouted directly into her ear. Serci was close now. Gusabu's forehead furrowed; she squinted. Tears streamed from her eyes and thick mucus flowed from her nose. Suddenly, Gusabu was thrown to the ground. She muttered, "Ah di, di, di, di, di, a dah, dah, dah, dah." Groaning, she squatted on the sand, her hands on her massive hips.

Serci had arrived. The drummers welcomed him, chanting, "Kubeyni, Kubeyni. Dungunda Kurnya. Garo Garo Kurnya" (Welcome. Welcome. Dugunda's husband. Garo Garo's husband.).

The two women behind Gusabu guided Serci to the edge of the dance ground and seated the deity on a straw mat. Meanwhile, another woman, whirling in front of the canopy, obliged the musicians to pick up the pace. The sorko shouted into her ear, and she too was taken by Mahamane Surgu (Mahamane the Tuareg), which prompted Serci to leave his attending mediums and join Mahamane in the dance area. They hugged one another in greeting and then pointed at the musicians.

"Play good music," they screamed.

The musicians responded, and the two spirits kicked, stomped, and grunted until the music momentarily died.

One of the attending mediums went to the spirit house to bring out the costumes. For Serci, the medium brought a white turban and white damask boubou, symbols of chiefly authority in Songhay. Mahamane Surgu was costumed in billowing black trousers and a long black boubou, both of which were made from thin Chinese cotton. A black turban was wrapped around Surgu's head—symbols of his Tuareg origin.

Preparations for this possession ceremony had begun several days before the musicians split the afternoon air in Tillaberi with their sacred sounds. Because Songhay marriages are full of uncertainties and often end in divorce, people contemplating marriage may seek the advice of the spirits. Plans for Serci's possession ceremony originated when the mother of a future groom visited Adamu Jenitongo.

"Zima," she said to Adamu Jenitongo, "I am fearful of my son's marriage. Will my son be happy with his new wife? Will the woman bring me grandchildren?"

"You must protect yourself on the path," the zima told her.

The woman nodded.

"We must stage a one-day White Spirit ceremony. We will look for Serci. Only Serci can answer these questions. Only Serci can tell you and your son how to protect yourselves."

A medium about to be possessed by Serci.

"Yes, Serci tells only the truth. We should have this ceremony, zima."

"Good," said Adamu Jenitongo. "Tomorrow bring me 2,500 CFA [roughly $10] and a white, a red, and a speckled chicken. We will hold the ceremony on a Thursday." (Thursday is the sacred day of the spirits, a day they are likely to swoop down from the heavens.)

Now Adamu Jenitongo would once again exercise his authority as the impresario of the Tillaberi possession troupe. He summoned his grandson: "Habi, go to Gusabu's compound [the head of the Tillaberi mediums] and tell her about our news of the Serci ceremony."

Adamu Jenitongo's grandson descended the dune on which his grandfather's compound perched. Marching through the deep sand, he came upon a dry riverbed strewn with the skeletons of cows and donkeys. He crossed the riverbed and climbed yet another dune, beyond which was the center of Tillaberi. As he reached the top of this second dune, he could see the Niger River stretching out before him. He walked toward the river on one of Tillaberi's wide dirt roads. He passed dry goods shops, parked trucks, a pharmacy, and a gas station. He crossed the single paved road of the town to pass the market and bus depot. Finally, as he came to the bank of the Niger, he arrived in Gusabu's neighborhood, Gunda Che.

Gusabu gave the boy water to drink in recognition of his long walk from the zima's compound. Like his colleagues in other villages, Adamu Jenitongo preferred to live close to the bush rather than in the center of town. "Near the bush," Adamu Jenitongo often told me, "one has peace. One is far from the treachery of the town."

Dressed in a black kaftan, Gusabu took another piece of black cloth and wrapped it around her head. Her brown-skinned brow was deeply furrowed and her eyebrows seemed perpetually raised as she assessed the zima's grandson. Fixing her watery eyes on the boy, she asked him questions about the upcoming possession ceremony.

"When is it to be staged?"

"They say Thursday," the boy answered.

"Will it last more than one day?"

"They say it is a one-afternoon ceremony."

"What is the purpose of the ceremony?"

"To bring Serci to Tillaberi."

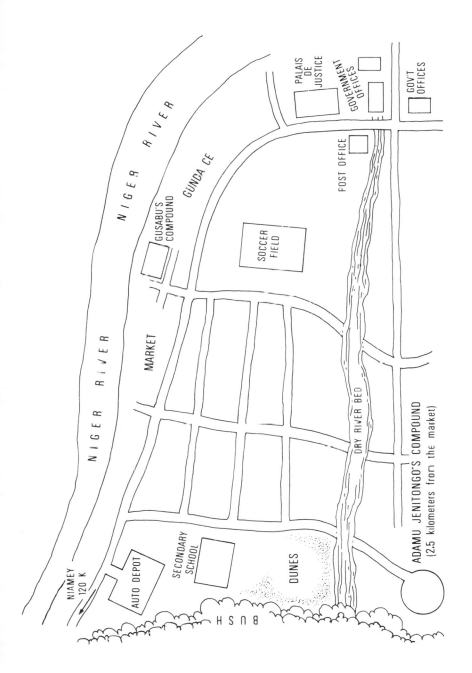

Map of Tillaberi.

"How much will the mediums be paid?"

"My mother," the boy protested, "I know nothing of money."

Gusabu was now ready to execute her plan of action. Calling to her own grandson, she asked the boy to go to the compounds of her associates to inform them about the scheduled possession ceremony. She herself would visit those mediums whose bodies alone could attract to earth the spirit Serci.

The next day, a full two days before the beginning of the festivities, a group of mediums trekked to Adamu Jenitongo's compound. Like the zima's grandson's journey the day before, the women's trip was like a march through time. They left their mud-brick compounds, which had neither electricity nor running water, and crossed a paved road. They walked past a secondary school, which, with its rows of one-story cement buildings, looked like a military base, and saw students who were dressed in European clothing. The students spoke French to one another. The women marched up the first of two dunes. Soon the moos of cows being led out to the bush overwhelmed the echoes of the French language. They passed through a cloud of dust raised by the cows and tramped across the dry riverbed. They climbed the second sand dune and caught their first glimpse of the zima's compound shimmering in the morning light. Behind them was the center of Tillaberi; ahead of them was the millet-stalk fence of Adamu Jenitongo's compound, and beyond it was the sun-baked bush dotted with occasional thorn trees. They stopped at the opening of the compound, where Adamu Jenitongo greeted them enthusiastically.

"Hadjo and Jemma," he called to his two wives, "bring out some straw mats for our guests. Put them under the tree."

Gusabu objected, however. "No, no, no. We don't want the mats there. Put them next to the spirit house," she ordered crisply.

Gusabu, Adamu Jenitongo, and the other mediums sat down to talk. Gusabu pointed to the canopy. "Is it ready?"

"Yes," Adamu Jenitongo replied. "I sanctified it yesterday."

"How much money will my mediums be paid?" Gusabu demanded.

In his usual soft voice Adamu Jenitongo explained, as he had a thousand times: "Sister, you know that the share of a medium depends on the size and generosity of the audience. Besides," he said, "you know that the fees of the musicians have been getting dearer."

"I don't care, brother. We want more money."

"May God provide it," Adamu Jenitongo proclaimed.

"Amen," the mediums responded. By now the lesser priests in Tillaberi, having heard the news about the scheduled possession ceremony, came to Adamu Jenitongo's compound to ask when it would begin. Meanwhile, apprentices to the lesser priests picked up debris and smoothed the sandy grounds of the compound with tree branches. The three drummers arrived. With shovels, they dug foot-deep holes just in front of the sacred canopy. They then placed a five-foot stick across each little crater. These provided support for the drums they put over the holes. In this way the drummers created for themselves deep resonating chambers—a key to the quality of the drum's sound. When they played their drums they struck the gourds with the flat of the hand or with bamboo drumsticks that are made like human hands, having a "palm" area (bands of tightly bound cloth) from which five "fingers" are extended.

Later in the afternoon, the violinist, Daouda Godji, strolled into Adamu Jenitongo's compound, carrying a cloth sack that protected his instrument from the elements. Daouda sauntered past the zima and his cronies and entered the spirit hut. Inside, he hung the violin sack on one of the wooden poles that supported the conical structure. Other ritual objects were there: the small leather sandals and clay jugs of the Atakurma (the elves of the bush); Dongo's (deity of thunder) black cap; a mirror embedded in a small hill of sand at the base of the hut's support poles (for the narcissistic Nyalia, a major deity of the Cold Spirits, which bring on sickness in women). Bottles of perfume and large clay jugs stocked with honey hung above the entrance to the hut, offerings for the Hausa Spirits who love the smell of perfume and adore the taste of honey. Wedged between two of the support poles was Dongo's weapon, a hatchet with a bell attached to its wooden head.

Daouda left the hut and rejoined Adamu Jenitongo and his cronies. The presence of the sacred violin, the central instrument in the mythic first possession ceremony, would draw the spirits from the bush to the spirit hut.

The clacks of the drums and the cries of the violin cut through the din of the crowd that surrounded the visiting spirits. Before the spirits were costumed, their heads were covered with white cloth, the Songhay symbol for nobility. Priests and mediums washed their feet, ankles, hands, and heads as if they were being prepared for Islamic prayer. The mediums then brought out soft leather pillows on which the robed spirits sat. They were now ready for an audience.

The woman who had commissioned the dance approached Serci and Mahamane Surgu with her son, who would soon marry. They sat on the sand at the feet of the spirits, with the sorko who was to serve as the intermediary.

"What must I do to protect the marriage of my son?" the woman asked the sorko.

The sorko posed the same question to Serci:

"Sorko, tell the woman she must acquire one white chicken, one red chicken, and one speckled chicken. These she must kill and then give the cooked meat to the poor." Serci paused a moment. "Do you understand, sorko? Do you understand my message?"

"Yes, yes, my chief. I understand."

Serci continued. "Sorko. This young man must acquire the egg of a white hen. He must dig a hole under the acacia at the crossroads on the Mangeize road—Sorko, do you hear my message?"

"I do, indeed, my chief."

"Sorko," Serci said, "if they follow my words the marriage will have peace and happiness only. Peace and happiness. Sorko, do you follow me?"

"I do, indeed, Serci." The sorko repeated the prescriptions to the mother and son.

Serci grabbed the young man by his head and screamed in each of his ears. Finished with his work, Serci waved away the mother and her son.

"Sorko. Sorko. Tell them they must never stray from the path of the ancestors and their spirits," Serci said.

Serci held his arms in front his body, grabbing his right wrist with his left hand. In this manner he presented his right hand to the mother and son and extended his forefinger in the air—the spirit gesture reminding the audience that there is but one path that connects the Songhay to their ancestors—the path of the spirits.

Meanwhile, the music echoed in the background. Suddenly, the audience scattered from the edge of the dance area, making room for a man whose thrashing covered the crowd with a shower of sand. Gondi, "the snake," had slid from the heavens into the body of his medium. Gondi slithered on the sand toward his masters, Serci and Mahamane Surgu, all the while darting his head and flicking his tongue. People in the audience tossed coins onto the straw mat where the spirits were seated.

The drums clacked and the violin droned. The deep orange light of the late afternoon seeped into the huts of the compound. But the possession ceremony was not yet finished. Suddenly, Baba Soro, the Fulan herder, took his medium—none other than the ninety-eight year old Adamu Jenitongo himself. He stripped off his black robe and rolled his trouser legs to just above the knees. He dashed toward the musicians, screaming:

"I am running. I am running."

He thumped his chest and hit his forehead repeatedly with his open hand. A medium gave him a tunic made of coarse white cotton, which he slipped over his head. Another medium presented him with a wooden staff covered with leather and decorated with scores of cowry shells.

"Play my music," he ordered. "Play my music."

They played and chanted:

> Doosa ana Bowsa. Doogu. Pula
> Maara mooda. Narra Balukuli.
> Gungun Naara [all names of Baba Sora].
> If all the spirits died,
> You would remain.

The coming of Baba Sora, the harbinger of good will, was a rare event. Excited by this good fortune, people gladly gave Baba Sora money, which he redistributed to children. He took 500 CFA and gave it to the musicians. He ran everywhere; he danced frenetically.

A lesser priest pulled Baba Soro from the dance area and shook him so the indefatigable young spirit would leave Adamu Jenitongo's tired, old body. Other priests did the same to Serci, Mahamane Surgu, and Gondi, "the snake." The sun slid toward the western horizon and, in the absence of possession music, stillness returned to the air above Tillaberi. Smoke from cooking fires rose in dusk clouds above the village. Headed for evening meals in their own homes, the audience poured out of Adamu Jenitongo's compound. The lead drummer gave Adamu Jenitongo all the money that had been collected. The zima put the money in a leather satchel.

"Today, was a great success," he announced. "Tomorrow, everyone must return, so that we can distribute the money."

The Songhay Universe

The Songhay universe consists of two domains: the social and spirit worlds. Although the spirit world is generally unseen and separate from the social world, its power and influence surface during possession ceremonies. In the ceremony described above, Serci, a spirit, enters and speaks through Gusabu, a spirit medium. This possession episode represents in Songhay the fusion of a spirit and a human being. More generally, possession is the fusion of the unseen and the seen, the supernatural and the natural; it is the fusion of the worlds, during which deities speak to mortals in Songhay communities. This pattern of communication has long enabled people in Songhay to comprehend the mysteries of their universe.

The Songhay people, who are primarily millet farmers in the republics of Benin, Mali, and Niger, trace their origins to the "first people" who were, according to legend, the Atakurma. The Atakurma were either small and thin or short and fat. While the Atakurma disappeared from Songhay more than a thousand years ago for reasons unknown, they remain a significant part of the "living tradition" of Songhay history.[1] Atakurma today are "guardians of the bush" who can inform their human interlocutors of future events. Ritual specialists often make offerings (candy, sesame, honey, and fresh milk) to the Atakurma. On several occasions Adamu Jenitongo and I left sesame and candy offerings at the base of an acacia in the bush. Adamu Jenitongo makes these offerings infrequently these days. Considering the Atakurma's prescience, Adamu Jenitongo says that "an old man does not want to know when he will die."[2]

Songhay oral history also speaks to the existence of two loosely organized social groups: *laabu koy,* or "masters of the earth" and *Do,* "Masters of water"—the Niger River. The laabu koy worshiped the gods of their lands and believed that if they did not stage rituals to the earth spirits, the land would become sterile.[3] Until 1953 laabu koy rites were staged yearly in Tera, Niger. The officiant, however, was Gurmantche rather than Songhay, and he spoke to the spirits in his own tongue, a Voltaique language unrelated to Songhay. These facts led Jean Rouch to speculate that the "masters of the earth" were Voltaique-language speakers who are perhaps today the Kurumba people of Burkina Faso.[4]

There are still many Do, masters of the water, who live along the Niger River.

> The origin of the Do can be traced to *N'Debbi*, the messenger of the Songhay magicians. One day he asked a group of fishermen for a volunteer who would lie on his stomach and offer his back as a point of support so that N'Debbi's iron dugout could be launched onto the river. The descendants of this volunteer became the Do. Due to this act of courage, the Do received from N'Debbi the power over water and that which it contains, and the mastery of water, under which they can remain for an entire day without surfacing.[5]

While the Do have been assimilated into Songhay society and culture, they are still consulted when, for example, a group of fisherman organizes a hippopotamus hunt. Without the Do's blessing, the hunter subjects himself to grave danger. In addition, Do do not eat the red flesh of the Niger River catfish (*desi*), which is their totem.

The sorko were also early inhabitants of Songhay. Mythically, the sorko are descendants of Faran Maka Bote, who was the son of Nisile Bote, a fisherman, and Maka, a river genie. Faran was the first possession priest. The sorko's historical past, though, is steeped in mystery. Rouch suggested that they migrated to the Niger River from the region of Lake Chad. Following the Benue River, they finally came upon the Niger in present-day Nigeria and migrated northward along the river into present-day Niger.

Songhay history begins with the coming of Aliaman Za, the founder of the first Songhay dynasty. Historians continue to debate Za's place of origin. Although a few historians think Za came from Yemen, the weight of historical evidence suggests that he was a Lempta Berber who migrated to the Niger bend (near Gao, Republic of Mali) from the Gharmantes in southern Libya. Za arrived sometime in the eighth century and found a local population consisting most likely of Do, sorko, and speakers of Voltaique languages—*gabibi*, or "black skins." Terrorized by a river demon, these peoples asked Za to kill it with his iron spear. In gratitude for Za's success, the local groups declared him king. Za quickly legitimized his newfound authority and established a dynasty situated at Koukya, an island in the Niger south of Gao.[6]

The first fourteen Zas were animists. In the eleventh century,

Za Kosoy converted to Islam.[7] During the early period, however, Islam remained a religion unknown to most of the Songhay population. Vestiges of the Zas remain in Songhay ritual life today. Among the most important Songhay possession deities is Za Beri, "the great Za," who might be a symbolic manifestation of Aliaman Za.[8]

During the epoch of the Zas, Songhay kings paid tribute to both Ghana and Mali. In the thirteenth century Ali Kolon, son of Za Yasiboy, fought a series of battles against the king of Mali and, as a result of his victories, gained momentary independence. He assumed the kingship, and his descendants, because of his bravery, considered themselves part of a new dynasty, the Sonnis. Independence was short-lived, however; soon the successors of Sonni (or Si) Kolon found themselves again the vassals to the king of Mali. Not until the ascendancy of Sonni Ali Ber (1464–91) did Songhay vanquish the Mali Empire. Beyond the fact that Sonni Ali Ber was nominally a Muslim, he was reputed to be the most powerful sorcerer in all of West Africa. His mother was of the Faru of what is now Nigeria, a people renowned for their sorcery. During his youth Sonni Ali Ber lived with his mother's people and learned their secrets. From his father, Sonni Seliman-Dam, he learned the regal magic of the Zas and the Sonnis, receiving as an adult the master world of power (*gind'ize gina*). From his mother's milk and his father's blood he inherited special magical powers—the ability to fly great distances and to kill people with incantations. In sum, Sonni Ali Ber became so powerful that he and his armies appeared to be invincible. Returning from a military campaign in 1491, Ali Ber died under mysterious circumstances.[9]

The Songhay Empire reached the height of its power during the reign of Sonni Ali's successor, Mohammed Touré, who, after defeating Ali Ber's son, Si Baru, established the Askiad (1493–1591), the third and last dynasty of Songhay. Except during the reign of Askia Daoud (1542–88), the power of Songhay was sapped through internecine rivalries. Sensing a Sudanese prize, Morocco's El Mansur sponsored a series of military expeditions against Songhay. Finally, in 1591, a relatively small Moroccan force defeated the Songhay army. After Gao "broke" in 1591, the nobility escaped to the south. Restraining their ambitions at first, the Songhay princes attempted to maintain the integrity of the empire. Soon, however, princely rivalries caused the empire to balkanize into five chiefdoms: Kokoro, Tera, Dargol, Garuol, and Anzuru. From the outset, the autonomy of these polities was threatened by ceaseless disputes among the princely family and by the rise of powerful and influential ethnic groups in neighboring regions: the Tuaregs in the north; the Moose in the west; the Fulan to the south in Torodi; and the Zerma and Hausa to the east.[10]

The splintering of Songhay and the increasing strength of its neighbors brought on a long period of incessant war, or what the French call *guerre intestin*. Garuol would form an alliance with the Tuareg to fight a war against Dargol, which, in defense of itself, would form an alliance with the Zerma. Tera would ally itself with Dargol to fight Kokoro. Kokoro would ally itself with Garuol to battle the Tuaregs. This pattern of alliance and warfare continued unabated from the seventeenth to the end of the nineteenth century, the onset of French-Songhay contact.[11]

Throughout the turmoil of *guerre intestin* Songhay remained a stratified patrilineal society in which slavery and preferential patterns of marriage produced a strong sense of social exclusivity. Nobles were the patrilineal descendants of Askia Mohammed Touré. Slaves were the patrilineal descendants of the prisoners of precolonial wars. Social exclusivity was reinforced further by strict codes of behavior. Nobles restrained their emotions and redistributed their wealth. Slaves acted like children and lived on the noble's dole.[12]

There was little contact between Songhay and Europe until the very end of the nineteenth century, during which the French colonial army conquered what was to become the French Soudan. Colonial policies, discussed at length in chapter 7, quickly undermined the fragile balance of the precolonial social order. The French transformed chiefs into tax collectors and conscripted young men to build roads. They introduced a money economy and educated a colonial elite.[13]

Despite the wholesale changes unleashed by colonialism, the social groups that comprise Songhay in the Republic of Niger still represent significant sociocultural vestiges of the precolonial era. Today, Songhay is comprised of the following groups:

1. Nobles (*maigey,* pl.). Nobles are the patrilineal descendants of Askia Mohammed Touré. They believe that their noble blood carries powers that give them a predisposition for local-level governance.[14]

2. Non-noble Songhay. Non-noble Songhay are comprised of Si Hamey, the patrilineal descendants of Sonni Ali Ber; the patrilineal descendants of Faran Maka Bote, who are called sorko; and commoners, who are patrilineal descendants of ancient peoples

long ago assimilated into Songhay (Gow, Do, Kurumba) or of slaves who bought their freedom. A small group of Si Hamey and sorkey (pl.) continue to practice sorcery and praise-singing to the spirits.

3. Former slaves and artisans. In the barter economy of precolonial Songhay, former slaves and artisans—the prisoners of precolonial wars—were clients to noble patrons. They are today civil servants, clients to economic patrons, as well as millet and rice farmers.[15]

4. Foreigners. Songhay is marked by ethnic diversity. Since precolonial times, Songhay have coexisted with Fulan, Tuareg, Gurmantche, and Moose people as well as the Songhay-speaking Zerma, Wogo, and Kurtey. Hausa-speaking peoples, who migrated to Songhay during the early part of this century, have become a major economic force in the region.

5. Civil servants. These are members of the educated elite who are professors, bureaucrats, and extension agents. Ideally, they place such national priorities as development above narrow ethnic interests.

Possession in Songhay

Songhay cosmology has expanded with historical experience. Prior to the Askiad, Songhay developed the central theme of their belief system: Human beings are powerless actors in a universe filled with powerful forces that can at any moment destroy society. Individuals attempted to control the powerful unseen forces through ritual offerings to their lineage altars (*tooru*). The historical patterns suggest, moreover, that prior to the Askiad, Songhay religion consisted of a series of localized and private rites during which sacrifices were made to the land, to the mountains, to the sky, and to the Niger River.[16]

With the onset of the Askiad and the Islamization of Songhay, Songhay ritual practices appear to have become more public: private offerings to the spirits of the *tooru* (altar) of a lineage became public offerings to the Tooru spirits that now spoke to mortals through the bodies of mediums. Like the old altar spirits, the Tooru controlled the most powerful forces of nature: the sky (wind, lightning, clouds, and rain) and the Niger River.[17]

What precipitated this transformation? The policies of the Askiad promoted Islamization, the dispersion of entire populations, and the dissolution of the lineage as a decision-making body.[18] In this climate of irrevocable change, the possession ceremony (*holle hori*) became a stage from which Songhay made sense of the changes confronting them.

The same patterns of incorporation emerged during other periods of Songhay historical contact and crisis. From contact with the non-Negroid Islamized Tuareg came the Genji Kwari or White Spirits, who are *kadi,* Islamic dispute arbitrators. From nineteenth-century contact with Hausa-speaking peoples, the Hausa deities became part of the Songhay pantheon. On the eve of the colonial period, there were five distinct "families" of spirits in Songhay (Tooru, Genji Kwari; Hausa, spirits of sickness and death; Genji Bi, spirits of the land; and Hargay, spirits of the cold, i.e., death and infertility). At the same time there emerged in Songhay villages possession troupes, consisting of priests, mediums, musicians, and praise-singers, which staged rites that created an interpenetration of the social and spirit worlds—the fusion of the worlds.

There are still many possession troupes in Songhay, and the possession ceremonies they stage continue to reflect symbolically themes of Songhay history. The Genji Bi, the spirits of the land, represent the earliest populations of Songhay; the musical instruments used during the ceremonies are mentioned in Songhay myths.

Possession ceremonies are also used by many Songhay to resolve various social problems. In the case of the mother and her son described earlier, the goal of the possession ceremony was to solicit the counsel of Serci, an expert on human affairs. Because of the care Adamu Jenitongo took in staging the rites, Serci did, indeed, swoop down from the heavens to visit Tillaberi and give his advice to mother and son. The mere presence of Serci and Mahamane Surgu, however, does not guarantee the son's successful marriage. If the son has "filth" in his heart, if he "walks two paths with one foot," to cite the wisdom of a Songhay proverb, the spirits will sabotage his marriage: his wife-to-be will be barren, or she will die in childbirth, or she will bear a dead child. Mother and son know this well. Because of his fear the son will follow Serci's advice. But if he should malign the spirits during the everyday routine of his life, he will pay dearly for it.

"Those who deviate from the path of the ancestors," Adamu Jenitongo was fond of saying, "suffer through life until they reach their untimely deaths."

The spirit hut in Adamu Jenitongo's compound.

PART ONE   ORGANIZATION OF THE
POSSESSION TROUPE

Adamu Jenitongo, sohanci and zima of Tillaberi.

2

ZIMAS FROM TILLABERI

Adamu Jenitongo was already an old man when he became the zima of Tillaberi in 1964. His government-issued identity card indicated that he was born in 1882 in the town of Jesse, which is roughly a hundred kilometers to the east and south of Tillaberi. He remembers when the first French soldiers came to Jesse, an event that occurred in 1898, according to historical records.[1] He lived through the famine of 1911–14, which the Songhay call *Gunda Beri* ("big stomach," lit.).

As a young man Adamu Jenitongo farmed for his father, who was the most powerful sohanci east of the Niger River. The sohanci are a clan of sorcerers who are direct patrilineal descendants of Sonni Ali Ber, king of the Songhay Empire in 1463–91. Before Soni Ali Ber's time, Songhay was a vassal state in both the Ghana and Mali empires. Ali Ber's great military skills liberated Songhay from Mali and extended considerably its hegemony. When he died in 1491, Ali Ber had made Songhay a West African empire.[2]

Sonni Ali Ber was also the greatest sorcerer of his day. "With his father's magic," Adamu Jenitongo said, "our ancestor Sonni Ali Ber made himself impervious to spears and arrows. With the magic of his mother's people, the Faru, Sonni Ali Ber learned how to fly. As a vulture [his totem], Sonni Ali soared high in the sky and traveled great distances."

Adamu Jenitongo, the son of a sohanci, listened to his father and gradually learned the secrets of his heritage. He memorized incantations. He mixed potions for natural and supernatural ailments. He experienced the spirits and their world.

When Adamu Jenitongo was thirty and had lived for a period of time in Accra, Ghana, his father taught him the speciality of circumcision. His father was a *guunu*, the sohanci practitioner who, because he is considered the most powerful sorcerer among the Songhay, is responsible for the sacred circumcision ceremonies.[3] A master of the operation, Adamu Jenitongo traveled throughout West Africa to perform it. On some occasions when he announced his readiness to operate in a village by planting in its soil his *lolo*, a long metal staff passed down in sohanci families from father to son, he performed one hundred circumcisions in

23

one afternoon. Afterward the elders would sacrifice a bull. "Those were good times," Adamu Jenitongo said. "I was strong and I ate well."

When his father grew old and tired, Adamu's days as an itinerant circumciser ended. Adamu assumed the burden of his father's responsibilities as a full-fledged sohanci. From miles around, people came to seek his advice, his magic, or his medicines. He now had little time for farming. Soon he was known as a powerful man.

And then the sky crashed. One week Adamu Jenitongo treated a person for spirit sickness and the next he was in prison in Tillaberi, accused of killing a man who coveted his wife. When the authorities came to arrest Adamu, he transformed himself into a vulture and flew away. He remained high in the sky beyond the reach and authority of colonial law. Frustrated, the colonial officials came to Jesse and threatened Adamu's father, Jenitongo.

"Jenitongo," a French military officer barked, "We want your son."

"But he is not here," Jenitongo protested.

"If he does not return, old man, we will arrest you instead."

Jenitongo ordered his son Yaye to play the sohanci drum. Soon the echo of methodical thumps filled the compound. The posse waited impatiently.

"What good is this drumming?" the French officer complained.

Jenitongo remained silent.

Soon a vulture landed in the compound.

Jenitongo pointed to the vulture. "There is my son Adamu. If you want to take him away, put the vulture in a sack."

The soldier captured the passive bird and put it in a large burlap sack. They left Jesse for Niamey.

Despite Adamu's protestations of innocence, the colonial judge condemned him to twenty years in prison. From 1940 to 1960 Adamu Jenitongo lived in three military prisons in Mali: Chidal, Bidon 5, and Tessalit.

After he had spent four years at hard labor, Adamu Jenitongo, a convicted murderer, was named the head chef of the officer's mess by the commandant of Chidal. Later, he was the caretaker of the officer's children.

When he was liberated from prison in 1960, Adamu Jenitongo was so fat that his sister Kedibo did not recognize him when he arrived in Tillaberi. His brother-in-law gave him money to marry

Hadjo, a Zerma woman living in Tillaberi. Leaving Hadjo in Tillaberi with her son Moussa, he returned to Jesse, his natal village and married a local woman, Jemma. He farmed in Jesse and resumed his practice as a sohanci. Once a month he traveled to Tillaberi to see Hadjo and Moussa. In 1964, the Tillaberi mediums summoned him to the riverain town and asked him to become their zima. He accepted and lived there until his death.[4]

The Zima and the Spirit World

The zima links the social and spirit worlds in the Songhay cosmos. A sohanci as well as a zima, Adamu Jenitongo was a particularly strong link between the Tillaberi community and the cosmos. For the past twenty-three years Adamu Jenitongo was the spiritual guardian of Tillaberi. I knew him for seventeen of those years. He introduced me to possession ceremonies in 1971. Since then, he gradually revealed to me many of the principles on which Songhay possession rests.

According to Adamu Jenitongo, the Songhay world consists of seven heavens, seven hells, and earth, on which there are four cardinal directions. There are also two elementary domains on earth: the world of social life and the world of eternal war, the spirit world. God lives in the most distant, seventh heaven. Since God is so distant, contact with him comes only through the good offices of N'Debbi, God's messenger, who inhabits the sixth heaven. Priests chant their magical incantations to N'Debbi, who then carries the message to God for a decision. Songhay elders are divided about which members of the spirit family reside in heavens two through five. Some elders, including Adamu Jenitongo, suggest that these heavens house the ancestors; others maintain that these heavens are the abode of angels. The first most proximate heaven is the domain of the spirits or *holle,* which are divided into spirit "families."

The Tooru

The Tooru are among the most ancient of the Songhay spirit "families." Members of the Tooru control the forces of the sky as well as the forces of the Niger River. The most important Tooru are the children of Harakoy Dikko, the goddess of the Niger River. These children comprise a multiethnic composite because Dikko was wife and/or concubine to numerous mortals of various ethnic groups. Her children are Cirey, the male deity of lightning, whose father was Songhay; Mahamane Surgu, the male deity of war, whose father was Tuareg; Moussa Nyori, the male deity of clouds, whose father was Gurmantche; Manda Hausakoy, the male deity of smithing, whose father was Hausa, and Faran Baru Koda, a female deity whose father was Tuareg.

There are other Tooru, but the most notorious of this group is Dongo, the adopted son of Harakoy Dikko. Along with Moussa Nyori and Cirey, Dongo is the deity who controls the heavens. He is considered the most powerful, mercurial, and dangerous deity in the Songhay pantheon. Of Dongo it is said:

> The *ka sah tobe* tree
> [a magical tree associated with Dongo].
> Dongo made the great rock in the skies.
> His power protects one from thunder.
> His power and knowledge are
> Greater than that of the sorko and
> Surpasses that of the sorko's slave.
> He strikes people and they fall forward,
> And then he returns to the clouds.
> He says the sun is his shadow and that
> His shadow covers the sun.
> Amen.[5]

In addition to the Tooru that have mediums, there are Tooru who never leave the heavens. Among these are Almajiri Fombo and Diga Fombo, who are Dongo's brothers, and Lombo Kambenya, Dongo's mother.[6] Many Tooru have no known names and are considered malicious.

The Genji Kwari

Genji Kwari or White Spirits are the Tooru's classificatory parallel cousins. They share the same apical ancestors, namely, Uwa and Uwatata, who brought forward two sons, Urufurma and Agam. Urufurma fathered a son, Dandu, who became the father of the Tooru. Agam became the ancestor of the Genji Kwari. The Genji Kwari are the Islamic clerics of the spirit world. Learned advisers who are experts on the human social condition, these spirits wear white costumes associated with Islamic purity. Serci, the "chief" of the spirit world, carries with him silver Islamic worry beads. Like the chief in the social world, Serci adjudicates disputes.

The Genji Bi

The Genji Bi spirits control the forces of the soil—soil quality, birds that eat ripening millet seeds, rats which eat young millet stalks, and the worms and grasshoppers which can destroy millet at any stage of its development. They are symbolic links to the masters of the earth (*laabu koy*)—the ancient Voltaique farmers (Kurumba, Gurmantche, and Moose) who tilled the soil before the coming of the Songhay. Some communities in Songhay stage annual possession ceremonies during which the Genji Bi receive offerings in exchange for protection from pestilence. Musicians sing the following song when they beckon the Genji Bi to earth.

> The masters of Willi Willa.
> The Masters of Tendema [names of ancient villages)
> They live under the earth and
> Cleanse themselves [with dirt].
> They are stubborn as dogs which
> Will not run even though they are afraid.
> Zatow, Jengo, Bada Mosi.
> Come among us and play.[7]

The term *Genji Bi* may well come from the extreme blackness of the Voltaique's skin. The father of the Genji Bi is Zubuda. When Zubuda became the master to a Fulan genie, Zatow, he married one of Zatow's two sisters. Their children became the Genji Bi. The numerous offspring ensconced themselves in the Garyel forest near Magadu (north of Ouallam in Zerma, some 180 kilometers northeast of Niamey [Niger]), which to this day is not generally frequented by humans. Being cool and inviting, the forest attracted deities from other spirit families. But Zatow admitted only a small number of spirits. In this way Moose, Gurmantche, Fulan and Hausa characters affiliated with the Genji Bi.[8]

The Hausa Genji (Doguwa)

The Hausa Genji are held responsible for misfortune and chronic illness, especially madness and paralysis. Costumed as herders and merchants, these spirits, which come from the Hausa-speaking regions of eastern Niger, entered the Songhay pantheon following a large Hausa migration to Songhay in the latter part of the nineteenth century. Adamu Jenitongo says that the first Hausa deities appeared in Songhay during Gunda Beri, the great drought of 1911–14. Doguwa possession ceremonies are staged when individuals are suffering from untreatable illnesses.

The Doguwa are undignified personalities. In the Songhay code of behavior, grace is achieved through the circumspect use of language. One who is dignified avoids the use of foul language. Not so the Hausa Genji, who specialize in what the French call *grossièreté*. In January of 1977 I saw the Doguwa spirit Hadjo greet the musicians of the Mehanna possession troupe: "Ni doonu kom sinda wah" (Your millet porridge which has no milk). This expression suggests that the musicians' semen has no sperm. Hadjo then added in Hausa: "Koy bani ci gatow gashi" (You have no sexual potency. You eat only vagina hair).[9]

The term *Doguwa* is borrowed from the Hausa *bori* cult. In the bori cult there are two deities, Doguwa Baka and Doguwa Fara, who paralyze their victims. Doguwa Baka paralyzes the left side of the body; Doguwa Fara paralyzes the right side.[10] In Songhay, Hausa spirits cause paralysis of the face, arms, and hands as well as leprosy, and some cases of male and female sterility.

The Hargay (Spirits of the Cold)

The Hargay are all the children of Nya Beri, the great mother. Nya Beri herself is the daughter of Harakoy Dikko and the genie of death who lives in cemetaries and holes. Sensing the wickedness of her daughter, Harakoy evicted Nya Beri from her village under the Niger River. Nya Beri flew to the heavens and asked her brother Cirey for comfort. Cirey rejected his sister and threw her back to earth, but she crash-landed and broke her arms and legs. Crippled, she returned to live with her father in cemeteries and holes. There, the genie of death taught his daughter the art of witchcraft (*cerkawtarey*) as well as death sorcery. Since mortals were afraid to visit Nya Beri's court, only fellow genies sought her company. She took three husbands with whom she had numerous offspring. These became the Hargay.[11] Most Hargay, in fact, are believed to be the ghosts of people who died under mysterious circumstances.

The image of Nya Beri and the Hargay is vividly depicted in the following song:

> She is something quite strong.
> She is something quite big.
> She is stronger than women.
> She is stronger than men.
> She looks into the sun and sees.
> She looks into the moon and sees.

In fresh milk she sees the future.
In blood she sees the past.
She sees all.
She knows all.
She is strong and lives in the place of death.
She is in front of a person.
She is behind a person.
She can wreak havoc.
Dara. Tubulo. Gunbi [trees associated with Nya Beri].
Masu's mother. Masusu's mother.
Jindi Ceri's [lit. "neck breaker"] mother.
Bong'ize's [lit. "the cripple"] mother.
Woah's mother.
Towey's mother.[12]

This song speaks of Nya Beri's malevolent powers.

Mother of the Hargay, Nya Beri.
The offspring of Wambata [Nya Beri] have no friends.
To you, one must talk of milk
Through which young men cannot see.
Pregnant women must fear you.
You will follow them and
Yank out their intestines.
You are the mother of Masusu.
She laughs.
She will make your head spin.
You are Fasio's mother.
Jindi Ceri's mother.
You strike those who deviate.
I shall have reverence for you.
I shall have reverence for your power.
In the name of god,
I shall pray to you.
I shall have reverence for the great mother.
You are the mother of Dargol's [place name] Hargay Spirits.
You live behind the village . . .
Waiting.[13]

The Hauka

The Hauka are the spirits of colonization, representing, from a purely Songhay point of view, the reincarnation of colonial characters (see chap. 7). The Hauka re-create colonial history with a

Songhay bias. In the bodies of their mediums, the Hauka seize burning bushes and brandish them like standards above their heads. They also plunge their hands into vats of boiling sauce.[14]

Each spirit family represents a period of Songhay experience. The Tooru, which are the most ancient of the spirit families, probably date back to the reign of Askia the Great (1493–1527) and are associated with the religion practiced by the *don borey,* the people of the past. The Genji Kwari too date from Askia's time. They represent the widespread Islamization during imperial Songhay. Conquering Songhay armies in the fourteenth, fifteenth, and sixteenth centuries vanquished Voltaique populations (Gurmantche, Moose and Kurumba), the first inhabitants of Songhay county, who are represented by the Genji Bi. The Hargay and the Hausa spirits are more recent phenomena. The Hargay represent recently deceased people renowned for their social deviance. The Hausa spirits came to Songhay with Hausa-speaking merchants who migrated west in the early part of the twentieth century. The Hauka, for their part, represent the colonial age. Each spirit family, then, signifies a distinct historical period during which there occurred a sociocultural crisis.

The proximity of social and spirit domains parallels a resemblance between spirits and human beings. Like human beings, spirits are members of various ethnic groups, marry one another, and have master-slave relationships. Unlike human beings, the spirits are invisible and live forever.[15]

The Songhay world is also affected by other forces, according to Adamu Jenitongo. After death, one can find oneself in either heaven or hell. Residence in the seven hells is greatly dictated by the nature of one's belief. The first hell is a way station. When a person dies, he or she waits in the first hell for God's decision. If God decides that an individual, during his or her lifetime, said prayers and gave to the poor, that person will ascend to the heavens; if not, the individual will be thrown down to a deeper level of hell. The second hell is for Jews, for their religion is closest to Islam. Christians are consigned to the third hell; Buddhists and Hindus to the fourth. Worse yet is the fate of nonbelievers in the fifth hell, a place of atheists, agnostics, and the ritually deficient individuals of the world. The offspring of Iblis, the devil, live in the sixth hell. They are thieves, murderers, and other perpetrators of evil. Munakuf'izey have reserved for them the deepest level of hell. These unfortunates are the offspring of Munakufa, the devil of discord—people who precipitate the kind of unending disharmony that undermines the unity of a community.[16]

The juxtaposition of the first heaven and earth creates in the world two contiguous domains: the world of social life and the world of the spirits. These worlds are fused during possession ceremonies when the spirits leave their world—the first heaven—to visit the social world by taking a medium's body—the fusion of the worlds.

How does a spirit take a medium's body? Adamu Jenitongo said that the human body consists of flesh, the life force, and the double (*bia*). Flesh, of course, is the material body. The life force resides in a person's heart; it is the energy of life. When a person dies, the life force immediately leaves her or his body and escapes into the heavens. Bia is the human double. Adamu Jenitongo said that a person can see his or her double in a pool of water. The same can be said when individuals see their shadows on the sand. When individuals sleep, the double leaves the body and travels about the village seeking adventure. Adamu Jenitongo believed that dreams are the results of the double's nocturnal travels. The double is the essence of a person's humanity. When a witch (*cerkaw*) attacks a person in a village, he or she steals the victim's double. Devoid of human essence, the victim becomes listless and suffers from nausea and dysentery. If a specialist cannot find and return the victim's double, the victim will die.[17]

Spirit mediumship results from the temporary displacement of a person's double by the force of a particular spirit. When the force of the spirit enters the medium's body, the person shakes uncontrollably. When the deity's double is firmly established in the dancer's body, the shaking becomes less violent. The deity screams and dances. The medium's body has become a deity.

There is widespread disagreement as to where the medium's double waits when it has been displaced. According to Adamu Jenitongo, the medium's double leaves the body and deposits itself in the sohanci's lolo, a tall iron staff. Other zimas suggest that the medium's double finds temporary residence in the sanctified wooden poles of the ritual canopy under which the musicians produce their mesmerizing sounds. A medium whose spirit has finished its performance—and left the body—is usually escorted to a hut, generally the spirit hut found in the compounds of most zimas, to rest and be reunited with his or her social double.

Adamu Jenitongo attending to a possessed medium.

Possession ceremonies are not everyday happenings in Songhay communities. During the rainy season (June–November) people are too busy with farm work to engage frequently in possession activities; the peak of the possession season is toward the end of the long dry season. From April to the beginning of June the zimas organize the farming and rain possession ceremonies which they believe are necessary for successful agriculture.

Zimas also stage ceremonies to protect the community, to resolve individual problems, to ensure a farmer's good crop, and to mourn or protect members of the troupe. Most possession ceremonies are organized to meet the needs of individuals in the community. Ceremonies are held, for example, to ask the advice of the spirits about an upcoming marriage, like the ceremony described in chapter 1. A woman who has suffered a miscarriage or a stillbirth may ask a zima to organize a ceremony to beckon Nya Beri, the mother of the Cold Spirits that bring on these horrors. The Cold Spirits also cause blindness. Adamu Jenitongo organized a Cold Spirit ceremony to treat a man so afflicted. Once the Cold Spirits, including Nya Beri, had taken their mediums, Adamu Jenitongo sacrificed three chickens and let their blood collect in a small gourd. The Cold Spirits bent over the gourd and spit into it. An attendant led the man to the spirit hut. There, Adamu Jenitongo put droplets of chicken blood into the man's eyes. On other occasions, Adamu Jenitongo summoned the Hausa spirits to treat people suffering from paralysis of the arm. Individuals about to take a trip may ask the zima to bring the spirits, who may tell the traveler to sacrifice a red chicken to ensure safe and successful travel.

Possession ceremonies for community protection are relatively infrequent. In 1971 village elders along the Niger River asked the zimas to organize possession ceremonies to protect their communities from a cholera epidemic. In 1983 and 1984 officials of the Nigerien government asked the Tillaberi priests to organize a series of possession ceremonies to bring rain to the drought-ravaged lands (see chap. 9).

In some Songhay-speaking communities, the chief's installation is celebrated with a possession ceremony. The spirits come to the social world to greet the new chief. They also ask him for gifts. In this way the chief assures the polity of his allegiance to the spirit world and to the ancestors.

In the rare instances that members of the community have been struck by lightning, the zima organizes a festival for Dongo, deity of thunder. An angry Dongo is known to kill people, and so the zima calls Dongo to the village to discover the cause of his wrath. In the only Dongo festival that I have witnessed, Dongo castigated the people of Tillaberi for deviating from the path of the spirits. He told the audience that the community should have great reverence for the power of the spirits and demonstrate it through sacrifices. Otherwise, Dongo said, he would continue to strike down Tillaberi farmers as they worked in their fields.

Three possession ceremonies are tied to farming activities. The first of these is called the Black Spirit festival (*genji bi hori*). The zimas organize this ceremony in April to pay homage to the spirits of the land, who control soil fertility and various forms of pestilence. If the ceremony is successful, said Adamu Jenitongo, the millet crop will be protected from rats, birds, and insects. "When these rites were widespread," Adamu Jenitongo insisted, "our fields were filled with millet. Today, today, just look at the fields. Nothing. Look."

The second farming ceremony is the *yenaandi* or rain dance, which is the reenactment of the first possession ceremony that took place in the ancestral past (see chaps. 4 and 6) and is still staged in most Songhay villages. In the rain dance, priests call to the social world four principal Tooru deities: Dongo, deity of thunder; Cirey, deity of lightning; Moussa Nyori, deity of clouds and wind; and Hausakoy, deity of smithing. If the rain dance is well staged (see chap. 6), the spirits are pleased and the community is assured of enough rain to produce a bountiful harvest.

Zimas organize a third farming ceremony after the harvest, called "eating the new millet." At this—a celebration of thanksgiving held by the possession troupe—the spirits are invited to sample the new millet.

The possession troupe also stages ceremonies for individual members who are severely ill. In January 1977 I witnessed a seven-day curing festival in the river town of Djamona. A zima in Mehanna, a town just across the river from Djamona, had organized it to cure the serious illness of one of her mediums. The afflicted woman remained in the spirit house of her village for the entire week as members of the troupe staged possession ceremonies. For six days the spirits possessed no one despite generous gifts from the people of Djamona. On the last day of the festival, however, the spirits "came outside" and took the bodies of their mediums. Even so, the woman died the next day. As Koda Mounmouni, the sorko of Mehanna said: "There can be no good work when there is dissension among the members of the troupe. When there is discord, there is death," a reference to dissension and duplicity in the Mehanna spirit troupe (see chap. 9).

Ceremonies of purification are held when a medium loses a parent, so that the priest can make the medium's body fit to be taken by the spirits. Death in the troupe itself requires a more elaborate ceremony. Especially important to the troupe is the mortuary ceremony held when a zima dies. In this event, all the mediums that a zima initiated are obligated to attend, for the purpose of the ceremony is at once to mourn the zima's death and to designate individuals who will take over the mediumship of the spirits that the zima carried. If the zima has surviving offspring, the spirits will possess them. A son or daughter to whom the zima taught magical incantations becomes the new zima. But if the priest has no obvious successor, the spirits themselves announce the name of the new zima.

The most significant possession troupe ceremony is the initiation of mediums (see chap. 3). Briefly, initiations are usually seven-day festivals during which novices learn how to carry their respective spirits. Initiation occurs whenever people suffering from spirit sickness organize a festival to appease the spirits. By the end of the seven days, the sick novice has become a healthy medium.

The pillar of the Songhay possession troupe is the zima. To borrow the terminology of the theater, zimas are the impresarios of the possession troupe. But their roles are not strictly defined; they can and do have other functions in the social and spirit worlds.[18] The title of zima can denote a healer, a sorcerer, or even a witch.

The measure of a zima has less to do with genealogical position and more to do with demonstration of organizational skill and knowledge of the various rites. The powerful knowledge that priests master and use inspires reverence in others. Adamu Jenitongo, the zima of Tillaberi, appeared to be a frail old man. Short of stature and slight of build, he walked with a slow deliberate gait. Like other Songhay elders, he had a manicured white beard. But in his weathered face were eyes that easily pierced the thin armor of a social personality to seize another person's inner self. He was a diviner, a seer, and a master sorcerer, and he used well-honed skills to direct Tillaberi's possession troupe.

Hamani Ayouta, sohanci and zima in Niamey.

A zima can be a member of any social grouping among the Songhay, and can be either a man or woman. Not a few priests inherited their positions from one of their parents. One of the several priests in Mehanna took control of that possession troupe when her mother died. Certain priests have descent links to specific groups of sorcerers. The zima of the Zerma town Simiri is a sorko. He organizes ceremonies and participates himself, on occasion, as the troupe sorko. We already know Adamu Jenitongo's story; he was both a sohanci and a zima. Like Adamu Jenitongo, Halidu Mossi, the zima of Wanzerbe, is both a sohanci and a zima. The principal zima of Ayoru, a Songhay town on the banks of the Niger River, was Howa Koda, a woman from a family of sorko. Some zimas have no genealogical connections to the spirit world; other zimas are not even Songhay. There is no one way, in sum, to become a zima other than by apprenticing oneself to an established priest or by extending one's magical expertise into the realm of the possession troupe.

Just as the spirit pantheon reflects the polyethnic experience of Songhay, so the multifaceted nature of the zima exemplifies the complexity of social life in multiethnic Songhay country. Most Songhay are subsistence millet farmers living among other ethnic groups. In addition to Songhay farmers, Fulan and Tuareg herders and the latter's former slaves, the Bella, who have been subsistence farmers, live in the region (western Niger). There are also the Wogo, Kurtey, and Zerma, all distinct ethnic groups, although they speak Songhay and share with the Songhay fundamental cultural values. Finally there are the Hausa merchants who, in many Songhay towns, control the local economy.

Given the impact of Islam in Songhay country, possession priests attempt to differentiate themselves from Islamic clerics. No matter their ethnic origin or genealogical position, possession priests generally wear black cloth to distinguish themselves from the rest of the their multiethnic counterparts and from the Islamic clerics, who wear white cloth—white being the Islamic symbol of purity. When I asked why zimas wear black, Adamu Jenitongo said, "Ce follo a si fonda hinka gana" (One foot cannot follow two paths). The zima's black cloth communicates to the community that he or she is the antithesis of the Islamic cleric. Since zimas follow the spirits' path, it would be hypocritical if they "followed two paths with one foot." As Sorko Djibo Mounmouni of Mehanna says: "When you follow two paths with one foot, your heart fills with filth. Filth brings death to the community."

Issifu Zima

Issifu is a young zima in Tillaberi. Like Adamu Jenitongo, he comes from Zerma country east of Tillaberi. When he was born, his zima uncle, Karimoun (mother's brother), took an interest in Issifu. Issifu attended the possession ceremonies that his uncle organized and traveled with his uncle to rites in other villages. As a teenager, Issifu moved into his uncle's compound. Karimoun taught him incantations and spirit praise-songs and made Issifu the caretaker of the ritual objects in his spirit house. The new caretaker learned about spirit costumes, and spirit colors, hatchets with bells, spears, walking staffs covered with red leather, small squash gourds decorated with dyed leather strips, and cowry shells.

One day Karimoun called Issifu into the spirit hut.

"My nephew. You have seen many ceremonies, and you have cared for my objects. You have learned my incantations and praise-poems. Alas, I have nothing more to teach you."

"Is that all there is to learn?" Issifu asked.

"No, my nephew. You must go to Loga and ask for Altinne Zima. He will teach you much more."

"Altinne Zima," Issifu repeated. "I'll get my things and be ready to go at once."

Issifu left that same day and headed south to Loga. He introduced himself to Altinne Zima and became his apprentice. Altinne Zima had two millet fields. His sons worked one field; Issifu cultivated the second. The young apprentice also scoured the bush around Loga for the herbs, barks, and roots that Altinne Zima requested. In this way, he mastered plant knowledge, distinguishing among medicinal, spirit, and magic plants. After the first harvest, Altinne taught Issifu how to mix potions. After the second harvest, Altinne revealed to Issifu his magic plant incantations. After the third harvest, Altinne asked Issifu to marry one of his daughters and remain with him in Loga.

Issifu refused the offer. "My path leads to the west. I want to be a great zima in a great town."

"So be it," said Altinne Zima with great regret. "But be sure to walk your path slowly. There are many dangers. And remember the Songhay proverb: Money resolves nothing."

Issifu arrived in Tillaberi in 1977, a young man of medium height with a round, unblemished face and beady brown eyes. He dressed flamboyantly in bright red and deep green boubous and, whenever he could, rode about town atop a black stallion whose ornate livery was decorated with cut glass that reflected the sun.

Although he was young and ambitious, Issifu Zima demonstrated respect for the older and wiser Adamu Jenitongo. He adhered to all the tenets of etiquette among zimas: he brought Adamu Jenitongo small gifts; he visited him frequently; he deferred to the older zima during important ceremonies; he sought Adamu Jenitongo's advice.

Adamu Jenitongo's presence, however, did not deter Issifu from charting his own course. Skilled at hiding his considerable ambition from the older zima, Issifu courted the Tillaberi mediums. He was young, attractive, and dynamic, and he flirted with the mediums, old and young alike. They liked him and, in return, recommended Issifu to their friends and family. The number of Issifu's clients increased. In exchange for appreciable fees, the young zima promised his clients quick miracle cures for their physiological and supernatural ailments. He staged ceremonies in his compound. He initiated mediums into the cult.

Attracted by Issifu's flamboyance, the Tillaberi mediums flocked to him. The old zima, they reasoned, was too conservative. He would not stage a ceremony unless conditions were correct: the right day, the right time, the right month, according to tradition. By contrast, Issifu was young and daring. He did not wait for the "right" conditions to stage ceremonies. Through his boldness Issifu amassed considerable sums of money for himself and his mediums.

Issifu's duplicity and the mediums' fickleness soured the heart of Adamu Jenitongo. The old zima feared for his community. Like his colleague Koda Mounmouni, the old zima knew that dissension caused death in a community (see also chap. 9).

Issifu's practice flourished. Rather than walking to Adamu Jenitongo's compound on the dune to seek treatment, people preferred the short trip to Issifu's in the center of Tillaberi. Although Issifu charged three times the old man's fees for his services, people continued to seek his cures.

When a number of Issifu's patients died, the local authorities investigated. They decreed that only registered traditional healers, like Adamu Jenitongo, could treat patients. The decree, however, did not deter the unregistered Issifu from treating patients. After all, what did the government know about zimas?

In 1985 Issifu traveled to the Niger River villages of Tillakaina,

Sakoire, Dai Beri, Dai Kayna, and Djamballa to offer his services. Encouraged by his therapeutic and financial successes, Issifu had the temerity to go to Sangara.

Sangara has history; Sangara has power. In the mythic past, a great hunter named Zoa founded the village of Sangara. Zoa possessed great powers. He could fly great distances. When he wanted to marry he flew to the Gobir (northern Nigeria) and married the king's daughter. The king's daughter bore him a son, Soumaila, to whom he taught his secrets. His words could kill people as well as animals. One day a bird ate Zoa's millet.

"That bird must die," he told his son.

The bird fell dead.

"Baba [father], I want to eat the bird."

A fire ignited on the ground and seared the bird to an inedible crisp.

Soumaila cried. "How can I eat the bird, Baba?"

"I have failed you, my son," Zoa said. He looked down at the seared bird. "Listen my son. The earth will soon open up on this very spot and no one will hear from me again."

"No, no, Baba."

"Be brave, my son. Go now and bring the people here."

Soumaila left and brought the people.

The earth opened up. "Listen people of Sangara. My son, Soumaila, will succeed me as chief."

The people pleaded with Zoa to remain with them.

Zoa ignored their entreaties. "People of Sangara, listen and listen well. When you have droughts, wars, and sicknesses, you must bring a white bull or a sheep, and cut its throat on this spot."

Zoa descended into the hole and disappeared. The earth closed. Soon thereafter four trees sprouted in the directions of the north, south, east, and west. The people of Sangara still sacrifice sheep or bulls on Zoa's tomb. And Zoa's descendants are great sorcerers whose words are transformed immediately into action.

When Issifu arrived in Sangara he announced his priestly intentions. While such insensitivity may have been tolerated in Tillaberi, the people of Sangara were much less forgiving. No one comes to Sangara and boasts of his great powers—without paying a dear price. Three days after his arrival, Issifu was deathly ill. Evacuated by Land Rover, he was admitted to the hospital in Tillaberi with severe abdominal pains and a severely distended stomach. Acute nausea sapped his appetite. Issifu remained in the hos-

Moussa Adamu, son of Adamu Jenitongo.

pital until some of his strength returned, two months after his admittance. The nurse said that Issifu might have been poisoned.

The Zima's Path

Issifu almost died. Even if zimas are courageous, they must have respect for other people and the spirits. "The path of zima-tarey [the craft of the zima] is a dangerous one," Adamu Jenitongo once told me. "If they have no respect, zimas die an early death." Moussa Adamu, the zima's son, says: "A few years ago Issifu would have died in Sangara, and everyone would have understood. To be a zima you have to be wise, patient, respectful. The power is developed slowly over time."

Yet there are today eleven young zimas in Tillaberi, all vying for money, prestige, and power. The backstabbing competition has broken the harmony of the Tillaberi troupe. In the view of Adamu Jenitongo, these new and ignorant zimas are ruining Tillaberi (see chap. 9). As he told them, "Children know haste; elders know patience." To misunderstand or to ignore this proverb, said Adamu Jenitongo, is to misunderstand the Songhay world, and the consequences are potentially catastrophic.

A medium in Mehanna.

3

GUSABU'S MEDIUMS

When she was a child in Filingue, a town some two hundred kilometers east of Tillaberi, Gusabu became very ill. She could neither sleep nor stand up. Her mother, Ramatu, took her to the Muslim doctor, but his cures did not help the girl. Then Ramatu took her to the local sohanci, but his remedies did not cure her. Finally, her mother took Gusabu to the local zima who said that the spirits had possessed the young girl.

"If you want your daughter to regain her health," he said, "she will have to be initiated into our spirit troupe. She must become a medium."

Gusabu's mother was not surprised by the zima's diagnosis; years before her sister had suffered from spirit sickness and had been initiated into a spirit possession troupe in Ouallam.

When Gusabu's parents had raised enough money, about $40, the zima staged a seven-day festival to welcome Gusabu's spirit, Serci, to the community. The ceremony was an occasion of great joy, for, as chief of the spirit world, Serci adjudicates disputes in the social world. A few years after the initiation, Gusabu married for the first time, but the union with her husband did not last long.

"We mediums are married to our spirits, not to our men, and our husbands do not like that," she said.

Tall and broad-shouldered with large almond eyes set deeply in her heart-shaped face, the young Gusabu soon attracted other men. After several unsuccessful marriages, and seven children lost to the custody of her husbands (in Songhay society, which is patrilineal, children belong to the father's lineage), Gusabu married a Tillaberi man and moved west to the banks of the Niger River.

She settled into Tillaberi's oldest neighborhood, Gunda Che. Constructed atop a sandy bluff, her husband's compound overlooked a deep green patchwork of small islands and rice fields chiseled out by the great river. From her vantage, water seemed to flow to the horizons. In Filingue, water, hard-won and husbanded, came from deep wells or from seasonal ponds. In Tillaberi, water was limitless; one could hear it gushing against the rocks day and night—such limitless power, controlled by the spirits. Eventually Gusabu, like other Tillaberi residents, got accustomed to having such an awe-inspiring natural neighbor.

Sensing Gusabu's respect for their home, the river, the Tooru spirits made her ill. She went through two additional initiations, one of which lasted seven years. Uncustomarily, her Tillaberi husband, Issaka, tolerated Gusabu's spirit-related activities into which she channeled much of her exceptional energy.

One day, however, Gusabu's husband died; no one could replace this tranquil man who supported her work in the spirit possession troupe. Rather than marrying again, she filled the void by devoting herself to the spirits.

Gusabu remained in the compound by the river, listening to the voices of the river. The presence and power of the Niger gave her the strength and determination to stand up to the zimas and musicians of the possession cult, making sure on countless occasions that her mediums were adequately paid. In patrilineal Songhay society, people considered Gusabu's assertive public behavior to be abnormal. Only a female witch, they said, would behave in this way. Such talk did not affect Gusabu's determination, and the mediums, in turn, urged her to become a zima. Soon she began to organize ceremonies, initiate mediums, and treat people for spirit sickness.

Spirit Mediums in Songhay

In the Songhay language it is said that "the child that you carry [on your back] will be the one who bites your back." As in most of Africa, women in Songhay country carry infants on their backs. Wherever one travels, to markets, private compounds, bush-taxi depots, or even on a lonely trail, one invariably sees women with babies tied to their backs. But as the proverb suggests, the fact that a woman carries a child does not guarantee that relations between the two will always be free of friction. The physical and perhaps emotional proximity of the caretaker and the child also means that the child's teething mouth is close to the mother's back. What is to prevent the child from biting that back? And what is to prevent a grown child from turning on the person who had carried it through infancy? Like life itself in Songhay country, all social relations are precarious, this most basic bond not excepted.

The precariousness of social relations reflects the fragility of Songhay being-in-the-world. Drought, disease, distress, and divorce are chronic features of life in Songhay country. In 1977 in Songhay country the millet harvest was bountiful; in 1980 and 1981 the millet harvests were poor. In 1984 there was widespread drought and consequent famine. Songhay families know that some years the harvest will yield food, health, and well-being, and that others will bring hunger, sickness, and possibly death.

While physical conditions in this exacting environment may fluctuate from year to year, many early Songhay social practices have persisted over time. Descent is still reckoned from a patrilineal ancestor. Rural families still live in large compounds of patrilineal relatives and affines. These households are the principal economic units of rural Songhay.[1]

During the time of the Songhay Empire (1463–1591) society was based on principles of social inequality. There were nobles or *maigey* (pl.) who were the patrilineal descendants of Askia Mohammed Touré, the greatest king of Songhay (1493–1528). There were also the free Songhay. These were either descendants of Sonni Ali Ber, whose regal line Askia Mohammed deposed in 1493, or descendants of freed slaves. Slaves, who constituted the bulk of the imperial population, were the descendants of prisoners captured during precolonial wars. *Banniya* is the Songhay term denoting "slave," a category that separated these precolonial populations from the *borcin* or "free man." Men who were recently captured slaves were called banniya; women of the same slave status were called *konyo*. When the captured slaves married and produced offspring, their children, called *horso,* could not be bought or sold; they were considered part of the families to which they were attached. Finally there were foreigners, members of ethnic groups who paid tribute to their Songhay masters.[2]

Vestiges of imperial social relations remain today. The nobles still carry great prestige in Songhay country, and the (former) slaves—the French abolished slavery in 1901—are still a stigmatized social group. The foreigners in Songhay regions are still considered strangers.[3]

Mediumship and Women

The social position of women in Songhay county is another vestige of the imperial past. Women of all social categories are equated with slaves or children. Like children, their minds are thought to be undeveloped. Like children, women are considered frivolous and untrustworthy. Women possess no jural rights: they

Fatouma Seyni, a medium and diviner in Mehanna.

can leave their husbands but cannot divorce them; they can nurse the children of their divorced husbands, but once these children are weaned, they have no legal claim to them.

The world of the possession troupe, however, is a refuge from a social world in which women are powerless. Women constitute the majority of the spirit mediums, and some are zimas. Men linked to the spirit world depend greatly on their women. Fatouma Seyni, a spirit medium in Mehanna, says:

> Women clean their husbands' paths. They pray to God for their husbands. They pray to prevent the devil's evil. They put money and perfume in their *baatas* [sacrificial container] to put the spirits behind their husbands. They sacrifice chickens and goats and watch the blood flow. Women take care of their husbands in many ways. Women are also the intermediaries between men and the spirits. Men ask women a question. Women then ask the question to the spirits. And then the spirit grants the wish. Without us, our men would be powerless. The sorko is the woman's slave. His strength comes from Dongo, but Dongo will not accept him unless he uses a woman as his intermediary. That is why sorko and zima call me "the chief." I am Dongo's intermediary.[4]

The Consequences of Mediumship

Despite the social strength many mediums derive from their mediumship, their path in the world is still precarious. The character of the relationship of infant to mother is not unlike that of the spirit to its medium. The relationship begins when the medium is initiated into the possession troupe. This initiation is the beginning of a long and close relationship between a human being, he or she who carries the spirit, and a *holle,* a being not of this world. Spirits are childlike in many ways. Like the infant, the spirit needs someone to "carry" it to make its way in the world of human affairs. Like the caretaker, mediums devote a large part of their lives to the spirits they carry. They wear clothing associated with their spirits. They make sacrifices to their spirits. They attend possession ceremonies. They suffer when their spirits take their bodies and speak to the community.

The spirits mediums carry are always with them. This continuous presence is at once their pride and their burden. It is their pride because it can give them importance in a Songhay community. It is their burden because their spirits, like the fickle child, may metaphorically bite their backs. While the relationship of child to caretaker may be precarious, that of spirit to medium can be life-threatening. Spirits may bring illness and ultimately death to their mediums.

Possession mediums are therefore in a kind of existential limbo. They are members of their communities, but unlike other people, they give part of themselves to a spirit. They are identities in the social world, but are also the ineluctable link between the social and spirit worlds. During possession ceremonies they are the living symbols of the fusion of the natural and the supernatural— the fusion of the worlds.[5]

What are the consequences of living on the border of the spirit and social worlds? Woman often have marital problems. Fundamentalist Muslims revile the mediums, considering them to be the devil's agents. Yet there is also a positive dimension to mediumship. The spirits, said Adamu Jenitongo, enrich the lives of those who carry them. This enrichment, according to the old zima, does not stem from an increased measure of social status in the community, but from a sense of well-being and completeness. Adamu Jenitongo said that most mediums display a joie de vivre that lets them rise above the conditions of hardship in which they live.

Although mediums do not recall their possession experiences, they must be keenly aware of the spirits they carry. Many Tooru mediums observe food taboos and make sure to eat regularly the plants associated with their particular spirit(s). Adamu Jenitongo said that these observances give mediums great physical and emotional strength, and that carelessness in such matters can bring sickness and death.

Spirit Sickness and Initiation

When people become ill in Songhay country they have several treatment alternatives. Religious Muslims seek the counsel of an Islamic cleric who has specialized in healing. The cleric may mix his client a potion. He may prescribe an amulet that carries either a passage from the Koran or a mystical combination of numbers. People not so inclined, however, will consult either the *dispensaire,* the smallest unit of the National Health Care Delivery System of the Republic of Niger, or a non-Islamic healer. Normally, the nurse, the non-Islamic healer, or the cleric can diagnose the cause of the illness and prescribe a cure. But there are times when an illness does not respond to any kind of treatment. Such resist-

Nana Ordana doing the *Gani*.

ance signifies that the sickness is extraordinary, precipitated by a spirit. This kind of "sickness" is work for the possession priest, the zima, who knows intimately the symptomology and treatment of spirit sickness. When a zima sees a person who is "sick," he or she suggests a number of alternatives. In some cases, the zima may determine that the "sickness" is untreatable because the victim has been invaded by pernicious spirits not part of the Songhay pantheon. In these cases the zima attempts—not always success-fully—to exorcise the spirit. In most cases the zima is able to divine the family of the invading spirit by listening to family mem-bers describe the symptomology of the "sickness." On rare occa-sions, the spirit will identify itself in a distant voice. Usually, how-ever, the identity of the possessing spirit is not revealed until the first night of an initiation ceremony which is the only treatment for "sickness." If the initiation ceremony is conducted flawlessly, novices are cured of their "sicknesses" but not of their spirits. Deities will return to the bodies of their mediums when the sounds of their sacred motifs—music and praise-poetry—beckon them.

The period between the diagnosis of spirit possession and the initiation ceremony depends on two factors: (1) the ability of the spirit-possessed person's family to pay for the ceremony; and (2) the season. In Mariama's case (see below), three months elapsed before the family of the future medium was able to finance the initiation. The ceremony involves many days' work of the zima, the sorko, the musicians, and the mediums, who must be paid, and up to seven sacrificial animals. In the interim, zimas prepare potions that diminish the effects of "sickness" until the initiation can be staged. As for the season, most initiations occur during the nonactive dry months of the agricultural cycle (November–May).

The foregoing exposition uncovers the skeleton of mediumship in Songhay. The following stories of Gusabu's mediums restore flesh to the bones of Songhay mediumship—its joys, pains, frus-trations, and fears.

Mariama

One night when she was a teenager Mariama woke up from a sound sleep in a cold sweat. Her neck was stiff, her back ached, her arms trembled, and her legs felt like lead. Dizzy from a fever-ish sleep, she slowly sat up. There were rumblings deep in her gut. She had to get outside before the walls fell in. Her scream shot through the light, dry night air.

Mariama's mother rushed into her room. She saw the shaking, crumpled figure of her daughter in a corner.

"Not you, too, Mariama," she cried, remembering how her recently deceased brother had suffered from a similar condition many years before.

She helped her daughter to her feet and led her into the open space of the compound. The moonless December sky sparkled with thousands of pinpoints of starlight. Mariama's wretching broke the starry tranquillity. When the vomit stopped flowing, she continued to heave.

"Not you, too, Mariama," Kadidja repeated. "Not you, too. Are the spirits going to take you, too?"

For the next few months Mariama suffered from chronic nausea and diarrhea. If her nausea subsided enough to offer a night's sleep, she might wake up screaming at invisible, unknown apparitions. People on the island wondered whether Mariama, formerly a cheerful, dutiful daughter, would recover from her illness.

Mariama's people were Kurtey, the people who have been living on the islands in the Tillaberi region for more than two hundred years. Although most Kurtey practiced Islam devoutly, the spirits did not spare them their unworldly afflictions. Still, most Kurtey did not like to involve their kin in local possession troupes. Because of these prejudices, Mariama's father sent her to local practitioners, Islamic and non–Islamic. Their remedies failed. Fearing for his daughter's life, Mariama's father insisted that she be taken to the hospital in Tillaberi, an administrative center in western Niger.

When they arrived at the hospital, Mariama trembled. She knew that the hospital village housed the dying and the dead. People went to the hospital village and did not return to their homes. In the hospital village were men and women in white coats who pricked villagers with needles. They forced villagers to drink mean water. Her uncle had stayed in the hospital village a few months earlier. Like the others, he died there, having laid on a bed for weeks with tubes in his body. Would she suffer the fate of all the others?

Like the other people who sought medical attention, Mariama and her mother sat in the shade of the main building's veranda. Like all rural hospitals in Niger, this facility was understaffed and poorly supplied. Mariama and Kadidja had heard that many of the nurses did not know what they were doing. "You go to the hospital for a shot," Mariama said, "and if you don't die, you leave a cripple"—a reference to botched injections in the thigh that sever the sciatic nerve.

After a day of waiting, a nurse examined Mariama and prescribed a course of nivaquin, an antimalarial drug.

"She should take two tablets now, two tonight at bedtime, and two tomorrow morning. Come back tomorrow afternoon and we'll see how she is."

Mother and daughter called upon a Tillaberi "brother" who reluctantly made them his guests.

"I like you, Kadidja, and I like Mariama, but I am afraid about Mariama's sickness. I don't want someone in my family to be taken by the spirits," he told his "sister."

"But where else can we stay," Kadidja implored. "We have no one else in Tillaberi. Please, 'brother' take pity on us. We did not choose this sickness."

Kadidja's "brother" reluctantly accepted his "sister's" request.

That night Mariama woke from her troubled sleep, moaning and groaning and speaking an incomprehensible language. Even her mother was terrified. Back at the hospital the next day, the nurses gave her a series of shots which made Mariama vomit.

Frustrated, Kadidja then took her to an Islamic healer who prescribed some plant remedies. Mariama drank medicinal decoctions three times a day for four days, four being the number in Islamic magic that corresponds to women. The decoctions seemed to aggravate Mariama's condition. One night, after the girl had finished taking the decoctions, Kadidja found her crumpled in the corner of their cubicle, her eyes fired by fever. Mariama muttered unintelligibly as she knocked her head against the mudbrick wall.

Accepting the inevitable, Kadidja took her daughter to see Adamu Jenitongo. The zima listened to Mariama's story and threw cowry shells to diagnose the problem. He saw immediately that a Hargay, a Cold Spirit, had possessed the young girl. He took some powders from his assorted cloth pouches and put them on hot coals in a brazier.

"Breathe the smoke," he told Mariama. "This will calm the spirit that has possessed you."

"Will she regain her health now?" Kadidja asked.

"She will not be cured completely," Adamu Jenitongo told them, "until she has been initiated into our possession troupe, until she becomes a spirit child. And you'll need to raise money for the ceremonies."

"You know, Baba," Kadidja said to the zima, "my brother held a Hargay spirit. Is it my brother's spirit that has possessed Mariama?"

"To know that, good woman," Adamu Jenitongo told her, "we must stage an initiation." At first Mariama's father refused to pay for the ceremony. But the implicit threat of death was persuasive, for it is widely known that spirits kill their mediums if they—or their families—refuse to stage an initiation.

It took three months for Mariama's family to raise the necessary money ($100) for the initiation. After seven days of festivities and sacrifices, Adamu Jenitongo initiated Mariama as a medium of the Cold Spirit Nyalia, the most narcissistic of all the Songhay spirits. Nyalia, however, was not the spirit that her late uncle had carried. Once its medium dies, a spirit often takes one of his or her kin, but sometimes it is enough to have had a medium as a relative to be highly susceptible to spirit possession.

The island family felt ambivalent about Mariama's spirit mediumship. Mariama felt like a stranger in her own compound. Uncomfortable, she moved to Tillaberi, and henceforth Mariama associated exclusively with other young mediums. They went to market together. They visited one another's compounds. They bathed together in the Niger.

Eventually Mariama married a young man from Tillaberi. Her "sisters" rejoiced. But Mariama's happiness was fleeting, for her husband quickly tired of her friends—her fellow mediums—who seemed always to be visiting her.

"Who are you married to?" he asked Mariama when she returned from her frequent visits. "A man must command his wife," he said. "But with you, I have no control. My friends laugh at me."

"I cannot help it if your friends laugh at you," she told him.

"My friends laugh at me," he repeated. "They think I'm not even a man. We have been married for one year, but you, Mariama, are not yet with belly. My friends say that my penis has died. They say my penis has died, Mariama. Do you hear that!"

Mariama remained silent.

"I'm married to a slave of the spirits. I want a real woman, Mariama."

Shortly thereafter, he left Mariama.

Mariama remained single for five years. She had soft brown eyes and black satin skin that covered an angelic face, a tempting lure for a future husband. But as a spirit medium, she had already "married" two spirits.

During those five years, Mariama lived collectively with other divorced women who were also spirit mediums. Like her "sisters," Mariama sold cooked foods at the market to support herself. Her father's people gave her rice and fish to supplement her budget.

In 1981 Mariama announced her marriage to a Wogo (a subethnic group, that, like the Kurtey, have lived on the islands in the Tillaberi region for two hundred years) fisherman who was a fundamentalist Muslim. The marriage festivities included a feast in Mariama's honor. She invited her "sisters" to her husband's compound. About seventy-five mediums, priests, musicians, and praise-singers pushed into the small compound on a hot afternoon in June of 1981. Daouda, the talented violinist, brought his instrument. Stoller brought his notebook. Mariama's "sisters" brought bowls of steaming rice topped with a spicy tomato and gumbo sauce. A male medium slaughtered chickens and roasted them for the guests. Daouda played his violin. A sorko chanted praise-songs to the spirits. The mediums clapped their hands and sang.

"Enough, enough!" cried Mariama's new husband. "Enough of this blasphemy. This is the devil's work, and I will not have it in my compound. Allah will strike you dead, and may He do so to rid our country of its demons."

The members of the possession troupe grumbled. Some of the men and women said that Islam was the scourge of Niger.

"Yes," one man said, "Islam has brought us disaster after disaster. In the old days, we had rain, we had food, we had health, and we had happiness. Back then we cleansed the ground where the Muslim prayed. Today we have nothing."

Adamu Jenitongo started for the opening of the compound and motioned for the others to follow. "One should not remain where one is not wanted," he said.

Mariama saw her guests out, apologizing for her husband's behavior. Her "sisters" consoled her.

"How long do you think this marriage will last?" one of the mediums wondered aloud.

"Not long," another medium opined, "for he [the husband] will pay the price for *his* blasphemey." That medium was correct, for within a year, Mariama's husband divorced her. One year after the divorce he was struck by lightning and died.

Rabi

Rabi was born to a Songhay mother and a Hausa father in Dakoro in the Adar, a Hausa-speaking region in south-central Niger. As a child, Rabi spoke Songhay to her mother and Hausa to her father. Before she reached adolescence, her family moved to Mehanna, a Songhay town along the Niger River in the region of Tillaberi. There, Rabi ripened into a beautiful young woman, the perfection of her oval face equaled by the shapeliness of her figure. Despite her beauty, men did not want her. She was quick-tempered, quarrelsome, and spiteful—the very antithesis of the ideal of women's behavior in the Songhay world, where women are supposed to be shy, dutiful, and demure.

Rabi fell into periods of illness. She was weak, moody, and refused to eat. She had nightmares. Her mother took her to Alfaggah Abdoulaye, a highly reputed Muslim healer. He prescribed for Rabi a course of herbal medicines, which did not improve her condition. Next Rabi was put under the care of the government nurse in Mehanna, where the public health facility consisted of one cement building that lacked electricity, sterile instruments, and essential medicines. Not knowing what had afflicted his new client, the nurse gave Rabi placebos. Rabi's mother, herself a spirit medium, took her daughter to Zeinabou, the local zima. Having seen these conditions before, Zeinabou divined that a Hargay (Cold Spirit) had possessed Rabi.

"Rabi must be initiated in Mehanna," Zeinabou announced. "We'll need to stage a seven-day ceremony. Rabi must learn to dance."

"We will do whatever is necessary," Rabi's mother said.

Rabi's family paid the initiation fee shortly after Zeinabou's diagnosis, and Rabi became a medium in the Mehanna possession troupe. She quickly resumed her normal quick-tempered, quarrelsome, spiteful state.

Rabi soon attracted other spirits, becoming the medium of Adam Hausa (a Doguwa or Hausa spirit that controls blindness) and of Cirey (the Tooru spirit that controls lightning). At possession ceremonies, Rabi was a standout dancer. People traveled great distances to see her sweep onto the dance ground and move with rhythmic grace. In this way Rabi's reputation grew—for her dancing as well as her hot temper. Well into her twenties, a late age for

A medium possessed by a Hausa (Doguwa) spirit.

a woman's first marriage in Songhay, she agreed to marry a Hausa-speaking man who was an Islamic cleric.

Rabi felt invincible. The spirits protected her from enemies, and now her husband's Muslim prayers increased her protection. But Rabi's sharp tongue and celebrated temper brought turmoil to her husband's compound. Every time her husband went to his other wife's bed, Rabi proclaimed his impotence to the entire neighborhood.

"How can a donkey copulate with a woman?" she would shout for the neighbor's benefit.

Rabi answered her own question. "The donkey can't copulate because its penis is limp."

Rabi's rhetorical tactic soon achieved its intended goal. To salvage his reputation as well as his marriages, the embarrassed husband, Hamidu, asked Rabi to leave Mehanna.

At dawn on a Friday in January, when the river was full and swift, Rabi boarded a dugout en route to Bonfebba. The air was cool and a mist hung over the river's smooth gray surface. The sun's rays skittered over the water as they pushed off, giving little comfort to the canoe's shivering passengers. The current carried them swiftly downstream in the direction of Wissili Island, the home of Wogo fisherman and cultivators. All the while, Rabi talked boldly.

"I am going to buy such fine cloth and soap in Tillaberi. That's where I'm going."

No one believed her, but no one wanted to pick a quarrel with quick-tempered Rabi. Before long the boat passed Wissili and the passengers waved to people in the harbor who were also preparing to go to Bonfebba market.

The river swept them toward Wissili rapids. Halidu, the canoe's owner, piloted his craft through the white water.

"Don't worry, people," Rabi said confidently, "I am here. Nothing can happen."

An unseen current catapulted the canoe against the rocks.

"We're taking on too much water," Halidu cried. "We're taking on water."

The canoe wedged between two boulders.

"Everyone out," Halidu ordered. "Everyone out." Tall and thin, Halidu's gaunt face tightened. "Everyone out."

Fortunately the rapids were located in a narrow branch of the Niger, and the passengers could easily scamper over the boulders to reach the shore. Halidu and his assistants disengaged the canoe and guided it through the remaining rapids. He then paddled the boat to shore and picked up his passengers.

Rabi was furious. "Don't you know how to pilot a canoe, Halidu! I'll never take your boat again."

Halidu's laughter masked his fury. He would never again take Rabi as his passenger.

They reached Bonfebba market at midmorning. Scores of dugouts were anchored in the harbor, which was only meters from market stalls fashioned from tree branches covered with woven straw. Rabi hired two young boys to carry her things to the bush taxi depot. Followed by her porters, Rabi, conspicuous in a purple, blue, and red tie-dyed cloth ensemble, walked through the market stalls, her head held high. When she emerged from the crowded stalls into the sandy square—the depot—that separated the town from its market, she hailed Duramane, the dispatcher. "Give me a seat in the cabin," Rabi ordered.

"I don't know, Rabi. Someone already has that place."

"I don't care. I want it, and that is all."

"In the name of God," Duramane said softly, "I do not want to offend you, Rabi."

"Good," Rabi said beaming as she took her seat in the cabin.

The ride to Tillaberi was a quick one. No people to drop off. No people to pick up. No flat tires. No engine trouble. No gasoline or oil leaks. And, as it was still morning, no need to stop to pray.

When she got to Tillaberi, she hired two boys to carry her things to her new home in her sister's compound, adjacent to Adamu Jenitongo's residence. Having long been separated from her only child, born out of wedlock, she became the "mother" to her sister's two small children, Hadjara and Saya. In Songhay, the mother's sister has all the rights and obligations of the biological mother.

Hamidu divided his time between Rabi and his other wife, who continued to live in Mehanna. Hamidu's first wife was pregnant, surely the result of his junior wife's absence. But distance did not bring harmony to his marriage, for Hamidu and Rabi argued frequently when he was in Tillaberi. People in the neighborhood soon knew her strident voice.

Rabi's behavior made people in Adamu Jenitongo's compound wary of her. Adamu Jenitongo once said that one should never trust a loud, boastful person—especially if he or she is young. One day Rabi strode into Adamu Jenitongo's compound to announce that she had become a zima. How could a zima and a marabout live as husband and wife? Adamu Jenitongo wondered. He cautioned his people to keep their distance from Rabi.

Hampsa

Hampsa was born into a famous family of Fulan marabouts in the region of Gao (Mali). Her grandfather, Alboubakar Alhinne, was a Fulan cleric known for his vast knowledge of Islamic law. Her grandmother, Asseta Lasahin, was also from a family of famous Islamic clerics. Hampsa's father, Hamadou Alboubakar, was a well-known healer and a strict Islamic cleric. He expected his sons to follow his unswerving religious path and his daughters to marry famous marabouts.

> I liked my life as a young child. I didn't live in Gao with my father's people. When I was little I lived in the Fulan camps with my mother's people. I liked the open spaces. I liked drinking milk every day and pouring butter into sauces and millet porridge. My friends and I played all the time. I was young and free.[6]

When Hampsa was twelve years old and living in Gao, she suddenly began to lose weight. She also refused to talk—even to her mother. Ramatu saw her daughter slowly withering away and, fearing that Hampsa would soon die, took the child to see a Songhay zima on the east bank of the Niger River.

> My father learned what my mother was going to do and sent a messenger. He told us that we should return to Gao at once. My mother ignored him. "I don't want my daughter to die. We stay here and that is all."[7]

Ramatu and Hampsa stayed in the zima's compound of straw huts while he prepared an initiation festival. Hampsa stayed in the spirit hut for seven days, during which time the zima fed her pastes made from sacred tree barks. He also burned aromatic resins in a brazier, filling the hut with fragrant smoke. On each of the seven days, Hampsa's spirit, Harakoy Dikko, the queen of the Niger River, took over her young body.

> Each day the spirit came into my body like a hot breeze. First, I felt it in my left toes, and left foot. Then my right toes and foot. Then up my left leg, then my right leg. Then through my waist and chest. Then I felt it in my left fingers and hand, and my right fingers and hand. And then my head boiled and . . .

and I can't remember any more. . . . On the seventh day the zima gave me a ring, and my illness was finished. My mother and I returned to Gao and my father married me off the next year.[8]

Since that time, Hampsa has never attended a possession ceremony and has never again been possessed. Her first husband, Mallam Zibbo, a major Islamic spiritual leader in Abidjan in the Ivory Cost, died in 1974. In 1976 she married Alfaggah Ibrahim of Mehanna, who disapproves of Songhay possession ceremonies. For this reason Hampsa keeps her possession ring hidden in her house.

Karimoun

Karimoun was born in Tillaberi in 1956. Like many of his contemporaries, he has no memory of the colonial period. When he was seven years old, Karimoun's parents enrolled him in primary school. This was exceptional during a period when many parents preferred that their sons work in the fields rather than attend school. (Girls generally did not go to school until the 1970s, and many remain strangers to the classroom even today). Karimoun's parents, however, thought he should learn to read and write the French language. Perhaps he would one day become a teacher. Karimoun did not disappoint his parents. He breezed through primary school and passed the entrance exam for secondary school. His French was fairly good, but science was his favorite subject.

While pursuing his studies at the secondary school in Tillaberi, Karimoun fell ill. During the nights he shivered with fever. Nervous tension gripped his body even as he slept. Sometimes he talked deliriously in his sleep; sometimes he woke up from a dream screaming about being devoured by a river demon.

His parents sent him to the Tillaberi hospital. A French physician and a Nigerien nurse examined him, but they could not diagnose his illness. They gave him nivaquin for malaria, but it did not improve his condition. Karimoun's parents took him to an Islamic healer. The marabout made a magic amulet for him, a piece of paper with magic numbers on it. But the charm was ineffective. Sensing the similarity of Karimoun's disorder to that of his cousin, who was a Hauka spirit medium, Karimoun's parents took their son to Adamu Jenitongo, who saw immediately that a Hauka spirit had possessed the boy. Accordingly, Adamu Jenitongo arranged a seven-day initiation ceremony for Karimoun. Being the most recent spirits, the Hauka, who first appeared in

1925, require less elaborate and therefore less expensive rites. At the end of the seven-day initiation, which cost $50, Adamu Jenitongo initiated Karimoun, a lanky youth whose habitual open-mouthed expression masked his intelligence, as Fadimata's medium. Thereafter, Karimoun's "sickness" disappeared.

Karimoun's membership in Tillaberi's possession troupe did not keep him from his studies. Having progressed steadily through the Tillaberi secondary school, Karimoun decided to become a fisheries agent. In his last year of secondary school, Karimoun passed the Fisheries School entrance examination and went to study in Kolo, a small town south of Niamey. After graduating with distinction after three years in Kolo, Karimoun was assigned by the government to a position in the Tillaberi fisheries office.

Karimoun returned to Tillaberi in triumph. Few of his contemporaries had become functionaries. Because of his steady government income, young Tillaberi women threw themselves at him. Eventually, he married a beautiful girl, sired three children, and built a compound for his family in a neighborhood close to Adamu Jenitongo's house.

One afternoon in February 1980, the clack of the calabash drum propelled me to a possession ceremony in Adamu Jenitongo's compound. Along the way I saw Karimoun, who had been a student of mine at the Tillaberi secondary school in 1970–71.

We exchanged greetings in Songhay.

"How is your health, Karimoun? And the health of your children? Your wife's health? And your wife's people?"

"I thank God every day for their health. And you, Monsieur Stoller? How is your body? How are the people on your land?"

"There are no problems, in the name of God."

"Are you going to the possession ceremony, Monsieur Stoller?" He insisted on referring to me as he had nine years earlier.

"Yes. Why don't you come along?"

"I can't," he said.

"Why not?"

"Because I have Fadimata [the name of his Hauka deity]."

"You do!" I gasped, having harbored the notion that only uneducated and socially stigmatized Songhay were spirit mediums.

"Yes. That is why I cannot go. If I hear the music, Fadimata will take my body. I'm a civil servant. I'm educated. I cannot participate."

There are scores of spirit mediums, male and female, who share Karimoun's predicament. They are educated civil servants, some of whom hold high positions in the Nigerien political and educational establishment.

How can this be? A spirit must find a new body when a medium dies and most often it chooses a person in the late medium's family. Thus, spirits have possessed many "relatives" who have become high-ranking civil servants. Although a person may change residence, clothing, and behavior during his or her rise through the ranks, a spirit possesses a person forever and a government official cannot change the fact of mediumship. Imagine an army officer, for example, taken by Hauka. He froths at the mouth and hurls insults at the crowd. He does backflips onto the sand and vomits black ink. To avoid this untenable humiliation, mediums who are civil servants avoid possession ceremonies. But their absence from public ceremonies is no indication of an absence of private belief or practice.

Halima's Initiation

Halima's initation ceremony took place December 9–16, 1979, in Tillaberi. She was a young woman of Songhay origin who had been "sick" for more than three months. Because of frequent nightmares during which she had uttered the name of her possessing spirits, Adamu Jenitongo had little trouble diagnosing double spirit possession. Halima had been taken by the Cold Spirit Fasio, and the Black Spirit Maalu.

The First Day

A violinist and two drummers sat under the ritual canopy, facing the spirit hut at the eastern end of Adamu Jenitongo's compound. Clack-roll-clack! The music shook the still afternoon air. The audience gradually filed into the compound, forming a circle around the dance area. Vendors sold cigarettes, kola nuts, chewing gum, and hard candy. Young men propositioned young women. The mediums strolled into the compound, hugging one another. They sat on straw mats to the right of the ritual canopy.

The ceremony was divided between two ritual frames: the *horey,* or having a good time, and the *tunaandi,* or raising of the spirit. In the horey anyone may dance while the musicians play random spirit rhythms, and the drummers choose the most syncopated rhythms to encourage dancing. At first, however, there was little or no dancing. Sensing the lull, the older women among the mediums took to the dance ground. The musicians picked up the tempo. The women formed a line at the opposite end of the ground, each one holding a length of cloth in front of her.

"Play some music, you lazy drummers. I've heard nothing so far. Play you lazy fools," the first dancer ordered.

Thus challenged, the musicians picked up the tempo even more. And then the women danced, stomping their bare feet on the sand. Their soft flesh shivered as they glided through the dust toward the canopy. Amid this pulsation, their blissful, wide-open eyes focused on the drummers. Tight-lipped smiles creased their faces.

After more than two hours of this dancing, Adamu Jenitongo told the musicians to play Hargay songs in honor of the Cold Spirit Fasio. The audience looked toward the spirit hut. At the first bars of Hargay music, Halima emerged, dressed in a white robe with a white shawl over her head. The white robe symbolized the Cold Spirits; the white shawl represented her status as a novice. She was led by her initiator, Fati, and followed by her protector, Fodie—both mediums of the troupe.[9] A black and white cord (black for Dongo and white for Harakoy Dikko, mother of the nobles of the spirit world) was lassoed around Halima's ribs. The protector, Fodie, gripped the end of the cord. The trio stopped just outside the opening of the hut. Then the initiator, Fati, gently pushed the novice back inside. This sequence, which represents crossing the threshold between the social and spirit worlds, was enacted three times, three being the sacred number for men among the Songhay.[10]

Now they approached the dance area. An overturned mortar stood directly in line with the violinist under the ritual canopy. The trio passed the mortar, walking toward the musicians. They bowed to the violinist and drummers. They turned and strolled back to the overturned mortar, where Fati seated the novice.

The musicians played a slow rhythm called the *windi* (the tour) and the initiation process began. Taking hold of Halima's hands, Fati demonstrated how to dance the windi. She moved her right foot forward and pressed her toes into the sand three times. She then brought her right foot back even with her left. Next Fati put her right foot forward again and brought up her left foot. Danced with arms swaying, the windi step represents an episode of the mythical history of the spirits—their emergence from water.[11]

At the prompting of Fati, Halima attempted the step to the ongoing beat of the music. Meanwhile, Fodie, the protector, always

A woman dancing at a possession ceremony.

behind the novice, prepared herself just in case the girl lost her balance. She held onto the cord firmly, making sure to give the girl enough slack for dancing. After five minutes of such practice, Fati again sat her charge on the mortar. While they rested, the music droned. Other mediums entered the dancing area, not to become possessed but to celebrate the arrival of a new spirit and medium. Adamu Jenitongo said that dancing is a testament to an individual's reverence for the spirits.[12]

The dance lessons lasted until the sun, low in the western sky, cast its golden glow on the dance ground. Shadows from the ritual canopy stretched over the dance ground, and it was time for the *fimbi*, the dance that brings on possession.[13] With her initiator and protector prodding her, Halima alternately shook her head and swayed her arms. The music was slow and melodious. The tempo quickened. Halima trembled. The trembling intensified to spasmodic shaking. She drooled; mucus bubbled from her nose. She stammered but did not articulate any comprehensible sounds. Then Fasio expressed himself, wailing "Wah, wah, wah, wah, way," flapping his arms up and down and turning his head left and right as though pulled by an invisible string. The tempo increased and Fasio, still reined in by the ever-present protector, retreated to a spot near the mortar. He was ready to dance. The drummers got up on their knees. Drum rolls and clacks filled the air. Fasio stomped on the sand for about five minutes and was led back to the mortar. Fasio got up and danced for another five minutes. Led to his seat, he rose to dance once again before letting himself be taken back to the spirit hut. There, a lesser zima, one of Adamu Jenitongo's many students, shook the spirit from his medium. The first day ended.

The Second Day

The second day proceeded much as the first, except that there were different musical rhythms. This day the ceremony honored the Black Spirit Maalu, the second spirit that had possessed Halima. Once the festive frame of the dance was completed, the musicians played Black Spirit music, and Halima emerged from the spirit hut dressed in an indigo-striped tunic over white fabric wrapped as a skirt. (The tunic, the major element of the Black Spirit costumes, is characteristic of Moose and Gurmantche clothing; the Moose and Gurmantche were the original inhabitants of Songhay country and therefore the ancestors of the land.) Fati and Fodie again made sure that Halima emerged and then reemerged from the hut twice. Again, there were the same windi sequences alternating with the vigorous dancing of the other mediums. Finally, Fati and Fodie readied themselves for the arrival of the spirit.

The musicians sang songs that honored the Black Spirits in general and Maalu in particular. Fati and Fodie coaxed their charge into the fimbi's swaying movements. Halima's body twitched and then trembled. She growled and groaned. Suddenly, the spirit threw her violently to the ground. She was no longer the initiate, but rather Maalu, a Black Spirit. Maalu growled like a dog. He hopped around like a frog and washed himself with dirt.

After Maalu refused to speak to the audience, Fati and Fodie led him back to the spirit hut to release him from his medium. The sun set, leaving in its wake a rosy sky streaked with bands of deep purple that momentarily folded into an oriental fan.

The Third Day

On the morning of the third day, Adamu Jenitongo organized the *hannandi* (to make clean). This rite cleanses the community of its "filth," bad faith, jealousy, and rivalries.[14]

First, Adamu Jenitongo collected five millet stalks and broke them into numerous small segments. He gave to the mediums the number of millet pieces that corresponded to the number of spirits they each carried. The novice, again dressed in a white robe and shawl, received two millet pieces for the two spirits she was carring.

The mediums filed behind the zima and marched toward the ritual canopy. Marching to the melodious "cries" of the violin, they circled the canopy three times. Then they followed Adamu Jenitongo out of the compound and walked until they reached a large ant hill at a crossroads outside the village. Adamu Jenitongo ordered everyone to stop. The crossroads, where one road ends and two new ones begin, represents the point where the social and spirit worlds are fused.[15] Adamu Jenitongo positioned the violinist to the east of the ant hill and told the mediums to place themselves behind the musician. The old zima moved Halima, the novice, who was flanked by her initiator and her protector, north of the ant hill. The zima placed himself to the west, between the ant hill and the village.

Adamu Jenitongo recited instructions to the mediums. "Throw your millet pieces into the ant hill, count to three, and run back to the village. Don't look back." All the mediums, even the old women, threw their millet into the ant hill and raced back to Adamu Jenitongo's compound.

The second day of festivities honored the Black Spirits; the third day reverted to the Cold Spirit Fasio's coming out. The old women had their moment once again. And once again the audience demonstrated its appreciation by contributing money to the musicians. After some two hours of dancing, the musicians played Cold Spirit rhythms. On cue, the trio emerged from the spirit hut. Halima, Fati, and Fodie advanced and then retreated. The trio repeated twice the emergence-reemergence sequence, as on days one and two. As on day one, Halima was dressed in a long white robe, her head covered by a white shawl. On this third day, Fati let her student dance longer. Fodie still kept Halima tethered to the black and white cord. The time came to raise the spirit. The initiator, Fati, took firm control of her student, prodding her into the swaying movements that bring a spirit to the social world. Fasio flailed and wailed but did not speak to the audience.

The Fourth Day

The fourth day, like the second, was staged for the Black Spirit Maalu. The ceremony proceeded much like those on the first three days. The attendants, who left Halima's head uncovered, had tied the girl's hair into ten plaits, each ending in a cowry shell.[16] Fati gave her student more license to dance. When Maalu arrived, the spirit again threw Halima's body to the ground. Maalu growled like a dog and hopped about like a frog for about ten minutes. Then Fati and Fodie accompanied Halima, the novice, back to the spirit hut.

The Fifth Day

On day five, Adamu Jenitongo staged a Cold Spirit celebration which began at midafternoon and ended at dusk. The novice again appeared with plaited hair. The initiator permitted her to dance for long periods. The protector, however, still "controlled" her charge. When the spirit Fasio came to take his medium, Fati and Fodie allowed the spirit time to express himself. Fasio wailed and thrashed his arms wildly in the air, but spoke in neither spirit nor human language.

The Sixth Day

On the afternoon of the sixth day, Adamu Jenitongo staged the *daarendi,* the ritual sacrifice of animals.[17] The daarendi differed in

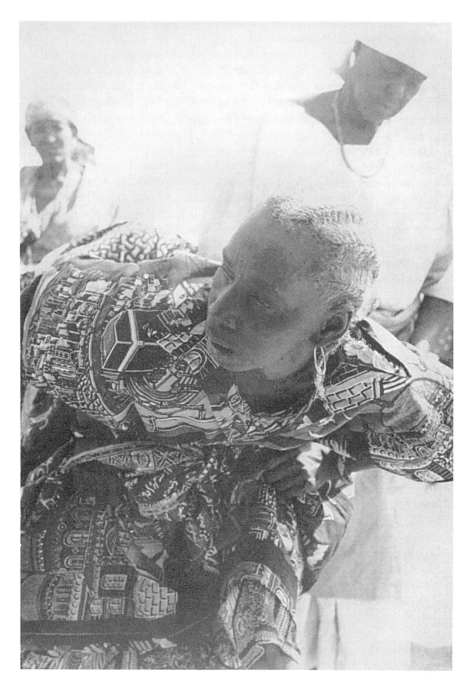

A medium possessed by a Hausa (Doguwa) spirit.

certain details from the preceeding ceremonies. First, the novice, Halima, danced without the black and white cord, which was no-where to be seen. Second, there were two sorkos in the audience. And third, the afternoon ceremony began earlier, for the daarendi had to be celebrated for Maalu as well as Fasio.

Halima and her initiator, Fati, walked directly to the ritual can-opy, bowed to the musicians, and remained there. The initiator gently pushed the head of the novice into the fimbi's rhythmic motion. The godji wailed. The drums clacked a slow beat. Grad-ually, they upped the tempo until the music reached its climax— violin crying and drum rhythms popping in the air. Maalu re-sponded by violently taking his medium's body and hopping around the dance area.

The musicians played Nya Beri's music, and one of the sorkos leapt from the audience to the dance ground to sing praise-poems. It is customary to bring to the social world the great spirits, Dongo and Nya Beri especially, to welcome new spirits to the community. Mediums carrying Black Spirits encircled Maalu, who was all the while hopping and groaning. Meanwhile, Nya Beri's medium danced the fimbi in front of the musicians. The sorko moved be-hind her and tapped his index finger on her shoulder. He chanted. Nya Beri's medium fell to her knees and shook. She extended her arms outward toward the musicians. She placed her palms on the sand. Her body convulsed uncontrollably. Tears fell from her eyes, and mucus ran from her nose. Nya Beri hopped about on the sand and beckoned Maalu to join her at the center of the dance ground. She drew Maalu to her breast, grabbed his head and screamed into his ears. At the edge of the dance ground, Gondi, the snake, took his medium, kicking up sand and scattering the crowd. Gondi slithered slowly across the sand, making his way toward Nya Beri and Maalu. Hissing and flicking his tongue, "the snake" reached the other spirits.

Holding by its tether a brown and white goat, the kind of ani-mal preferred by the Black Spirits, Adamu Jenitongo stood among the deities. He presented the goat to Nya Beri. The "Great Mother" caressed the goat's testicles. "This goat will do," Nya Beri an-nounced.

Nonpossessed members of the troupe led Maalu and Gondi back to the spirit hut, where a lesser zima shook the spirits loose from their mediums. Left alone, Nya Beri crept to the musicians' area. She greeted the violinist and the gourd drummers.

"Ay ga ni fo" (I am greeting you), she croaked, extending her hand, "Ay ga ni fo."

The musicians responded: "Fofo, Ay nya, kubeyni" (Hello, my mother. Welcome.).

The greeting was intended to do more than satisfy etiquette; it also had a mercenary function. Nya Beri wanted money. She greeted me and refused my initiation donation.

"You'd better give her more money, Paul," someone suggested.

Not wanting to anger Nya Beri, I increased the ante. She shook my hand. Eventually the "Great Mother" gave her large collection of coins to the musicians and was led away toward the spirit hut.

Only the first part of the daarendi had been performed at this point. By changing the music the violinist and drummers transformed what had been a Black Spirit celebration into a Cold Spirit festival. Fati led the novice, Halima, to a spot just in front of the musicians. Halima swayed herself into the fimbi movements. Before long, Fasio had arrived, flapping the arms of his medium up and down and jerking Halima's head to the left and right. Mediums carrying Cold Spirits came forward and danced. Nyalia descended on her medium with violent paroxysms. The medium had to be restrained from pulling off all of her clothing. While one attendant held the convulsing figure, a second tied a strip of white cloth around Nyalia's ribs—an ample restraint. Arms at each other's waists, as if they were friends out on a stroll, the two spirits retreated to the edge of the dance ground. The musicians picked up the tempo. The spirits danced frenetically. They kicked their legs high in the air and stomped their feet on the sand. Spotting another medium of a Cold Spirit, Fasio grabbed the woman's hand and pulled her into the center of the dance area. Nyalia screamed into the woman's ears. Chanting praise-songs, the sorko thumped the woman's shoulder with his forefinger. Unable to resist such overpowering stimuli, the woman yielded to the violent presence of Dundo.

The three spirits took to the center of the dance area, greeting one another as long lost friends. Absorbed in this activity, they did not greet members of the audience.

Adamu Jenitongo talked to the three Cold Spirits, but, still absorbed in one another, they did not respond. The zima and his assistant guided the spirits to the southern edge of the dance ground. The sorko brought forward the brown and white goat, which the spirits inspected. They squeezed the goat's testicles.

"Zima," said Dundo, "this goat has no testicles."

The sacred canopy in Adamu Jenitongo's compound.

"That is right, zima," Nyalia said. "Drummer, this is not a goat. You are not playing with children."

Adamu Jenitongo pleaded with the irrascible spirits, claiming that only the best goat had been selected for sacrifice.

Dundo, who was carried by a sixty-year-old woman, left the dance ground. Mumbling to himself, he stormed off toward the spirit hut. He scaled the thatched roof and reached for the hut's center post. Growling, he shook the post violently. A lesser zima coaxed Dundo off the roof and led him back to the dance area. The three Cold Spirits again inspected the goat.

"It will do," Nyalia proclaimed.

The sorko pulled the goat to a spot just in front of the spirit hut entrance. Wielding a large knife, Adamu Jenitongo slit the goat's throat. The spirits jumped up and down. Gushing blood splattered their costumes.

The Seventh Day

Before the seven-day initiation ceremony, the novice had been suffering from general lethargy, abdominal cramps, and nausea. These symptoms vanished during the first six days of the initiation festival. On the seventh day, Adamu Jenitongo examined his new medium to see whether the spirit had returned her fully to health.

He found the new medium energetic on the morning of the seventh day.

"Baba, I feel strong, strong enough to work in the compound of my family."

A week later the healthy Halima visited Adamu Jenitongo. Satisfied that his work had gone well, he asked her for five hundred francs in exchange for a small brass ring.

"Put this ring on the third finger of your left hand and never remove it." Adamu Jenitongo touched the girl's ring finger. "This is the finger of power, the finger through which the spirit enters the body."

Mounkaila's Initiation

Mounkaila, a twenty-year-old Bella man who had been ill for more than three months, consulted Adamu Jenitongo about his disorder. The old zima said that Mounkaila's suffering could be the result of "sickness," or prepossession malady.

"Baba, I can't sleep. As soon as I fall off to sleep a nightmare wakes me up. In the night I can't stop shaking, and I can't catch

Mounkaila's initiation, Tillaberi, 1981.

my breath. One night, Baba, my brother found me in the cemetery. I was digging up corpses! On another night, my brother found me next to a dead dog that I had strangled."

"Mounkaila," the old zima said, "you have been possessed by a Hauka deity [one of the colonial spirits]. There must be an initiation," he told the young man.

Three months later Mounkaila's family had raised the 25,000 francs CFA ($100) necessary to produce the ceremony.

Days One through Five

Hauka initiations are generally not elaborate. During days one through five of Mounkaila's initiation, the drummers and violinist played their possession music. A prominent sorko, Djimba, sang praise-poetry and danced. The novice was not costumed, and he was not placed in the spirit hut until the final two days of his initiation. This lack of pomp devolves from two sources, according to Adamu Jenitongo: first, there is a general impoverishment of possession ritual in contemporary Songhay; and second, the Hauka, being the most recently arrived spirits (ca. 1925), do not merit elaborate ceremonies.[18]

During the first five days of the initiation, an entourage of Hauka mediums—mostly men—escorted Mounkaila to Adamu Jenitongo's compound. Unlike the previous initiation, the mediums did not instruct the novice on the subtleties of possession dancing; instead, the musicians played Hauka music and the Hauka mediums simply marched counterclockwise in a loosely formed circle. Some of the mediums carried bullwhips, which they snapped from time to time. A few of the mediums wore pith helmets, symbols of the French colonial rule which the Hauka deities burlesque. Occasionally, the Hauka mediums jerked Mounkaila's arm, prodding him to march more rapidly. Soon, a Hauka entered Mounkaila's body. Like other Hauka, this nameless spirit groaned and clenched his fists. He thrust his right arm in the air. The new Hauka roared like a lion. Saliva foamed from his mouth. Meanwhile, the other Hauka mediums marched on.

This same sequence of music, dancing, and novice possession was repeated for the next four days of the festival. On the first day Adamu Jenitongo allowed the spirit to remain in Mounkaila's body for five minutes; on day five he let the spirit express himself for twenty minutes.

The Sixth Day—Daarendi

Dressed in a black robe, Adamu Jenitongo left his compound in the morning and went to an anthill at a crossroads. He cleaned debris from the ant hill and returned to his compound ready for the sixth day of the Hauka initiation.

In the late afternoon, the zima took the novice by the hand and led him out of the spirit hut. Followed by the other Hauka mediums and the violinist, they walked to the crossroads. Adamu Jenitongo stuck his forked stick—which represents the fusion of the spirit and social worlds—into the ant hill. With their feet, other mediums traced a circle around the ant hill. They then traced two lines that intersected where the zima had inserted his forked stick, indicating the cardinal directions.

The violinist sat to the east of the circle. Adamu Jenitongo put one egg, corn kernels, millet seeds, and sorghum seeds in the ant hill. He recited the *genji how,* the ritual incantation that harmonizes the forces of the bush.[19] In this way the zima nourished the earth at the point where it meets the sky. The sorko, Djimba, led Mounkaila to the circle and walked around it left to right. The violin's cries pierced the air. Djimba recited his praise-poetry, and, as if on cue, the unnamed Hauka entered Mounkaila's body. Because it is on the sixth day of the initiation cycle that the other Hauka must greet the new deity, the Hauka mediums walked left to right around the circle, a circle that is symbolically the edge of the social and spirit worlds, so that they too were taken by their Hauka spirits. The spirits remained inside the circle. Djimba prepared the sacrifices of the day: three chickens. He rubbed the chickens over the head, arms, and legs of the novice. "These sacrifices will help protect you from the fickleness of your spirit." Adamu Jenitongo placed Mounkaila on the west side of the forked stick. He then cut the chickens' throats, and their blood spurted into the mouth of the ant hill. In the background the Hauka screamed. They moaned. They launched themselves into the air and landed on their backs. The sorko approached the new Hauka.

Sorko: We have made sacrifices and everyone is listening. What is your name?

Spirit: [groans].

Sorko: We want you to speak, and only the truth—no lies

Spirit: Ah! Ah!! [Groan] Ceferi.

Sorko: You are lying! That is not true.

Two other Hauka approached the novice-spirit and shook his body violently.

> *Sorko*: Quickly, the night is falling. We want to know who you are. What is your name?
> *Spirit*: Ceferi.
> *Sorko*: You are still lying. We are not afraid of you. We want to know your name. This is the last time we will ask.

The spirit uttered his name three times. The sorko, Djimba, was satisfied. The Hauka spirit, Ceferi, "the nonbeliever," had taken Mounkaila's body. Darkness swept over the compound. Shaken loose from their spirits, the Hauka mediums returned home.

The Seventh Day

The spirit had revealed his name to the community on the sixth day. He was Ceferi, the Hauka who neither fasts (during the Ramadan) nor prays. In Songhay it is said that the *bakillo,* or stingy nonbeliever, neither fasts nor prays. When he goes to the shithouse, being so stingy, he will not shit. These base attributes notwithstanding, the troupe joyfully staged Ceferi's formal welcome on the seventh day of the initiation.

The ceremony differed greatly from other possession ceremonies: there was no casual dancing. Instead, the musicians played only Hauka music. The Hauka mediums formed a circle on the dance ground and marched stiff-legged to the pulsing beat of the drums.[20] Dressed in a billowing black robe, Djimba Sorko burst through the circle of Hauka mediums. He blew an ear-piercing whistle and chanted praise-poetry. The musicians upped the tempo. Mounkaila, the novice, was the first medium to be taken. Standing absolutely still, he hyperventilated. Saliva oozed from his mouth. He bellowed. He thumped his chest. Ceferi's arrival inspired the other Hauka to enter the bodies of their mediums. Commandant Mugu and Istanbula, the chief of the Hauka, threw their mediums wildy in the air. They thumped onto the sand and then leaped to their feet.

Dongo, considered the Hauka protector, arrived to bless his new son. Dongo hopped to the spot where Ceferi stood. Ceferi dropped to his knees. Dongo caressed his new son's head and screamed into his ears, all of which sanctified the arrival of the new Hauka. An attendant led Dongo away.

Ceferi's reception was by no means over. Since the new Hauka had to be greeted by the other Hauka mediums in town, the priests coerced the more reluctant Hauka mediums into the dance circle. They forced the mediums to march to the beat of the music. One by one their spirits took them: Lieutenant Marseille, Commandant Gomno, Fadimata. Like most Hauka, they did back flips, groaned, moaned, and foamed at the mouth. They greeted one another and then goose-stepped into the audience to greet the people. Meanwhile, Adamu Jenitongo had prepared a special porridge for Ceferi, an offering from the community. An attendant brought forward black and white sacrificial chickens.

The music clacked and rolled. The Hauka formed a line and stood at military attention. The sorko placed himself just in front of the drummers, holding the two sacrificial chickens behind his back. He called to Ceferi. The spirit marched forward a few steps, threw himself in the air, and landed on his back with a thud. He picked himself up and dove forward, landing on his chest. He quickly pulled himself up and stood at military attention. The sorko rubbed the chickens over Ceferi's head, ears, mouth, arms, and knees. Annointed, Ceferi marched back to his spirit cronies. The sorko held the calabash bowl of porridge high over his head, and Ceferi advanced once more. He took the gourd and drank. This action excited the Hauka standing in the background. They jumped, strutted, and goose-stepped around the dance ground. Some threw their bodies in the air, allowing them to hit the ground heavily. Commandant Mugu did leg splits. The sinking sun reddened the sky.[21]

Spirit Mediumship in Songhay

Most mediums in a Songhay troupe are women who constitute a sisterhood that tolerates the participation of the occasional male medium. In the social world of the possession troupe, women enjoy unaccustomed power and social license, and for good reason. Without mediums, there is no possession troupe. Without mediums, there is no rapport between the social and spirit worlds. Without mediums, the world becomes fully susceptible to the powerful forces of nature.

In the 1950s and 1960s it was said that Songhay possession was a doomed phenomenon. Most young Songhay men and women, after all, had been exposed to Western influences, French language and culture. And Islamic clerics, of course, had long warned that people associated with possession would never ascend to heaven; they were the devil's agents, were they not?

Despite the popularity of Islam and the impact of French language and culture in Songhay, there is today no lack of mediums in possession troupes throughout western Niger. True, all mediums suffer from prepossession malady, and they must all be initiated into the possession troupe. But why the plethora of mediums today? As in the case of Mariama and her uncle, the answer derives from kinship. Spirits search for mediums in certain families.

In this way the spirits become the foundation of a subset of social relations that are bound by rights and obligations in the spirit world. This fact has two major ramifications. First, spirit mediumship is generally a genealogical inheritance. Second, spirit mediumship affects the social relations of the medium's family, which becomes obligated to spirit as well as social kin. Since Mounkaila carries Ceferi, a Hauka spirit, his family is expected to engage in "kin" relations with the families of other Hauka mediums—all of whose members are at the mercy of the spirits. Out of fear and respect for the spirits' power—to maim and kill—family members participate and support various sacrifices to the spirits. They are also obliged to support the activities of the possession troupe, both directly through attendance and indirectly through financial contribution. Spirit mediumship therefore creates a subset of social relations in Songhay society, the major social manifestation of which is the possesion troupe. It is for this reason that Fatouma Seyni, Dongo's medium in Mehanna, said to me: "No matter how bad the times become, no matter the number of Imams and other clerics, no matter the number of [black] anasaras [Europeans—a reference to the educated elite], there will always be spirit mediums here. Mediumship is in our blood.[22]"

Mounmouni Koda, sorko of Mehanna.

4

PRAISE-SINGERS FROM THE RIVER

Mounmouni Koda, a master sorko, initiated his son Djibo more than twenty years ago. In his youth, Djibo, a tall and muscular boy whose angular brown face was dominated by black, darting eyes, lived with his family in Ouallam (a town one hundred kilometers east of Tillaberi). Early on, he memorized his father's incantations and scoured the bush in search of his father's medicines. Djibo revered his father but was an undisciplined son. Against his father's advice, he married at a young age, but his marriage lasted only a short time. He boasted of his great powers. He was duplicitous, often betraying his friends and his relatives. Djibo's behavior displeased his father. And so Mounmouni Koda sent his son to "sit" with Adamu Jenitongo in Tillaberi. Djibo served Adamu Jenitongo for three years, increasing substantially his knowledge of plants. Toward the end of his apprenticeship in Tillaberi, he received word that his family had moved to Mehanna, a village on the Niger's west bank some sixty kilometers north of Tillaberi.

Djibo boarded a bush taxi in Tillaberi. The driver skillfully negotiated rock-strewn tracks, deep sand, and the fallen branches of thorn trees. They passed Sakoire, Djamballa, Namarigungu, finally reaching Bonfebba—on market day. Scores of Mehanna boatmen were there who would take people and their cargo home that afternoon.

The people on Djibo's boat asked him: "Who are you? Where are you headed?"

Djibo replied, "I'm Djibo Sorko, son of Mounmouni Koda Sorko. I am going to Mehanna."

When the boat reached the Wissili rapids, the passengers cringed. One old man recited an Islamic prayer for protection.

"That won't help you, old man," Djibo said. "But don't worry. I am a sorko. I am of the river, and you have nothing to worry about."

They passed through Wissili rapids without incident.

Djibo reached Mehanna in late afternoon and asked after his family. He was directed to the western outskirts of town. Walking along a sandy road bordered by high mud-brick compound walls, he proceeded up toward the dune that towered over Mehanna. The walls that protected small rectangular mud-brick houses from public inspection soon gave way to low fences made of millet stalks tied to tree branches. These defined compounds of conical straw huts. Although the stalk fences afforded little privacy, they at least kept stray donkeys out of the compounds.

When the path came to its end, Djibo saw one last cluster, the home of the most recent arrivals, his family. The compound consisted of three huts set off from the bush by a circular millet-stalk fence. The first house was for his younger brother, Zakaribaba. The second house belonged to Hampsa, his sister. The third house, which faced the west, the direction of danger, was his father's.

His family greeted him with great delight.

"Baba," Djibo asked his father, "why did we move here from Ouallam? We liked Ouallam, did we not? We had respect in Ouallam. This is a Songhay town, and the Songhay do not like strangers, even if the strangers are sorkos."

"What you say is true, my son. But I am old, and an old sorko should be close to his river. Is there not truth in my words, my son?"

"There is indeed, Baba."

And so Djibo installed himself in Mehanna and took up his work as a sorko. His words compelled the spirits to swoop down from the heavens to take the bodies of their mediums. Like his patron spirit, Dongo, he resuscitated people who had been struck by lightning. His successes made Djibo all the more boastful. Wary of his bravado, Mehanna people preferred to seek the cures of Djibo's father, who, like the wise sorkos of the past, let his substantial deeds speak for him.

In 1976, Djibo Mounmouni made me his student. I memorized incantations and learned about plants sorkos use in their potions. People warned me about Djibo.

"People with swollen heads," I was told, "have nothing in them."

Others said: "Beware of Djibo. He will betray you. He doesn't like you; he likes your money."

Despite these warnings, I continued my studies with Djibo until I left Mehanna in June of 1977.

In 1979 Mounmouni Koda died at the age of seventy-seven. Death came to him swiftly. One day he took to his bed, sick, suffering from severe abdominal pains and nausea. He breathed with difficulty. Knowing that his time had come, he called his oldest son, Djibo, now a man of forty, to his deathbed. It was time to reveal to his son his greatest secrets. He gave Djibo his most prized medicines, including a powder that, like the sorko, could be submerged in water without becoming wet. He told Djibo how to get this powder from the river. He taught Djibo his most prized magic incantations. He warned Djibo about boastfulness and made him promise to keep these great secrets until it was time to pass them on to his own son. And then Mounmouni Koda died. Soon Djibo, like his father, would walk into the Niger River.

Djibo descended into the Niger River for the first time in 1981, when the spirits beckoned him to the water a full two years after his father's death. He was ready.

> Seven months ago, the king of the sky [Dongo] came to me in a dream. He said that my time had come. He said that I must now enter the river and walk to Harakoy's village. I left Mehanna on a Thursday evening and walked north all night along the riverbank. I approached Ayoru. There, the river is wide and deep. This is where the spirits have their village under the water. I was looking for a smooth black boulder. This boulder marks the spot where the sorko enters the river. Just before sunrise I found the boulder and I entered the river.
>
> I went into the river, but I did not become wet. I followed a path of smooth white sand. The more I walked, the whiter the sand became. I walked on. To my right and left I saw the river. I saw crocodiles and fishes, but whirlpools kept us separated.
>
> When the sand changed from white to dark gray, I saw three large jugs in a line. Sadyara, a large black snake with a horn on its head, was coiled next to the first jug. Frightened, I recited the Tooru's praise-poetry. Sadyara opened his mouth, hissed, and flicked his forked tongue. Harakoy Dikko sat to the other side of the first jug, swaying back and forth, back and forth, back and forth. Her eyes were covered with long white hair that touched the ground. She brushed her hair back and motioned for me to approach.
>
> I sang more Tooru praise-songs and came closer to the jugs. I saw a sacred tree and a sacred vine growing out of the dark gray ground. I removed some bark and broke off part of the vine. With these plants, I could save people whom lightning had

Djibo Mounmouni, sorko of Namarigungu and son of Mounmouni Koda.

struck. Behind the first jug, I saw the sacred kobe tree. If I could get some of its bark, I could enter the river any time. I took out my knife, but before I could get beyond the first jug, a force knocked me down. A voice said: "You cannot yet cut away the bark of the kobe tree."

The first jug was filled with fresh milk, which I drank. It was sweet. I moved ten feet to the second jug. It was filled with special sorko medicines: *sah nya, dugu nya, wali belinga.* I put a little bit of each powder in cloth pouches and put the pouches in my pockets. The third jug was filled with blood. There was a special vine floating on the surface. I recited an incantation and took it.

I sat down on the ground of the spirit village and scooped some of the dark gray soil into my pockets. I stood up to leave, but I could not find the white sandy path leading to our world. And so I recited the Tooru praise-poems again. The Tooru surrounded me. I screamed. They gave me a powder I had never seen and made the white sandy path reappear. A wind caught me from behind and pushed me away from the village of the spirits. Soon, I emerged from the river completely dry. A voice told me that I could return next year, but not before.[1]

Djibo collected the dark gray powder in Harakoy's village in January 1981. In his house six months later Djibo molded a hill of the dark gray powder on a flat piece of slate.

"Watch this," he told me.

He took the slate and powder and immersed it in a bowl filled with water. The form of the powder remained intact under water. He removed the powder and asked me to touch it. It was completely dry.

"This powder and the sorko," Djibo said, "are the same. When we enter the river, we emerge completely dry."

Origins of the Sorko

Sometime in the ancestral past, Nisile Bote and his wife, the river genie, Maka, celebrated the birth of a son. Faran Maka Bote, their son, grew up in Kare Kaptu, a village on the Niger River located near the border of present-day Niger and Benin.

Near Kare Kaptu, the Niger narrows and deepens as it cuts its way through the surrounding hills. Kare Kaptu was a few hundred meters from an island choked with green vines and creepers that entwined a thick assortment of island trees. River spirits lived on

Cendaaji, a sacred site on the Niger River.

the island of tangled vegetation. One of these was Zirbin Sangay Moyo, a spirit that transformed itself into a crocodile which delighted in killing local fisherman.

Distraught, Maka visited Harakoy Dikko, spirit queen of the Niger.

"My mother," she said, can you kill this terrible crocodile who is killing our sons?"

"Yes, my daughter," Harakoy agreed. "I'll take care of Zirbin Sangay Moyo."

Using her great powers in the river, Harakoy transformed Zirbin Sangay Moyo into a strip of iron which then sank to the bottom of the Niger. Maka entered the Niger and found the iron strip and brought it back to Kare Kaptu.

"My son," she said to Faran Maka Bote, "take his iron strip and use it for your hunting on the river."

From the strip, Faran made the first harpoon with which he became a great fisherman, killing more crocodiles, hippos, and manatees than he could count.

One day Faran announced his departure from Kare Kaptu.

"My mother," he told Maka, "I leave today to go to Gao. The river has many riches in the north."

In Faran's absence, Zinkibaru, a blind river genie, went to live on the river spirit island near Kare Kaptu. Through his magic charms and the sonority of his guitar, Zinkibaru mesmerized the river spirits and made them his captives. In this manner he took control of the Niger River. But Zinkibaru's victory was short-lived, for Faran Maka Bote, armed with his magic, his resolve, and his knowledge of the river, soon challenged Zinkibaru for control of the river spirits.[2]

"I will not allow that blind genie to control the Niger," he said to Santama, his companion.

But Zinkibaru made the first move in the battle between himself and Faran Maka Bote. Faran lived in Gao, where the the green of his rice fields stretched to the towering dune on the west bank of the Niger. Every night Zinkibaru came to those copious rice fields to play his guitar. The sounds of the guitar forced the fish of the Niger to devour Faran's rice. Zinkibaru also drove away from Gao the hippos—Faran's favorite food.

One day Faran went fishing and could find only two hippos.

"How can I bring home only two hippos from this hunt?" he complained to his aide, Santama.

"Something is terribly wrong, great one," Santama said.

"It must be that Zinkibaru," Faran suggested. "We must find him and kill his power."

So Faran and Santama left Gao to fight Zinkibaru. Faran soon found him on an island at the junction of seven rivers. Zinkibaru strummed his guitar; two river spirits beat drums made from gourds, and another river spirit played a one-string violin. The Tooru river spirits danced to the sweet music.

Faran said to Zinkibaru: "Give me your guitar."

Zinkibaru said: "You will have to fight for it. If you win, you will have my guitar and my river spirit captives. If I win I will take your dugout canoe."

Faran agreed to the duel.

Faran's compact body was topped by a head as big and round as Niger River squash. Zinkibaru's face, as pale as the midday Niger sky, sat atop a body that was stringy as Niger River grass.

The battle commenced. Faran came toward Zinkibaru, but Zinkibaru said: "The palm leaf will never capture the hippo."

This spell overcame Faran, who fell to the ground.

Zinkibaru took Faran's dugout and left.

Faran laid limply on the ground.

"Santama," he cried, "I have been shamed. We must go to Kare Kaptu and seek my mother's advice. She'll tell us what is to be done."

Faran called for his mother, who, being a genie, appeared shortly thereafter.

On seeing Maka, Faran wept.

His mother asked him: "Why are you crying?"

"My mother, I have been vanquished by Zinkibaru," Faran explained.

His mother said to him: "Faran, you have a big head, with nothing in it. To fight a spell you need a counterspell. If Zinkibaru said, 'The palm leaf will never capture a hippo,' you have only to reply, 'And if the rays of the sun are in front of the leaf?'"

Thus armed with powerful words, Faran and Santama took a large dugout and headed south in search of Zinkibaru. Faran was swifter than the river's current. He left Gao in the evening and by morning he was already at Sinder. He fished as he traveled, but on this trip the fishing was not good. Faran, who had a voracious appetite, captured a manatee, which he ate all by himself. Had he caught a hippo, he would have eaten most of it himself, giving only a small portion to Santama. All the while they searched for Zinkibaru, whom they could not find.

When Faran came to Runkuma, he saw the willowy figure of Zinkibaru, and the battle began. Faran went after the genie, but Zinkibaru escaped. Faran came to Duskogye and saw Zinkibaru. The battle began again and went on and on. But Zinkibaru escaped. The battle continued.

Faran went to throw Zinkibaru to the ground, but Zinkibaru said: "The palm leaf will never capture a hippo."

But this time Faran quickly replied: "And if the sun's rays are in front of the palm leaf?"

Zinkibaru fell to the ground. The genie musicians escaped, leaving the violin and the drums. Only the Tooru remained. Faran took Zinibaru's guitar. He took Zinibaru's Tooru captives and put them into his dugout. Santama took the violin and drums. Faran and Santama got in the dugout and returned up the river to Gao.[3]

With the powers of the Tooru under his control, Faran was better able to exploit the riches of the Niger River. Soon, however, Faran's control over the increasingly assertive river spirits weakened. Despite Faran's repertoire of magic, the quick-tempered Dongo, the deity of thunder, threatened the Niger fishermen.

One day Dongo set a village on fire with lightning, killing many people.

Dongo said: "I am angry that there is no bard to sing praises to me."

Harakoy Dikko spoke to her temperamental adopted son (Dongo): "My son, Sorko Faran Maka Bote will be your bard."

Taking with him a large clay vase, Dongo paid a visit to Faran, who had gone to inspect the burned village. Sensing his powerlessness in the wake of Dongo's destructive capacities, Faran begged Dongo's forgiveness: "King of the sky, I have wronged you. From this day on, I will honor you and submit to your powers."

Dongo gave Faran the clay vase and taught him the spirits' praise-poetry.

"Fill the vase with water," Dongo ordered.

Faran filled the vase with water. Dongo plunged his head into it. Slowly he lifted his head from the vase. Water dripping from his chin, he stared at the bodies strewn throughout the village. Dongo swaggered through the village, spitting water on the bodies. The dead became the living. And Dongo spoke to the audience of spirits and human beings:

> Now you are too old, Dikko [reference to Harakoy]. You should
> go back to the river. Cirey, Moussa, Hausakoy [other river spir-

its] and me, Dongo, we shall go up to the heavens. But you, Faran Baru [the youngest of the river spirits], you are still too young. You must remain with your mother, Dikko. Every year, we will come down to the river to see whether all is going well. . . . As for me, Dongo, I like no one, and I do not want to be pitied by anyone. . . . But if there is pain in my heart, I will kill someone.[4]

Called the *yene,* this mythic ritual was the first possession ceremony—a ceremony at which human beings could see the spirits.[5] Thereafter the spirits became invisible to most human eyes. At the second possession ceremony the following year, Faran recited his praise-poetry, and the musicians produced their clacks, rolls, and cries. As promised, the spirits swooped down from the heavens and took the bodies of human dancers.

Sorko in Songhay

Faran Maka Bote is the ancestor of the sorko, most of whom still live in the vicinity of the Niger River, which remains the Songhay spirits' source of life and power. Since that fateful day when Faran Maka Bote staged the first yene, many of his descendants through the patriline have been praise-singers to the spirits, playing the same role in possession ceremonies that bards play in political events. Some of the sorko along the Niger are also "masters of the river," or Do. When a man is "master of the water," it is said that he is of the water and can enter the Niger River and remain under water for long periods of time.

Abdou Kano of Mehanna told the following sorko story in December of 1985.

> My friend, a merchant like myself, had just bought a Swiss watch—a genuine one—at the Ayoru market. He was proud of it and was showing it to me and the other people on Mamadu's motor dugout. We had just left Ayoru. We were going to Mehanna. The boat was running with the current of the Niger, and as we came to the Cendaaji bend, a rapid pitched the boat up. The watch dropped overboard. He cried out in grief: "I took my watch off to show to Boubakar, and then the river swallowed it up."
>
> As it was the day of the market, our boat docked at Cendaaji. Although saddened by his loss, my friend went to the market. He told his sad tale to some of his cronies. "Wait a minute," one

of them said. "Something can be done." This man went into the center of the market and brought back with him two young men. "These men are sorkos, and they can help you."

After my friend described to the two sorkos his watch, they walked off toward the Niger. Sometime later they returned to our group. One of them thrust his open palm toward my friend. We all saw a beautiful Swiss watch.

"Is this not your watch?" the sorko asked smiling. My friend examined the watch. It was his indeed, and it was working perfectly. And do you know, those sorkos were completely dry.[6]

There are hundreds of similar stories about the superhuman feats of sorkos. From the river they recover watches, sewing machines, and the snagged bodies of drowning victims. They talk with certain fish, and they visit Harakoy's village for weeks, months, or years. Some people say that rather than dying, the spirits of old sorkos enter the bodies of certain fish, manatees, or crocodiles.

Central to the mission of the sorkos—no matter the domain of each one's expertise—is their relationship to the spirits, from whom they receive their powers. Without the blessing of their spirit father, Dongo, the patron of Faran Maka Bote, sorkos are powerless. And so sorkos wear black, an homage to Dongo, and they eat plants and barks associated with Dongo. At possession ceremonies they sing praises to the spirits, hoping to coax them into the body of a medium. Praise-singing reinforces the link between sorkos and their spirits; it also reinforces their powers in and out of water.

Zakaribaba

Zakaribaba Mounmouni has been a practicing sorko for more than fifteen years. Like his brother Djibo, Zakaribaba was initiated by his father, Mounmouni Koda. Unlike his brother, he is short and pudgy. His round face and soft eyes immediately put his interlocutor at ease. Since adolescence the two brothers have walked different paths. Manipulation of the spirits' power fascinated Djibo; herbalism impassioned Zakaribaba. Djibo boasted about his increasing powers; Zakaribaba practiced his craft quietly. The two brothers lived with other brothers and sisters in a large compound in Mehanna. Djibo's grass hut was always in disarray; Zakaribaba's house had been built with deliberation. It was round, like a traditional grass hut, but larger. Indeed, from the outside it appeared to be an ordinary grass structure, but once inside one could see the difference. The floor and the lower portion of the walls were baked mud—at once cool and clean.

People summoned Djibo from far away to treat their supernaturally induced disorders. Zakaribaba remained in Mehanna for the most part to care for people suffering from worldly ailments. If one showed Zakaribaba a plant, he named it easily. Then he might describe the medicinal uses, if any, of its root, bark, leaves, and stems.

"How do you know which part of the plant to use?" I asked him in 1984.

"I'm glad you asked. I will open your head to this," he said, taking delight in my question. "You choose the root of a plant for one kind of illnesses, like skin sores, and the leaves for another sickness, say intestinal worms."

"Is there more to it?"

Zakaribaba beamed. "Of course there is. The stem of a plant has one application if picked during the day and another if picked at night."

Unlike his brother, Zakaribaba did not expect to travel to Harakoy's under-river village. His mission was on earth with his clients.

One afternoon in July of 1984 a mother brought her wheezing child to Zakaribaba's hut: "Zakaribaba, do something. My child is going to die. Do something!"

"Calm yourself, mother," he told the woman. "We will care for your child."

He held the child in his strong hands and massaged her congested chest.

"The child has a closed heart [asthma]."

"Will she die?"

Zakaribaba smiled. "Not today."

He fanned the charcoal in his brazier and put on them an array of aromatic roots. The hut filled with acrid smoke. He mixed an assortment of green, beige, and copper powders with clarified butter and rubbed the gritty pomade on the girl's chest.

"Maymouna," he called to his wife who was preparing dinner, "bring me a pot of boiled water."

Minutes later a woman as thin and knotty as a drought-ravaged acacia root appeared with a steaming pot of water. After searching through his medicines for a moment, Zakaribaba pulled from a sack a short root, which he put in the pot.

"We'll wait a little while and then your daughter will drink this tea."

Although she continued to wheeze, the little girl seemed to be out of danger. The mother was relieved.

"Does she have to drink the tea now?"

"Oh, yes. She must." Zakaribaba poured some of the tea into a plastic cup.

"Drink this, little one."

The girl drank the tea.

Zakaribaba poured the rest of the tea into a metal pot.

"Take this home with you. She should drink another cup at dinner, and another before she goes to bed. By tomorrow, she should be completely cured."

"How much do I owe you?"

"If she is better, come back tomorrow and bring me five hundred francs [$2]."

The next day the woman returned the metal pot and gave Zakaribaba five hundred francs.

Djingarey

Dressed in green fatigues that did not camouflage his puffy face and small black eyes, Djingarey surveyed the auto depot, a dusty square adjacent to the Tillaberi market. Djingarey's huge head sat directly on his massive shoulders; his enormous belly extended beyond his barrel chest. Each day Djingarey rifled through bush taxi and truck cargo in search of contraband—the primary task of the Nigerien border patrol. Despite his status as a civil servant, Djingarey practiced as a sorko.

Highly respected as a sorko—he was a good organizer—and as a soldier—he had diligently served the government for more than twenty years—Djingarey treated his friends with unmilitary kindness. When I arrived in Tillaberi in 1983, I had been cramped with twenty other people in the carrier of the Peugeot 404 for three hours in 120 degree heat. I stumbled out of the carrier and stood in the searing sunlight as two boys untied my baggage from the taxi's roof. My hair was dry as straw. Sweat stains spotted my shirt. Salt had caked on my forehead.

"Hello, Monsieur Paul," Djingarey said. "Welcome back."

"Thank you, *sodje* [the Songhay term for modern soldiers]."

"A long trip?"

"Two flat tires and many police stops."

Djingarey nodded. "Are you staying with the old man [a reference to Adamu Jenitongo]?"

"Yes."

Djingarey knew well that I would have to hire two boys to carry my things to the zima's compound, a distance of two and a half kilometers over dunes. He must have taken pity on my sorry condition. "Come, Monsieur Paul. I'll drive you there." We hopped into his ancient Citroen Deux Chevaux and drove to Adamu Jenitongo's. Had his superior found him absent from his auto depot assignment, Djingarey would have been disciplined. To Djingarey, the extension of graciousness to a weary guest, an important Songhay tradition, was more important than his immediate civic responsibilities.

Unlike Djibo and his brother Zakaribaba, Djingarey is strictly a praise-singing sorko. From 1981 to 1985, his primary focus was the Tillaberi possession troupe. Given his dual status, Djingarey offered his services as an intermediary between the local government administrator, the *sous-préfet,* and the Tillaberi possession troupe. He always informed the sous-préfet, for example, about upcoming possession ceremonies. Sometimes Djingarey organized possession ceremonies himself. In 1981 he organized a second rain dance in Tillaberi. The first rain ceremony, which had been organized by Adamu Jenitongo, had been spoiled by dissension in the possession troupe and the rains had not come. Fearing for the harvest, Djingarey decided to organize a second, remedial ceremony. Three days after the ceremony, the rains came. During the peak of the drought in 1984 Djingarey organized a series of ceremonies—some in Tillaberi and some at sacred sites in the bush—to bring rain to the parched fields. But these efforts resulted only in dust storms; dissension in the community had spoiled the ceremonies.

"When there is dissension in a community," Adamu Jenitongo once said, "the spirits take the rain away from us."

Djingarey was transferred from Tillaberi in 1985.

Djimba

Djimba was born in Ouallam, a town in Zerma country that is a major center of possession activity. Djimba's grandmother's brother, Seku Godji, was among the most famous of all sorkos of the last several generations. Because of his affection for his sister's offspring (*nyaize*), Seku Godji taught his secrets to Hamadu, his

A sorko reciting praise-poetry during a Hauka ceremony in Tillaberi.

sister's son, and to Hamadu's children Ide, Hamani, Djimba, and Mounkaila, all of whom became practicing sorkos.

Djimba's brothers worked in the Ouallam region. As the youngest and least experienced brother, Djimba decided to leave Ouallam for a new beginning in Tera. By the time he went to Tera he was as towering and tough as an acacia.

In Tera, a center of Songhay tradition and culture, Djimba became the resident sorko. There were other sorkos in town, but no one dared to compete with the man from Ouallam. Djimba's services as a praise-singer and a healer were therefore in high demand in Tera and the surrounding countryside. During the dry season he traveled frequently to other Songhay towns to perform—an itinerant sorko.

In December of 1982 Djimba came to Tillaberi while I was in residence. He frequently visited Adamu Jenitongo's compound, and when he learned that I, like Jean Rouch, asked questions about the spirits, Djimba attempted to become my informant. He taught me a few of his incantations and showed me his altar, several vials of perfume, a mirror, and a *baata,* or sacred box in which blood offerings are made.

"I am of a great sorko family, the family of Seku Godji," he explained. "I know more about possession than any of these fools in Tillaberi. You cannot find a better person, Monsieur Paul. Even when you go away, you will write me your questions, and I will answer them. My brothers and I understand what the European is after."

I was intrigued but suspicious. "But, Djimba," I told him. "I already have a teacher in Tillaberi."

"You mean the old man?" he asked, referring to Adamu Jenitongo.

"Yes."

"Ah, he has power, yes. But he will not tell you what you want to know. I will. I know more than he does about the spirits."

This man, I thought at the time, had the gall to insult a revered zima, Adamu Jenitongo, in his own compound. How could I ever work with such a man?

Djimba spent two weeks in Tillaberi in December of 1982. On the last day of his stay, he knocked on my door, disturbing my siesta.

"Oh, Djimba. How are you?"

"Fine, Monsieur Paul. And your health?"

"No complaints, Djimba."

"I am leaving tomorrow, Monsieur Paul."

"So soon?"

"The work in Tillaberi is finished. We sorko must move on. Tomorrow I'll be in Sakoire. In two markets, I'll move on to Djamballa."

"May God protect you on your journey, Djimba."

"Amen. Thank you Monsieur Paul."

Djimba took his leave and I went back to my bed. Two hours later I left my house only to discover Djimba biding his time under the canopy in Adamu Jenitongo's compound. I walked to the next house in the compound and greeted Jemma, Adamu Jenitongo's second wife.

"What is he doing here, my mother?"

"He says he's waiting for you."

Suddenly, I realized that I had unwittingly become Djimba's patron and that he would not leave until I had given him a going-away gift. Dressed in his black robe and fondling his cane, Djimba seemed anything but an obsequious client. Knowing him to be stubborn, I reconciled myself to offering him a cash gift.

"Djimba," I began. "You are still here?"

"I've been waiting for you, Monsieur Paul."

I gave him five-thousand francs ($20). He smiled. "Now, I can move forward, Monsieur Paul. Now we can work together. Send me your letters."

"I will, Djimba."

He gave me his cane, the wooden base of which had been covered in red leather.

"Take the cane to America, Monsieur Paul. Put it in your house or walk with it. This way, you will not forget Djimba. Next year, when you return, we will work together."

Djimba's offer was a tempting one, but I never had the opportunity to continue our relationship. In 1984 Djimba died under tragic circumstances, the victim of his own hubris.

In 1983 Djimba's activities in Tera brought him into competition with the Tera sohancis, sorcerers who were direct patrilineal descendants of Sonni Ali Ber. Reputed to be among the most powerful and vengeful families of sohancis, the Tera group resented Djimba's intrusion in their affairs. In the hope of cornering an even greater share of the Tera market in traditional medicine, Djimba boasted of great personal power which exceeded that of the local sohancis. In most circumstances, the Tera sohancis would have "fixed" Djimba by placing a spell on him to teach him a lesson in humility. The chief of the sohancis, however, had great respect for Djimba's father and would not allow a spell to be cast.

But Djimba's quest for money and prestige knew no bounds. In 1984 he attended a sohanci ceremony in Tera. At the ceremony, sohancis dance to the tam-tam beat to enter into trance. In trance, some sohancis become clairvoyant; others vomit their magic chain (*sisiri*) which repels all evil. The sohanci trance, however, is a difficult one to achieve. And so the sohancis danced and danced as the considerable audience contributed money to a kitty.

Since the Tera sohancis had invited the public to witness their ceremony, Djimba attended the dance.

"I am the greatest sorcerer in Tera," he proclaimed to the throng. Then he swaggered up to the sohancis' kitty, took all of their money, and returned home.

Although the leader of Tera sohancis had been tolerant before, he could not ignore such an insult. Three days later a serious illness swept into Djimba's body. He suspected that the Tera sohanci had "fixed" him as punishment for his affront (*sambeli*—throwing the magic arrow). Knowing that Western medicine could not cure him, he rushed to Ouallam so that his brothers might save him. He died en route, however, having defecated his intestines onto the sand.

Sorko and Their Words

As do many peoples of the world, most Songhay believe that words are not merely neutral instruments of reference. Words can be dangerously charged with the power of the heavens and of the ancestors. In Songhay country there are three domains of word power: sorcery, poetry, and possession. Sorcerers in Songhay country control secret words that can heal, maim, or kill people. The power-laden words are transmitted from the sorcerer's mouth into various substances—pastes, roots, barks, ablutions—which are ingested or rubbed onto the body. Sometimes the words are simply spoken into the wind. These can become to borrow Jeanne Favret-Saada's memorable phrase, "deadly words." [7]

The importance of words is denoted in Songhay myths. The myths about Faran Maka Bote highlight the culture hero's control of two interconnected resources: magic and the words that make magic possible. According to other Songhay myths, the spirits revealed the words of magic incantations to the ancestors who taught those words to their sons, and their sons to their sons, and so on, passing them on to the current generation. [8]

The bard's world is the second domain of word power. Bards or griots generally recite their praise-poetry at formal ceremonies: births, weddings, homecomings, initiations of chiefs, and other political festivals (national holidays in the republic of Niger, Islamic holidays). Praise-poetry may encompass genealogy, historical events, and a living person's accomplishments. The bard's recitation of the name of a person's celebrated ancestor is believed to imbue that person with the force of that ancestor. Here the sound of the ancestor's name is sacred and powerful. When the sound enters the body of the descendant, it is transformative.[9]

> Words do not just have meaning—they are breath and vibrations of air, constituted and shaped by the body and motives of the speaker, physically contacting and influencing the addressee. Some informants liken the effort of a *griot's* praise-song on his addressee to the effect of wind on fire (both metaphorically and literally, since air and fire are supposed to be basic constituents of the body).[10]

This kind of word power is especially important during possession ceremonies. Adamu Jenitongo explained that it is the praise-poetry directed to the spirits that obliges the spirits to take the bodies of their mediums. The sound of the powerful ancient words penetrates the bodies of the dancers as they prepare to receive their respective spirits. Sorkos are the owners of this dynamic praise-poetry. Sometimes the sorko will place his forefinger on the medium's shoulder as he recites praise-poetry. This gesture ensures the passage of ancestral energy from past to present, from heaven to earth, from sorko to medium.

Because of their word-power, sorkos do not give their praise-poetry to scholars in exchange for money. To record possession praise-poetry, scholars must learn it themselves.[11] And so Djibo Sorko of Mehanna made me his student. In this way, I learned spirit praise-poetry. We sat in his house and I memorized the poetry line by line. When I had learned a verse, I etched a small straight line in the sand. We progressed verse by verse and line by line until I had memorized the praise-poem. Memorization is easy. Not so, however, is understanding the full meaning of a praise-poem. The most powerful sorkos, in fact, spend their adult lives studying the praise-poems they committed to memory in their youth.

The most important praise-poem of the sorko is called "Tooru che," or the Tooru spirits' chant. The poem recounts in an oblique

and mysterious way both the origin and the particular character-
istics of the Tooru spirits.

> She gave birth to Sentenga.
> She gave birth to Mantenga.
> She gave birth to Banio and then
> Gave birth to Red Banio.
> The Sah tree.
> The Dugu tree.
> The Wali Belinga tree.
> The Kasaa Tobe tree.
> The queen of the great festival,
> Dikko [queen of the river].
> The queen of the little festival,
> Dikko.
>
> The great river's bulenga tree.
> It has a Kwomo Kosi tree.
> Its hand leaves the Sami tree.
> Its hand returns to the Sami tree.
> Wandu will heal and make one strong.
> There is Wandu. It stands in pure white sand.
> The sand has food and water.
> If the uninitiated take from this Tooru sand,
> They will go mad.
> Those who know the Tooru will
> Eat this special food and laugh.
>
> Mala's [spirit of lightning] work is quiet and forceful.
> Health and God's blessing.
> They ask: "What have you taken?"
> They say: "Sorcery."
> When they speak the words of magic,
> They eat magic cake.
> The sorcery is strong.
> The mother chicken does not
> Clean dirt from her chick's eyes.
>
> Nya Beri has power in and
> Out of water.
> She is the guardian of the
> Tooru behind the house.
> For them there are prayers only
> To the spirits, not to Allah.

They killed 150 people with their spell.
Their sister also killed 150 people with her spell.

Moussa Nyori.
Men are carried on his shoulder.
He carries a man and steals a
Man's body fibers,
Changing them into black eggs.
This is how he takes a man and
Slings him over his shoulder.
If he should take a man's head, the
Man's head fibers will bubble like boiling water.
If he stops in a man's body, the
Man must not lift his ankle.
He is Moussa Nyori.
He awakened the angels and sees them.
One must not hurt oneself by
Doing bad deeds.
When you take a cowry shell for magic, it
Is lost to the spirits.
The spirits feel sadness from their loss.
There is ever more sadness in the
Sorko's N'Debbi chant.

There is strength of body.
There is strength of eye.
He is the master of strength, power, and
Force. Dongo knows more than any
Sorko and any sorko's slave.
He strikes and they fall to the left.
He strikes and they fall to the right.
He says that his shadow covers the sun
And that the sun is his shadow.[12]

Being the deity of thunder, Dongo is a principal in the most important possession ceremony of the Songhay year, the *yena-andi*, or the rain dance (see chap. 6). Besides being the most feared of the Songhay deities, Dongo is also considered the patriarch of the sorko. Sorkos wear black, which is Dongo's color of choice. They burn resins, which are Dongo's scents of choice. In their huts they keep small hatchets to which are attached bells—Dongo's weapon of choice. In some of their compounds they keep black goats—Dongo's familiar. To pay homage to their master,

Sorko Djibo Mounmouni and his sacred rock (*wanzam*).

they burn the dried fat of a black goat. Throughout the year, they eat plants and pastes that Dongo prescribes. Every Friday they make a sacrifice to Dongo: a black chicken, a sheep, a goat. In exchange, Dongo gives the sorko supernatural powers. In the powerful shadow of Dongo sorkos heal, maim, or kill. They dwell under the river and emerge from it completely dry.

A sorko's most precious possessions, however, are his words, the very sounds that Dongo taught Faran Maka Bote in the distant past. Without these words, a sorko cannot heal, maim, or kill. Without these words, he cannot dwell under the Niger River. Without these words, he cannot visit Harakoy's village. Without these words he cannot sing praises to the Tooru. Without these words the powerful link between present and past would be broken and Songhay would be doomed.

Ali Godji of Garie.

5

CRIES OF THE VIOLIN, RHYTHMS OF THE DRUM

He was afraid the first time he went to Niamey. Having spent all of his fifteen years in his father's compound in Kowra Ceeri ("broken spoon," lit.), a village 180 kilometers northeast of Niamey, Mamadu did not know what to expect from life in the city.

"I was afraid of Niamey. There were so many people, and so many cars. What did I know about the city?"

He was a slight boy with bulging eyes, who preferred to listen rather than speak to his elders. His father, a drummer in Kowra Ceeri, had sent him to Niamey to find work. Since farming and drumming did not provide the necessary cash to pay taxes to the colonial government, the family needed additional income.

Too poor to pay for motorized transport to Niamey, young Mamadu walked to the colonial capital, carrying only a small cloth satchel that contained his worldly belongings—two tattered cloth shirts, a pair of underpants, and one bar of lye soap. These things complemented his traveling outfit: a pair of white *tumbalaagi*, the balloon drawstring trousers that leave ample room in the crotch for the swelling heat of Niger, a shirt cut from a burlap sack, and a pair of leather thongs.

And so he walked and walked, following paths through forests of thorn trees, trails around dried-up water holes, and tracks over dunes. Some nights he slept in the bush. In Ouallum he spent the night with his older brother. In Simiri he stayed with his cousin. Finally he reached Niamey; it was everything he thought it would be: crowded streets, large markets, dust in the air kicked up by the unending passage of donkeys, camels, and cars. He walked into the center of town, passing open sewers where vultures huddled and soapy water puddles where children frolicked. The stench in Niamey, more pungent than the garbage pit of his family's compound, made his head spin.

He walked into a large market and asked a spice vendor for directions to Gamkalle, his paternal uncle's neighborhood. The vendor directed him toward the Niger River. He walked a bit more to the west and then saw the Niger, snaking its way south through the dry bush. In the shallows, women washed their family's clothing; men washed themselves. He slid down an embankment and asked a group of male bathers the way to Gamkalle.

"Just walk downstream for awhile. You'll see it."

Thirty minutes later, he finally came upon Gamkalle and asked a man for directions to his uncle's compound.

"Ah, so you are Mounkaila's nephew? His godji speaks to the heavens; it is sweet." The man directed young Mamadu to the compound.

Mamadu's uncle was a gaunt man who seemed never to smile. His walled compound was a large rectangular space at the western end of which stood a thatched canopy, a place to shade oneself at midday. Constructed against three of the compound walls were four drab-brown mudbrick houses. Three connected houses for Mounkaila's wives and their children were attached to the northern wall. A large single dwelling, Mounkaila's, was attached to the eastern wall.

"As soon as I arrived my uncle told me to put my things in his house. He told me he didn't like lazy boys. He said that if I wanted to stay in Niamey, I had to work. My job in the compound was to wash the cooking pots and sweep the courtyards. In time, my uncle expected me to find work in the city."

Mamadu soon found work as a cleanup man at the Niamey slaughterhouse. He worked from dawn to noon and returned to work in the late afternoon after a siesta. One afternoon a man who identified himself as a violinist confronted Mamadu as he dozed under his uncle's canopy.

"Do you know me?" the violinist asked.

"I don't," Mamadu responded.

"You don't?"

"No," Mamadu reaffirmed.

"Well, I *know* you. The spirits have directed me to you. You must make a godji for yourself. Go find kubu. Go get nails. Go and get horsehair."

"Horsehair?"

"Get either sobe or guru horsehair."

Mamadu went to his boss, a young Frenchman. For some reason the French liked horsemeat, and as a consequence there was no lack of horsetails at the slaughterhouse. He asked the director for horsetails.

"Horsetails? Why horsetails?" the baffled Frenchman asked.

"To make violin," Mamadu answered in his Pidgin French.

"Yes, go ahead. Take as many as you want."

"Yes, I take one."

And so Mamadu found a sobe horsetail.

"I went there and got a sobe horsetail. Then I found kubu for the neck and a small gourd for the body. I took these things to my family's house. My uncle gave me lizard skin which I stretched over the gourd. I fastened the skin to the gourd with nails and cut a small hole in the skin. I attached the neck to the gourd and placed my horsehair string on the instrument. I asked my uncle to "open" the godji. He cut the throat of a black chicken and let its blood drip into the cavity. Night fell and I slept under the canopy. Morning came. Noon. And when the sun began to descend in the sky, they came to me and said:

"'Come. We have a problem and we need a godji player.'"

Although he had heard possession music since childhood, no one had taught him how to play the godji. He wondered what would happen. His uncle gave him a bow and Mamadu went to a man's compound in Niamey and played for the first time. His music was sweet. He played for seven days and received 15,000 CFA ($60).

"And that's how I came to be called Mamadu Godji."

Since the time of his salad years in Niamey, Mamadu Godji has been an itinerant musician. He spent the early years of his career in the Zerma areas of the Republic of Niger (Ouallam, Simiri, Dosso, Loga). Between 1969 and 1980 he lived in Songhay areas, spending the longest amount of time in the village of Koro Gusu, (the hyena's hole). The village, located on the road between Tera and Wanzerbe, lies in a deep depression next to a permanent pond. Cooled by the shade of tall trees, the village, in lush green, contrasts markedly with the parched dunes that rise to the village's north, east, and south. West of Koro Gusu a treeless plain pancakes to the horizon. While he was in Koro Gusu, Mamadu often traveled to Wanzerbe to play his violin for the possession troupe of the famed village of sorcerers. Mamadu prospered and was able to marry a Koro Gusu woman, who in 1980 gave birth to a boy. In 1984, the year of famine in Niger, hunger drove Mamadu and his family to Tillaberi, where he lives now in a decrepit grass hut, five hundred meters from Adamu Jenitongo's compound.

Usually the arrival of a violinist in a village is a welcome event. Most villages must send for violinists—at great cost. But there was already an established violinist, Daouda, in Tillaberi, which severely limited Mamadu Godji's bookings. To feed his family, he worked in the rice fields. But Mamadu did not complain about

Halidu Yaya (on gasi), Mamadou Godji, and Moru Adamu (on gasi) of
Tillaberi.

being second fiddle in Tillaberi. He attended possession ceremonies and played his violin only when he was asked to do so.

Sound in the Songhay World

Sound is a powerful sensation in Songhay cultural experience. It is the only force that can penetrate the body—hence, the emotive power of music in the world.[1] Just as the sounds of words are important in the practice of sorcery and praise-singing in Songhay, so the sounds of certain musical instruments are central to Songhay possession ceremonies. These instruments are the monochord violin (*godji*) and the calabash drum (*gasi*).

The resonating cavity of the godji consists of half of a large hard gourd that has been cut along the axis. The opening of the resonating cavity is parallel to the neck of the violin, and its diameter averages about twenty-eight centimeters.[2] The violin's cavity is covered by *bo* lizard skin (*Varanus nilotica*), which is stretched over the opening and fastened to the instrument with either small nails or the thorns of the *garbey* tree (*Balanites aegyptica*). The instrument's neck is a simple stick of wood, generally seventy-five centimeters in length, cut from the *kubu* tree (*Combretum micantrum*). The neck is inserted into the resonating cavity about three centimeters below the point where the gourd was cut in half. The violin string consists of black hair clipped from a horse's tail. This hair can come only from one of two kinds of horses: *sobe,* a black horse with white hoofs and a black tail, or *guro,* a dark-brown horse with a white face, brown hoofs, and a black tail. The horsehair is tied to the end of the neck and to a piece of wood attached at the far end of the resonating cavity. The violinist pulls the string taut by pushing a small wooden bridge into position. The bow is an arc of wood to which is attached more black hair clipped from the correct horse's tail.

When the violinist plays the godji he produces a sound similar to a high-pitched wail. In Songhay one says that the godji "cries" (*a ga he*). Adamu Jenitongo often said: "The godji cries for me, it cries for you; it cries for the people of Tillaberi; it cries for all our people."[3]

Mentioned in the Faran Maka Bote myths, the godji is at least as old as the Songhay people. But it is more than an instrument linking Songhay with their ancestors. Adamu Jenitongo told me that "the sound of the godji penetrates us and makes us feel the presence of the ancestors [*don borey*]. We hear the sound and know that we are on the path of the ancestors. The sound is irresistible. We cannot be unaffected by it and neither can the spirits. When they hear it 'cry,' it penetrates them. Then they become excited and swoop down and take the body of a medium."[4] The godji's sound links the Songhay present and past. Its wailing reinforces deep-seated cultural themes about the nature of life and death, the origin of Songhay, and the juxtaposition of the social and spirit worlds.

In the very process of constructing his instrument, the violinist infuses it with the force of the ancestors. At the kubu tree from which he will cut the wood for the fret, he recites:

> In the name of God the merciful,
> I come to cut the wood for the violin.
> Today is Wednesday, a sacred day.
> In the name of God the merciful.
> I testify to the heavens.
> I testify to the east.
> I testify to the north.
> I testify to the south.
> N'Debbi venerates God.
> I do not have white eyes.
> Ndebbi came and gave knowledge to the ancestors.
> The ancestors came and transmitted the knowledge to Maade.
> Maade transmitted it to Gunabo.
> Gunabo transmitted it to Sibto.
> Sibto came and transmitted it to me.
> Sibto gave to me my burden.
> I have come today to cut the
> Wood of the violin on this Wednesday.
> In the name of God.[5]

In the first part of the text the musician announces his task to the social and spirit worlds: to cut the sacred wood for the violin, which can be undertaken only on a Wednesday. When specialists take something from the earth—in this case wood from a tree—they must restore to the universe the harmony they have disturbed. The musician therefore speaks (testifies) to the heavens.

> He speaks to the earth.
> He speaks to the east.
> He speaks to the west.
> He speaks to the north.
> He speaks to the south.

This testimony, in effect, brings into balance the violent forces of the universe. He talks then of N'Debbi, the intermediary between the distant High God and the mortals who inhabit the earth. The musician, who does not have "white eyes" (a reference to the spirits), is brave, as must be anyone who seeks the power to contact or beckon the spirits. The spirits can easily kill a man or a woman who displeases them.[6]

Even with its neck of kubu the godji is not yet ready to be played. First, it must be "opened" so that the force of the spirits can flow through its cavity. On a Thursday, the sacred day of the spirits, the musician sacrifices over his violin a white, a red, and a black chicken (the colors correspond to the major figures of the spirit world: Harakoy Dikko [white], Cirey [red], and Dongo [black]).[7] As the chicken blood runs into the cavity of the violin, the musician chants the following text.

> I pray to God.
> I pray to God and his messenger.
> I pray to the ancestors and their descendants
> In the name of God.
> I have come to pray to you, Dandu Urufurma [father of all the
>   spirits].
> Dandu liked having children so much that he engendered Uwata.
> She engendered "plait-to-the-thighs."
> She engendered "sweep-water-with-his beard."
> She engendered "pull-up-the-baobab-to-pick-your-teeth."
> When trust goes away, life slips away.
> When trust returns, life also returns.[8]

This text reinforces the links between past and present, the ancestors and the moderns, the powerful and the powerless. The names, "plait-to-the-thighs," "sweep-water-with-his-beard," and "pull-up-the-baobab-to-pick-his-teeth," protect the true identities of the offspring of Uwata, the Tooru's ancestor. They also suggest that the deities are superhuman and powerful. If there is no trust in the power of the spirits and the ancestors, the force of life slips away. But the force of life can return when human beings demonstrate their trust in the spirits. The godji is a material link between the Songhay past and present, between the powerful and powerless. The violinist is the human link between social and spirit worlds. The sounds he produces with his violin call the spirits to the social world.

Daouda Godji of Tillaberi.

Daouda

Daouda Godji was born in the Zermagunda town of Fagel Kaabey in 1953, the oldest among three brothers and four sisters. As a child, Daouda declined to do household chores. As a young man, Daouda refused to work in his father's millet fields and instead played with his friends, although on occasion he helped his father weed and harvest.

Daouda's behavior disgusted his father, Idrissa.

"You, my son, are an Anasara [European]," he told him.

"You're just like those Europeans who rule us; you think you're too good to work with your hands."

Daouda never responded to his father's frequent exhortations.

"I spit on your laziness," his father fumed.

At fifteen Daouda married, an act that also exasperated his father.

"How could a boy so young get married?" he wondered aloud to his wife. "Most Songhay men don't marry until they are in their thirties."

As his father predicted, the marriage soon ended in divorce. Daouda grew bored in Fegel Kabey, a small village near Filingue, about two-hundred kilometers north and east of Niamey. A year after his divorce, Daouda left his village for Maradi, a major commercial center in the Hausa-speaking region of Niger. He worked for two years in the Maradi peanut fields before tiring of it and returning to Fegel Kaabey.

Having grown used to life in the city, however, Daouda did not last long in Fegel Kabey. This time he headed west for Niamey, capital of the Niger republic. Although he liked the life in Niamey's Bar Moustache, his drinking and womanizing soon depleted his resources. Three months after his arrival in Niamey, Daouda was back in Fegel Kabey. He began to sell kola nuts in his and other villages.

"When I sold kola then, I was a mean son [izo foutu]. I made a lot of money, but gave none of it to my father. I killed all my money on women."

Although 1974 was a lean year, Daouda's father threw him out again. Having heard that there was food and work along the Niger River, Daouda left for Tillaberi. He had just enough money to pay for his transport. But Daouda's truck broke down en route to Tillaberi. Since Daouda had no money left, he did not eat for two days. When he finally got to Tillaberi he begged for some rice at the market. Would he find work in town? Would he be able to eat? Where would he sleep?

Like all recent arrivals in town, Daouda settled in the neighborhood of strangers which was close to Adamu Jenitongo's compound. He soon found periodic work in the rice fields. Sometimes he made mudbricks, receiving a few francs for each brick he produced. In his spare time, Daouda attended possession ceremonies in Adamu Jenitongo's compound.

Beaten down by the climate, hunger, and his social circumstances, Daouda lumbered around Tillaberi for several years. He lived in a run-down grass hut. He worked sporadically, ate irregularly, and bathed infrequently. Women took no interest in him. Men pitied him. One day Daouda asked a neighbor for rice.

"I reserve my rice for true beggars. You can work. You can feed yourself. You are a lazy worthless child."

During a possession ceremony in 1977, the spirit Fulan, a Hausa deity, took the head of Adamu Jenitongo. Fulan ran up to Daouda, who was seated on the ground, and yanked him to his feet.

"Daouda," Fulan said. "Daouda, I want you to play the godji."

Daouda had never played the violin.

"Take that godji," Fulan ordered, pointing to the instrument being played by the musician in residence, Ali Godji, "and play for me."

Ali Godji gave Daouda his violin and bow. Daouda sat on a stool and played the violin.

"Daouda's godji is sweet," proclaimed Altinne, a zima. "It comes from the heavens."

Since that day to the present, Daouda Godji has been the principal violinist in Tillaberi. He says, "The spirits saved me from myself."

Because he is a talented musician, Daouda is often asked to play at ceremonies in distant villages. At first, the music made him happy. In 1978 he married Amina, a woman from Filingue. She bore him two sons and and one daughter. Since Amina was a civil servant, Daouda's family was relatively prosperous. Daouda worked regularly, ate heartily every day, and washed with scented soap.

Daouda's carefree spirit returned. He spent months away from home in search of possession ceremonies. He earned "not a little amount of money," as he put it, which, despite his happy marriage, he "killed" on women and clothes. Amina tolerated Daouda's frequent absences and continuous philandering. She had her job with the government, her children, and her many friends. Besides, there were spirit mediums in her family too; she knew the great spiritual significance of Daouda's gift. The spirits had commanded him to play. His music came directly from the heavens— a blessing.

But the spirits keep an unforgiving watch on those they bless. If the blessed do not make the necessary offerings to the spirits, they are punished. In 1984 Amina died of hepatitis. Daouda knew well that hepatitis is a viral disease that can attack anyone. But why had it attacked Amina? Daouda was convinced that his behavior had provoked the spirits' retribution; he was to blame for his wife's untimely death. Morose, he sank into a deep depression. Unable to care for his children, Daouda sent them to live with his affines in Filingue. Months passed. Daouda refused to play his godji; he refused to eat. Instead of working, he sat despondent in his compound wallowing in his own filth.

A young woman, Alzouma, began to visit him. She brought him food and looked after him during his period of mourning, which lasted well beyond the forty days stipulated in Islam. Despite the attentions of Alzouma, Daouda had regressed to the beggar he had been before he took up the violin.

Paying no heed to Adamu Jenitongo's advice, Daouda married Alzouma. Daouda stopped looking for women with whom to "kill" his money, but his new wife continued to see her former lovers. When Daouda complained about her infidelity, she moved to her mother's house. When he begged her to come back, she returned, and their domestic life was peaceful until Alzouma began to see her lovers again. Daouda complained. Alzouma left. He begged her to come back, and so on.

By 1985 Daouda, still a young man, had lost much of his hair. His deeply wrinkled face and his stooped posture belied his relative youth. When he visited me that year, I expressed my sympathies.

"Fonda tilas, Daouda." (The obligatory road leads to death.)

"Tilas, walla." (It is obligatory, indeed.)

"Daouda," I said. "You know how much I liked Amina."

"She's gone. It will never be the same, Paul. One day she was healthy, and then she was sick. She returned home to Filingue, and died there."

"You've suffered, my friend."

"Yes. I am sad all the time."

Daouda exaggerated a bit. Yes, he was sad except when he played his godji, the sound of which brought a smile to his face. When I saw him in January of 1986, Daouda was frequently ill, sometimes too ill to play at possession ceremonies. And yet, music is his life. Even if his remuneration is a pittance, he still played for Adamu Jenitongo. And when he did, his music was still sweet.

"It's the spirits that compel me to play. I have no choice."

The Gasi

The construction of the possession drum or gasi is not steeped in ritual. The gasi is made from gourds that grow in the extreme southern regions of western Niger and northern Benin; they are much larger than those used for the godji. The gourds are ready to be played after they are cut along the axis and dried. Drummers use their hands or drumsticks made from bamboo to strike their drums. The drumsticks resemble the human hand, consisting of five "fingers" of bamboo tied together at a point called the "palm," in such a way that each "finger" can hit the drum separately. When the drummer hits the gourd with the "palm" of the drumstick, it produces a "clack." When the drummer turns his wrist so that the "fingers" hit the gourd individually, a "roll" is produced. The possession rhythms therefore consist of a series of clacks and rolls. Each of these series corresponds to the praise-song of a specific spirit. The tempo shifts with the type of dance being performed. It is slow for the *windi* ("the tour"), rapid for the *gani* (fast dancing), and slow, building to rapid, for the *fimbi* ("shaking").

Adamu Jenitongo said that the sound of the drums reminds the dancers, audience, and spirits of the battlefield heroics of the Songhay past. Ancestral drummers played their rhythms just before important battles. The beat infused the troops with courage.[9] "The sound of the drums explodes from the gasi and reminds us of the ancestors and their strength."[10]

And so the sound of this special drum—its clack and roll—intoxicates the dancers and the spirits, creating for them a context in sound which they find irresistible.

Moru

Moru Adamu, the twenty-seven-year-old son of Adamu Jenitongo, has heard the cries of the godji and the beat of the gasi for his entire life. Once or twice a week Moru saw a possession ceremony in his compound. Although his father encouraged Moru to

Dukio Gasi of Mehanna.

learn a trade, Moru was born to be a musician. As a child, Moru used a hundred-liter water barrel as his drum, beating out deep syncopated possession rhythms. Gradually, Moru took up the drum. He apprenticed with Seyni Gasi of Tillaberi, and eventually his father invited him to drum at Tillaberi possession ceremonies.

As a teenager, Moru was often called away to other towns to play the drum. On one occasion he lived in Ayoru for two months. He made a good deal of money there and spent it all on the local prostitutes and teenagers. Moru was a good musician, but he was nonetheless an irresponsible person who felt stigmatized in his community. The Muslims in Tillaberi labeled him the devil's child.

"You and your kind are savages," townspeople would often tell him. They also laughed at the elaborate checkerboard scarification on his cheeks, the sign of his membership in the Jenitongo family of sohancis.

"We don't carve the cheeks of our children anymore. But you! Look at you, Moru."

Moru's sohanci heritage shamed him. To compensate for his social insecurity, Moru lavished his "friends" with gifts, which they never reciprocated. When Moru had money, his friends descended on him like locusts. They fed upon him until the money was devoured. And then they ignored him until he played at another possession ceremony and once again had money.

Short like his father, Moru is a muscular man who walks with a swagger. One day he swaggered up to his father, Adamu Jenitongo, and jutted his strong square jaw in his father's face.

"Baba, I'm going to marry my girlfriend, Djebo, and I don't care what you or my mothers think."

Five months earlier Moru had impregnated Djebo, a copper-skinned Fulan girl whose incessant scowl threw out of kilter the symmetry of her finely chiseled face. Adamu Jenitongo wanted him to marry a sohanci girl from his hometown. There were heated arguments, but Moru finally married Djebo.

Djebo bore him a daughter, Djamilla, who drowned during a flash flood in the summer of 1985, and a son, Hamadu, who is still alive.

In 1985 three drummers sat under the ritual canopy during most ceremonies in Adamu Jenitongo's compound. The drummer in the center, usually Halidu, the son of Yaye, Adamu Jenitongo's younger brother, was the lead percussionist. He chanted risqué spirit songs unrelated to those of the sorko. As long as Halidu remained in Tillaberi, Moru would not become the lead drummer.

Moru made very little money from his music, and his earnings during the past few years of drought and famine were especially meager. To help support his family, he farmed for his father and worked as an occasional laborer. He would travel great distances to perform his music for a fee.

On one of those trips he was asked to play in a small village northwest of Tillaberi. Before the dance, he set up his instrument, placing it over a meter-deep hole he had dug to increase the drum's resonating cavity. He then left the ceremonial area to eat some rice. He returned and struck his drum once. But something was strange. Had he heard a noise under the calabash? Had something moved under it? With a long stick, Moru lifted his calabash, and then sprang from his spot behind the drum. In his absence, someone had put a viper under the drum. He killed the snake.

"What the hell are you people doing here? What kind of people are you?"

Halidu calmed Moru, who quickly regained his composure and played his drum until sunset.

"There are mean people everywhere. There are people who wish me harm, and I do not even know why. That day, I wanted to leave that damn place, but I could not. As a drummer I have a responsibility to myself and to the spirits."

Cries of the Violin, Rhythms of the Drum

Any man living in Songhay country can become a violinist or drummer. Usually the musicians are members of families that are linked to possession troupes. A musician may be the son of a priest or a priestess, the son of a sorko or of a sorko's sister. He may be the descendant of sohancis. Sometimes there are no genealogical links between the musician and the spirit world. No matter their social origin, musicians do share a sense of duty: they are the sensual bridge that links the social and spirit worlds. The sounds they produce so artfully come from another age, a distant place. Without their cries, clacks, and rolls the spirits would not leave their domain and travel to the social world. They realize their importance and devote their energies to their music even when they are mistreated. Even when they are cheated of money, the musicians play. Because they devote much of their time and energies to possession activities without substantive remuneration, most of the possession musicians I have met are exceedingly poor. For food and shelter, they rely on the generosity of relatively poor peasant farmers. In desperate times like the famine of 1984, however, most musicians played their violins and drums for free. When I asked Moru Adamu why he played day after day without payment, he answered: "We have been called by the spirits. We must play for them and for the welfare of the community. What else can we do? The music is part of us."

The Possession Troupe

Few people willingly join a possession troupe; they are chosen by forces beyond their control and cannot refuse. Most zimas inherit their roles from someone in their lineage. The dying zima usually selects a successor from a group of relatives. Like the dying zima, spirits usually select their mediums from the lineages of their former mediums. The spirits give their novice mediums a "sickness" that can be cured only by initiation into the possession troupe. From that point, mediums are "married" to their spirit(s). Sorkos are also chosen. Being born into a sorko family is no guarantee that a person will become a praise-singer. Practicing sorkos study the characters of their younger relatives to decide carefully which young men can be entrusted with the family secrets—powerful words and powerful things. Sometimes, a man of non-sorko origin will be pointed out to a master; he too will receive training. In my case a sorko was witness to a bird—a familar of Dongo— that defecated on my head as I typed my field notes in February of 1977. As a *sorko benya* (lit., "the sorko's slave")—my classification—one learns praise-poetry and incantations, but one's knowledge will never compare to that of a full-blooded sorko. Musicians are also selected by the spirits. Many of them have genealogical ties to zimas or sorkos; a few do not. Some of them study with master players and learn to play their instruments; others, like Daouda Godji, are inspired, so they simply pick up the instrument and begin to play.

Members of possession troupes derive their great strength and joie de vivre from their "ownership" of specialized knowledge. Zimas are masters of spirit knowledge. They diagnose and treat spirit sicknesses. They make sacrifices to the spirits and they organize possession ceremonies. Mediums are masters of movement. They carry themselves in ways that entice the spirits to take their bodies; they are the intermediaries of the spirit and social worlds. Sorkos are masters of the word. Like bards, sorkos learn words that have been passed on from father to son since the time of Faran Make Bote. These words can heal, maim, or kill. During possession ceremonies these words compel the spirits to take the bodies of mediums. The musicians are masters of sound. They reproduce ancient cries, clacks, and rolls that excite human beings and the spirits. Their sounds are a sensible link between past and present, between the spirit and social worlds.

But the great joy that is derived from owning powerful knowledge is complemented by a sense of vulnerability. Zimas know that their path is fraught with personal dangers: spiteful spirits who sometimes kill their priests; jealous competitors whose intrigues dangerously complicate the mission of the troupe—and its zima—in the community. Zimas must continuously protect themselves from the vicissitudes of their spirits and colleagues. Mediums, too, walk a dangerous tightrope. To please their spirits, they must always wear the correct clothing and objects and eat special foods at special times. Possession is physically exhausting, especially for the older mediums. It is also work for which the mediums are rarely appreciated. The sorko's path is an exceedingly dangerous one.[11] The river spirits may take a sorko from the earth at any time. The mercurial Dongo often sends sicknesses to his ardent followers even though they chant his praise-poetry from their hearts. Musicians, too, bear the burden of their knowledge. If musicians fail to perform required sacrifices, the spirits strike down the men who produce intoxicating sounds. I have known several drummers, all of whom were seemingly healthy and under twenty-five years of age, who died after brief but violent illnesses. In one case, the young man complained of numbness in his fingers, which spread to his hands, arms, legs, and chest. He died three days after the onset of symptoms.

Participation in the Songhay possession troupe frequently exacts high personal and social costs. Most of the priests, praise-singers, and musicians are subsistence farmers. The majority of the mediums who are women sell cooked foods in the market. These activities generate little money, and as a consequence many members of the Tillaberi troupe need to supplement their incomes with the proceeds of possession ceremonies. In good times, these sums can be substantial. In bad times, possession specialists may be paid only a paltry fee.

Despite these considerable hardships, the possession troupe is a viable social institution in Songhay. In recent years officially sanctioned Islamic Committees have destroyed sacred possession altars and have disrupted ceremonies. In some villages these committees have blocked initiation and rain ceremonies.

The troupe in Tillaberi fends off these attacks. Its members are bound by a set of rights and obligations—to one another and to the spirits—which transcends local-level politics. Despite the presence of Islamic fundamentalists bent on wiping out the "devil worshipers," few people in Tillaberi can be unaffected by possession. Who in Tillaberi can claim, after all, to be part of a lineage in which no one is a spirit medium? Few indeed. And if a person's relative is a spirit medium, he or she must also pay homage, directly or indirectly, to the spirits, or pay the consequences. And so the possession troupe is resistant to the breezes that bring change to Songhay. In the end, the possession troupe bears its burden, refusing to "walk two paths with one foot."[12]

PART TWO   THEATERS OF SONGHAY
EXPERIENCE

The Tillaberi yenaandi (1977).

6

RAIN DANCE: RITES OF THE ANCESTORS

In the month of May the arid earth of Songhay country forms a dusty crust. The Sahelian sun casts little or no shadow at midday, and even the most vigorous Songhay avoid its rays. When the rays of the afternoon sun sear the parched land, people leave their sweltering houses and seek shaded areas: the east side of a straw hut, the east side of a compound wall. Intense even in the shade, the heat reduces activities to sitting, talking, drinking water, and watching for clouds. The most knowledgeable people are able to divine whether the fleecy cumulus clouds that form on the eastern horizon will bring nothing, wind and dust only, or, with the grace of the spirits, wind and dust followed by rain.

A band of storm clouds rouses the village to urgent activity. The expanding band has a deep orange-brown color close to the hue of the baked laterite of the Songhay steppe. Before the wind direction changes, people scurry about, tethering their animals, putting their beds inside their houses or huts. The dust cloud looms large as it approaches the community, until, like an ocean wave about to crash onto a beach, the wave inundates the village, blocking the sun. The sky becomes thick with reddish brown dust. The light of late afternoon is filtered out. The fierce sun now glows a dim red like a fire burning in the distant sky. The temperature drops precipitously, and the scent of rain is in the air. If the community is fortunate, the wind and dust will be followed by a downpour. If not, the dust will blow for hours, bringing with it discomfort, disease, and another day of drought.

Of Rain and Life in Songhay

In Songhay, people are powerless actors in a universe controlled by the spirits. The spirits control the invisible forces that determine soil fertility, pestilence, birth, health, and death. The greatest threat facing a Songhay community, however, is drought, a recurring event in Songhay history. The rains, like other natural events in Songhay, are controlled by the Tooru spirits, which as masters of clouds, wind, lightning, and thunder are masters of the heavens.

Songhay country is dry and rocky. In the south of Songhay

127

there are vast clay plains broken by rocky mesas. Here rainfall levels are relatively good (600–850 millimeters per year). Farther north, rainfall levels drop off sharply. The soil becomes more sandy, and there are many dunes that extend in ranges from north to south. In the Tera region rainfall levels have fallen below 400 millimeters per annum, a level that imperils a rain-fed millet crop. In Gao and Timbuktu, rainfall levels are consistently below 300 millimeters, a level too low for millet cultivation.[1]

Rainfall levels present only the surface of the Songhay farmer's reality. By following the yearly activities of one farmer, Soumana Yacouba, a sixty-year-old spirit medium in Tillaberi, we can fully comprehend what rain means to people in Songhay.

In 1983 Soumana Yacouba, whose millet fields are seven kilometers east of Tillaberi, planted his crop just after the onset of the rains in late May, which began with dust storms and were followed by tornadoes and downpours. Like other Songhay farmers, Soumana sowed his field and waited for the next rain, which came two weeks after the sowing. Like the first rain, the second storm produced a heavy downpour. Soumana's seeds sprouted, and three weeks after the planting, green millet shoots emerged from the sandy soil.

"When the shoots come out," Soumana says, "they are very delicate. If it rains too much and too hard, the shoots can be damaged. If the rains stop, the shoots shrivel and die."[2]

In 1983 the violent storms abated in July, and Soumana's millet grew taller and taller. The ample rains also sprouted weeds in Soumana's fields, and so Soumana, a conscientious farmer, had to move through rows of millet stalks with his weeder (*kumbaw*)—back breaking work. "We usually weed twice during the planting season. Once in July, and once about a month before the harvest [September]."[3] In July it rained three times, just enough to keep the young millet plants alive.

In June and July of 1983 the rains were sporadic, which is normal. In August it rained seven times in Tillaberi. Soumana's millet plants grew tall and strong, resembling corn. In late August Soumana weeded his field for the second time and inspected his crop. Green millet seeds protected by husks swelled at the top of his healthy stalks. One or two more rains in September would ensure a fine harvest. But Soumana, like most Songhay farmers, did not immediately expect a bumper crop. What if the rains did not come in September? What if the rains continued into the October harvest season? Soumana says: "If the rains do not fall in September, we lose much of our crop. If the rains continue into October, they rot the millet plants."[4]

In September, Soumana, more concerned about pests than about the rains, went to his field every day. Even if the rains fell in September and abated in October—as is the norm—birds, rats, or locusts could easily ravage his maturing crop. To protect his produce Soumana built a scarecrow in the center of his field. "It worked a bit," he said, "but the birds still ate some of my crop. No matter how hard you work, the birds always eat some of the crop."[5] In 1983, Soumana did not have to fight off packs of rats or swarms of locust.

Now it was harvest time, which began in mid-October. The rains stopped, and the temperatures increased. In Tillaberi the average high temperature is thirty-three degrees Centigrade in September; in October it rises to thirty-seven degrees.[6] In 1983, the hot October sun browned the green millet until it was ripe for harvesting.

Soumana hired two young boys to help him harvest his crop. For four days, Soumana and his helpers rode donkeys to the field. Morning and night they cut the golden seeded part of the plant, leaving for the cows, sheep, and goats the fibrous stalk. They bundled the millet and tied it onto the donkeys for the trip back to Tillaberi. In 1983, Soumana harvested 173 bundles, which would feed his people for the rest of that year. "That year [1983] was a good one, a miraculous one."

But the season soon changed. November marked the beginning of the cool-dry season, which stretches to mid-February. Cumulus clouds were replaced by high cirrus and strata-cirrus clouds, a sign of the approaching cool-dry season. In the cool-dry season the afternoons continued to be hot, but the temperatures plummeted at night. As he got older, Soumana found the cold more and more penetrating. Drafted as a soldier in World War II, he served in Europe, had seen snow, and had known much colder temperatures. "But that was a long time ago, when I was young and strong." Each night and morning Soumana built a fire in his compound to keep warm. Despite his aching joints, Soumana liked the cool season better than any other time of year.

In 1983 the cool-dry season was festive in Tillaberi. Their stomachs full of food, people in Tillaberi enjoyed their good fortune—celebrating marriages, naming ceremonies, and tam-tam dances.

They attended possession ceremonies. Soumana spent most of his time visiting his friends. He and I conversed for hours in Adamu Jenitongo's compound.

The cool-dry season ended in mid-February. The sun moved higher and higher in the sky, and the hot-dry season unfolded, with temperatures reaching their peak in late April. In March, before it became too hot to work, Soumana cleared his field. Foraging cows, sheep, and goats had devoured the millet stalks, leaving in their wake inedible stumps, which Soumana uprooted on two successive mornings. His field now ready for planting, Soumana remained at home during the peak of the hot season (April–May). "No one goes out to the fields during the hot season." With good reason. Shimmering with heat, the air burns one's skin. Hot-season temperatures often exceed forty degrees Centigrade (102 degrees Fahrenheit), and in Tillaberi, one of the hottest villages in Niger, they often climb well above forty-five degrees.[7]

Something strange occurred in April of 1984: it rained, and rained hard. These early downpours, called mango rains because they fall when mangoes are ripe for picking, are blessings. The early rains remove disease-carrying dust from the air, wiping out, for example, meningitis, which strikes Songhay in March and April. Some Tillaberi farmers, convinced of a good season of rain, sowed their fields. Thinking the early rain a fluke, Soumana remained at home to wait for the later rains, which came, in fact, in early May—also early for Tillaberi farmers. This time Soumana planted his field. Perhaps 1984 would be an extraordinary year. Two weeks after the May sowing, Soumana's millet germinated and emerged from the sandy soil.

Confident Tillaberi farmers spoke about record harvests. The chief felt no need to arrange a *yenaandi* or rain dance during which a village makes offerings to the spirits that control the rain. Deprived of a major source of financial support, the Tillaberi possession troupe staged an incomplete rain dance (see chap. 8).

Overconfidence soon gave way to worry. The young millet plants needed additional rain to survive the intense May heat. The sky, however, remained cloudless, and hot, dry desert breezes swept across Tillaberi east to west, ensuring rainless days. Their millet plants dying in the dry heat, Tillaberi farmers watched the sky for rain, which, in 1984, did not come.

In 1984, Soumana's field yielded no millet. As an army veteran, Soumana received retirement benefits four times a year and could buy grain for his family in lean years. Most people in Tillaberi went hungry; some starved to death.

> When I was younger in Nemega, we always had good harvests. That's because we followed our ancestors' path. Every year, we sacrificed a black bull to the genie of Nemega Mountain. Every year, we staged a rain dance to appease the spirits. We respected our ancestors. We respected the spirits. And now, look at our fields. People today have no respect. They prefer to save the expense of sacrifice. But what does this stinginess bring? Look at our fields. Look![8]

The character of the land and the climate is a central part of the Songhay story. The slightest deviation in rainfall patterns can result in crop failure. For centuries Songhay sages like Adamu Jenitongo have recognized the vulnerability of disrespectful human beings to the retribution of the spirits. How common it is for the Songhay farmer to labor for months only to lose his crop. How common it is for that farmer's family to feel pangs of hunger and the pain of disease during the ensuing year. As Adamu Jenitongo said in 1984: "Without the spirits, there can be no rain. Without the rain, the millet dries and dies. Without millet we Songhay dry up and die."[9]

In Songhay, rainfall, which is controlled by invisible forces, is associated with the spirit world. When rain falls it comes as scattered thunderstorms, dropping torrents of water on one village, leaving an adjacent town untouched. The spirits control the path of rain—Dongo's path—and can prevent it from falling on non-observant villages.[10]

To protect their fields from pestilence, some farmers make private offerings to the spirits. In most Songhay communities, Tillaberi included, the possession troupe stages elaborate rain ceremonies, *yenaandi*, which are human attempts to control the rain by making offerings to the spirits.

Yenaandi, which means "the act of cooling off," is organized at the end of the hot-dry season. It is a Tooru festival, for the Tooru, especially Dongo (thunder), Cirey (lightning), and Moussa Nyori (wind and clouds), control the natural forces that bring rain. Rain dances are generally held on a Thursday, the Tooru's sacred day, in an open space that is usually ancestral land. In Tillaberi, the yenaandi space is a sandy plaza that sits on a bluff overlooking the Niger River.

Yenaandi in Tillaberi (1977)

By midday the still air was blistering, and an occasional breeze was the draft of a blast furnace. Rain seemed far away on that Thursday (June 16, 1977) in Tillaberi, the day of that year's yenaandi.[11]

Adamu Jenitongo arrived at the yenaandi space in his sohanci garb of black cap and billowing black robe. He greeted his people and told a young man to go to the river to fetch water: "Get the water and splash it on the dance ground; our dancers must not burn their feet on the hot sand."

People dressed in brightly colored print cloth, strolled onto the plaza. Carrying their calabashes and their violins, the musicians greeted the growing throng. Four drummers dug resonating cavities in the shade of a canopy. Three violinists sat down on low stools behind the drummers. But the first sounds heard that day were not the clack of the drums or the whine of the violins; rather, they were the pulsating thumps of the double-headed tam-tam.

"Why the tam-tams?" I asked Salou, an elder in the audience.

"Listen to that sound," he said. "That's Dongo's music from Dongo's instrument."

Ready at last the drummers struck their instruments. Clack-roll-clacks counterpointed the thumps. The high-pitched whine of the violin completed the suite. The crowd thickened; it murmured with expectation. Some old women glided onto the damp dance ground to display their prowess and demonstrate their reverence for the spirits. More clacks, rolls, thumps, and cries burst from the instruments. Adamu Jenitongo stood up and waved his arms.

"Dance! Dance, you women! Are you lazy? Are you full of shame?"

Seated to the left of the ritual canopy, the mediums seemed not to hear Adamu Jenitongo's exhortations. One of the younger women, however, stood up and pulled on her "sister's" arm, prompting the latter to stand up. They strolled to the dance ground. The entire contingent of mediums followed them. They formed a circle and sauntered along the sand, moving counterclockwise. They were a stream of reds, greens, oranges, blacks, whites, and silver lamé. The colors flowed and the women flapped their left hands over their open mouths, turning their patter into "wa-wa-wa-wa." The sounds—clack-roll-clacks, echoing thumps, high-pitched wails, and now the mediums' "wa-wa-wa-wa" chorus—combined with the colors to hypnotize the audience. And then, as they circled, the women raised their right arms skyward and extended their forefingers toward the heavens—a gesture indicating that there was but one path to follow, the path of the spirits.[12]

Adamu Jenitongo rushed into the midst of the sound, color and, movement, ordering the uninitiated to leave.

"Women," he said, "sit down near the canopy."

"Why aren't the women going to dance?" I asked Salou.

"They don't dance in the yenaandi. They sit and wait for their spirits to come."

The three tam-tam drummers kneeled at the feet of the Tooru mediums, overwhelming the mediums with their resonating thumps. Dressed in black, the sorko shook a hatchet with a bell attached to it (Dongo's hatchet). "Ping, ping," the bell tolled for Dongo. The Tooru mediums winced in pain—too much sound. But the musicians and sorko pursued the mediums relentlessly. The spirits had to come. Tillaberi needed rain. Tears splashed from the Tooru mediums' eyes, their faces patchworks of pain. More music. More praise-poetry. More pings, thumps, clack-roll-clacks, cries. The spirits were close but not yet in the mediums' bodies. Then screams escaped from their bodies. There was Moussa Nyori's (deity of wind and clouds) nasal scream. There was Cirey's (deity of lightning) high-pitched quavering scream. More music and then Dongo's powerful roar, which dominated all the other sounds. The Tooru had come to Tillaberi that day. Dongo, Cirey, and Moussa Nyori dropped to their knees in front of the ritual canopy. They furrowed the earth.[13]

The presence of the Tooru triggered the arrival of the Black Spirits. Two of them, Zatow and Moss'izey, took their mediums and rolled in the sand. They crouched in front of the musicians, took handfuls of sand and rubbed it into their hair and onto their bodies. Completing these ablutions, they hopped toward their Tooru masters (in the spirit world, the Black Spirits are Tooru captives) and licked the Tooru's feet.

The presence of the Tooru also prompted the Hauka to come to earth (see chap. 7). For this rain dance, Zeneral Malia (the general of the Red Sea), Medina, Lieutenant Marseille, and Commandant Bashiru swept past the audience into the bodies of their respective mediums. They somersaulted, did back flips on the sand, and foamed at the mouth like rabid dogs. They saluted the audience and took up positions as Tooru guards, protecting the nobles of the spirit world from the intrusions of mortals.

A lesser zima guided the three Tooru to a house bordering the plaza. They returned shortly thereafter, fully costumed. Wearing a full black robe and a black cap, Dongo carried his hatchet. Cirey wore a bright red robe and a red fez, and carried a long metal staff (a *lolo*). Moussa Nyori sported a blue-and-white-striped tunic and a cap made from heavy cotton spun by the Moose of Burkina Faso.

The Tooru deities marched in short deliberate steps, a sign of nobility. The lesser spirits greeted them obsequiously, some bowing deeply, others prostrating themselves at their feet. Adamu Jenitongo led the Tooru to three overturned mortars—the Tooru thrones. One by one the audience greeted the spirits. In exchange for small bits of food and money, the Tooru shook hands, grunted, screamed, and gestured at their mortal interlocuters. They did not speak directly to the people.

Meanwhile a sorko swept the ground to prepare it for sacrifice. He then stirred millet gruel in a ritual vase (*hampi*) at the center of the plaza. The ritual vase is a material representation of the world.[14] For the sacrifice, the sorko directed four women to separate millet seeds from seven stalks of the grain. The sorko then traced with his foot a large crossroads in the sand. Mixing the seeds with dried grass, he put the mixture on both sides of the lines of the crossroads.

I asked Adamu Jenitongo about the significance of the dried grass.

"The dried grass is the old millet crop; the seeds stand for the future harvest." [15]

Lesser zimas brought the Tooru to the edge of the crossroads. Adamu Jenitongo took a match and lit the millet-grass mixture—a fire to fuse the old with the new. The bright orange of the leaping flames contrasted sharply with the dull violet of the fading sky. At first the spirits watched the fire passively. Then Dongo roared. He leapt from his seat and ran to the crossroads. Swinging his hatchet over his head, he stomped his bare feet on the fire, quickly extinguishing it. The blackened crossroads would now receive sacrificial blood.

The sorko gave Adamu Jenitongo four chickens: one white, one red, one black, and one speckled. He killed them one at a time, cutting their throats at the point of the crossroads. He let their blood soak into the earth, then threw them to the east.

"Why throw them to the east?" I asked a zima in the crowd.

"Does the rain not come from the east?"

The sorko brought Adamu Jenitongo a black kid to be sacrificed to Dongo. He cut its throat and the blood gushed onto the sand. The animal writhed and died. The spirits jumped up and down like excited children.

Meanwhile, another sorko had readied the spirit porridge in the ritual vase. He gestured for the audience to form a circle at the center of the plaza. Once again, the Tooru sat down on their mortars. Behind them stood the other spirits. The sorko recited the *genji how* (the incantation that harmonizes the bush) and added seven special spirit powders—various pounded tree barks and plants—to the mixture in the vase.

"Raise your right arms, Tillaberi people," he ordered.

They raised their right arms and pointed to the sky, the ultimate sign of spirit reverence.

Salu, the Tillaberi elder who was sitting next to me, poked my arm.

"Raise your arm, Tillaberi person. Raise it high. Show your respect."

I raised my arm.

The Tooru screamed with satisfaction.

"Ah, Monsieur Paul," said Salou. "When they scream like that, it is good. They will bring us much rain this year. Much rain."

"That's right," a woman chimed in. "Our bellies will be full of millet in October."

As the sun set, the priests led the Tooru back to their dressing room. One of the tam-tam drummers approached me. He was tall and thin as a millet stalk.

"Ah, Monsieur Paul. You saw something today."

"It was really something," I said.

"You saw something truly special."

"Yes?"

"What you saw is Songhay work. We will have rain in three days."

Three days after the ceremony, it poured. The morning after the rain, Tillaberi farmers planted their millet. There was a good harvest that year.

Yenaandi in Tillaberi (1981)

In 1981 the Tillaberi yenaandi was a failure. Although it was staged at the right time in mid-May, it brought no rain to Tillaberi. Rain drenched the communities surrounding Tillaberi in May and early June, but there was none to enable the Tillaberi farmers to sow their millet crop.

In other years the yenaandi had been successful. What happened this year? According to Adamu Jenitongo, a dispute had erupted between the yenaandi organizers and the performers. Disputes bring disharmony.

"Even if the sacrifices are good," Adamu Jenitongo told me once, "if the community is not united, the spirits will not be satisfied."

This disharmony resulted in continued drought. The local troupe consequently decided to stage a second yenaandi that year on a Sunday (June 24, 1981).

On the day of the second yenaandi Djingarey Sorko invited us to his compound, for *sodje,* as he was called, had organized the ceremony. Far from the sacred plaza, Djingarey lived near the local prison on the northern fringe of town.

Adamu Jenitongo and I walked across dusty tracks and paths in the midday sun, passing well-wishers along the way.

"May the High God be with you today, *albora* [a term of respect signifying 'the old man']," one woman said to Adamu Jenitongo.

"May the spirits follow you to the yenaandi," an old man said.

"Amen," said Adamu Jenitongo.

"May God agree to it," I said.

After a ten-minute walk, we reached Djingarey's, a large compound with a big three-room mudbrick house protected from the sun by a corrugated tin roof. In the distance to the west under a tall acacia, I saw Moru and Halidu preparing their drums at the edge of the dance ground.

Djingarey greeted us at his compound's door and escorted us into his house. Altinne Zima, Issifu Zima, and Douda Godji sat in Djingarey's "parlor" on two splintery benches on either side of an aluminum card table covered with some Dutch Wax cloth faded from exposure to the Sahelian sun.

"Sohanci, come in and eat. Monsieur Paul, join our table. There is rice with black sauce and mutton. Eat, my friends."

Djingarey's servants brought us plates heaped with steaming rice and sauce. I ate with gusto. Adamu Jenitongo chewed on a kola nut.

Djingarey pointed out the animals that he had bought for sacrifice: four chickens (black, red, white, and red and white), and a black goat.

"These are good for sacrifice," Issifu Zima, the officiant for this ceremony, said.

While we ate, Djingarey's servants brought in two bundles of kola nuts and a bale of tobacco. Issifu Zima inspected these gifts.

"Okay, the drummers get two bundles of kola nuts, and one portion of tobacco. The violinist gets three bundles of kola and two portions of tobacco."

"What about the mediums?" Altinne Zima asked.

"They should get one bundle of kola and one portion of tobacco," Djingarey interjected.

"That should satisfy everyone," Altinne Zima said.

"But we also need to talk about money. I spent five-thousand francs [$20] on the kola, animals, and tobacco. If we should take in much more than five-thousand francs today, we'll return here tomorrow for the money distribution. Zimas and sorkos get the first cut. Musicians get the second cut, and mediums the third. Does that sound okay?"

Everyone agreed. Adamu Jenitongo remained silent.

When the June sun blanched the sky, the godji cried. The drums clack-roll-clacked. The tam-tams thumped. Young dancers coaxed older women onto the dance ground. Members of the audience threw money at the musicians or presented money to a particularly inspired dancer. The possession sounds drew more and more onlookers. Harakoy Dikko's medium arrived and greeted people.

"How is your health?" Adamu Jenitongo asked.

"I thank God for it," she responded.

"Now you must leave," he insisted.

Although the old woman protested, Adamu Jenitongo pressed two-hundred francs into her hand. Reluctantly, she agreed to leave.

"I sent her away," he said later, "because the presence of Harakoy's medium spoils the rain ceremony." Due to longstanding jealousy, the principal yenaandi Tooru—Dongo, Cirey, and Moussa Nyori—will not take their mediums if Harakoy's medium is present.

Daouda Godji played Tooru rhythms and the mediums entered the dance area. Dressed in a black caftan of thin cotton, Gusabu led her mediums in the slow *windi* movement. They danced counterclockwise, thrusting their clenched fists skyward repeatedly as they cried "woo, woo, woo," flapping the palms of their left hands over their open mouths. Two sorkos burst into the dance area, each shaking a Dongo hatchet.

The lead sorko directed the tam-tam drummers to one of Cirey's mediums, the hot-tempered Rabi. The tam-tam players flooded her with drum thumps. The sorko sang praise-poetry. In the background, Daouda's godji cried sweetly, and Moru and Halidu's drums clacked. Rabi turned her back to the drummers and walked away. She rubbed her forehead. The sorko followed her. Rabi sat down. The drummers crouched next to her. Rabi grimaced and covered her ears. She pushed the sorko away, but he refused to leave. He shook his hatchet and browbeat her with praise-poems. Rabi's left hand twitched. She played with the ring on the third finger of her left hand. She rested her cheek on the palm of her left hand, staring emptily into space. Rabi slapped her face with her right hand. The drummers were still on her, sweat pouring off their bodies. Rabi dropped to her hands and knees. Tears gathered at the corners of her eyes. Cirey was close but had not mounted his medium.

Suddenly Dongo took his medium, Adamu Jenitongo. Flapping his arms, Dongo dashed toward the musicians. He bellowed, thrusting his clenched fists to the left and then to the right. Dongo grabbed one of the violins and screamed into its cavity three times. Dongo turned and ran to the tam-tam drummers. He threw his aged medium to the ground right next to Cirey's medium. Dongo screamed into Rabi's ear. Intoxicated with sound, Cirey, Dongo's older brother, entered Rabi's body. On their knees, Dongo and Cirey hopped to the center of the dance ground.

The sorko and his tam-tam entourage left these deities and searched for other Tooru mediums in the crowd. They brought to center stage a big-boned woman. She sank to her knees. Cocking her head to the left, she listened to the words and the rhythms. Dongo hopped to her left and Cirey to her right. They screamed in her ears. Mahamane Surgu (the Tuareg warrior) took his medium.

The tam-tam drummers dogged other Tooru mediums in the crowd. At most rain dances three or four Tooru—all children of Harakoy Dikko—take their mediums. Given the poor millet harvest the year before, the organizers wanted all six of Harakoy's children to take their mediums' bodies. In rapid succession, Moussa Nyori (deity of clouds), Hausakoy (deity of smithing), and Faran Baru Koda, the youngest of Harakoy's children, mounted their mediums.

The air above the dance ground echoed now with shrieks, bellows, screams, and roars. Like the Songhay nobles of yore, the Tooru did not speak to mere mortals. Instead they vocalized and gestured. They pointed to the sky, indicating the true path of the spirits. They put their forefingers just under their right eyes, demonstrating their true identity as the spirit world's nobility.

Moru and Halidu picked up the tempo. It was time to bring the lesser spirits to the earth. Zatow, Harakoy's slave, took her medium, violently throwing her to the ground. A Black Spirit, Zatow thrashed in the sand and drank blood from a dish.

And then the Hauka came: Gomno (the governor), Lieutenant Marseille, Fadimata, Istanbula (chief of the Hauka). Commandant Bashiru mounted his medium without warning. One minute Bashiru's medium watched the ceremony passively. The next minute his body shuddered, and he vomited a black liquid.

"What the hell was that?" I asked Karimoun, an elder among the Hauka mediums.

"That's *duwa*," he said, chuckling.

"Ink?"

"Yes, of course," Karimoun replied. "Many Hauka vomit duwa when they take their mediums' bodies."

The Hauka moaned. He performed a leg split and then backflipped onto the sand.

Djingarey Sorko and Issifu Zima formed a line with the Tooru in the center and the lesser deities at either end. They led the spirits to Djingarey's compound, where they would be costumed.

Properly clothed, the spirits were ushered into the open-air portion of Djingarey's compound. They gathered around a ritual vase in which there was a mixture of water and seven sacred powders. They drank from the vase. Properly fed, the spirits returned to the dance ground. Dongo walked stiff-legged in his billowing black robe and his black cap. Cirey wore his red robe and red fez. Moussa Nyori had on his blue-and-white striped tunic. Hausakoy, dressed in his filmy black cape and black cap, carried an iron staff. Mahamane Surgu sported his black and white robes and his black turban. Clothed in a light blue robe, Faran Baru Koda carried a small doll. Led by the Tooru, the procession of spirits returned to the dance ground.

"Ay ga ni fo. Ay ga ni fo" (I greet you. I greet you), the various

Hauka possession at the Tillaberi yenaandi (1977).

spirits repeated as they passed people in the audience—the first words the spirits had uttered. The air filled again with spirit music. The spirits readied themselves to dance in full costume. Meanwhile, the lesser spirits greeted the audience with a combination of salutations and insults. Noticing me in the crowd, one Hargay spirit wagged her finger in my face.

"All of you white people are dumb; you have no ideas in your head. But you in particular, I like."

Faran Baru Koda strode up to the musicians' area and etched in the sand two intersecting lines, a sign that is the equivalent of the genji how, the incantation that harmonizes the forces of the universe.[16]

Then Issifu Zima nodded his head, a signal for the beginning of the sacrifices. The carnival subsided and everyone—spirits and audience—left the dance ground and walked five-hundred meters to a small hill just outside the town limit. One of Issifu's assistants had dug a cubic-meter pit and four shallow canals, each one extending about one meter in a cardinal direction. These emptied into the pit.

The violinists and tam-tam drummers placed themselves between the south and west canals. They played their music. The zimas faced the spirits from the west end of the pit. Issifu Zima took an egg and rolled it between his thumb and first two fingers. He recited three times his version of the genji how. He broke the egg and threw it into the pit. Meanwhile, the spirits stood stiffly to the east of the pit. Attendants brought Issifu Zima two vials of perfume. He opened them and threw them into the pit. Two other attendants brought a large mortar filled with *doonu* (millet porridge) and poured some of it into each canal. The muddy brown liquid flowed like lava into the pit.

"The spirits are getting hot now," a man in the audience commented.

"They have risen, have they not?" a woman said.

Zatow, a Black Spirit, rolled in the sand near the pit. Clamoring, the entire group of spirits bounded over the pit. Issifu Zima then cut the throat of a white chicken, spurting its blood into the pit. He threw the carcass over the pit toward the east. He dispatched the three other chickens in the same manner. Attendants brought the black goat to the sacrificial space. Issifu Zima cut its throat. Blood gushed into the pit. An attendant cut the goat open and threw its viscera into the hole. Several attendants threw the carcass to the east toward the dead chickens.

Exhilarated by these offerings, the spirits got very hot indeed. Black Spirits rolled in the sand like jackals; Hauka did back flips, landing hard and flat on the ground. The spirits advanced toward the pit once again, and they leapt to its east side. Attendants led the spirits back to the dance ground. Lesser zimas filled the pit with sand.

"The earth has drunk," one of zimas said, "and now we pray that the sky will cry."

Back at dance ground, the spirits circulated among the audience. Attendants brought thrones—overturned mortars—for Dongo, Moussa Nyori, Cirey, and Hausakoy. Mahamane Surgu and Faran Baru Koda flanked their older brothers.

Music still filled the air some five hours after the beginning of the festivities. More spirits took their mediums. Kong'izey, Hadjo, Hamsu Belley, and Mumay Wanzerbe—all female deities—strutted around the dance ground looking for people to insult. Commandant Bashiru and Lieutenant Marseille, two Hauka, stood guard over the Tooru entourage.

The Tooru held a town meeting, speaking to the community entirely through intermediaries—the sorkos. Gesturing toward the crowd, they summoned people from the audience.

Mounkaila Alhassane, a millet farmer, was summoned before the deities.

"Please, my family was hungry this year. Please help me to protect my fields."

Dongo put his finger under his right eye and roared.

A sorko interpreted the gesture and vocalization. "You must take a black chicken and sacrifice it in the center of your field."

"But when?" asked Mounkaila.

"Next Thursday."

"Is that all?"

"No. You must find some iron shit [prehistoric slag] and bury it at the four corners of your field." [17]

Mounkaila Alhassane nodded his head. Dongo held out his hand.

"He wants to be paid," the sorko informed Mounkaila.

Mounkaila put a hundred-franc piece in Dongo's hand.

Dongo pointed his forefinger skyward.

The town meeting lasted about forty-five minutes. The sun had slipped behind purple and blue bands of dusk clouds. In full view of the audience, zimas sat the spirits down on straw mats and gently shook them from the bodies of their mediums. The Tooru mediums returned to the social world. They drank water. After a few moments of rest, they went home. No one thanked them for their efforts.

Adamu Jenitongo and I returned to his compound. Dust, kicked up by cows returning from the bush, hung like fog in the air. Women carried small bundles of wood, fuel for their cooking fires, into their compounds. Adamu Jenitongo yawned. Although he was well over ninety years old and had been possessed for more than four hours, he glided across the sand.

"Paul, it was a good yenaandi," he said. "All of Harakoy's children came today. That is good."

Rain came three days after the ceremony. The earth's thirst had been quenched and now the sky was crying.

Spirits, Human Beings, and Power

Power comes from the distant past in the Songhay world. The spirits, who inhabited the earth long before social beings, have great power over the forces of the universe. They shared some of this power with the ancestors. They gave some power to the original inhabitants of the Songhay bush—the "owners" of the land. The original "owners" of the land were most likely such Voltaique-speaking populations as the Gurmantche and Kurumba, both of whom live today primarily in Burkina Faso. Having been granted power over the land, these groups prospered as farmers in a harsh environment. When Songhay warriors came to live in present-day Niger in the late fifteenth-century, they found Gurmantche and Kurumba villages. Since the warriors knew little about millet cultivation, they allowed the Gurmantche and the Kurumba to celebrate their land and millet rites. When the fields filled with ripening millet, the warriors took what they needed. Finding cohabitation with the Songhay unbearable, many of the Kurumba and Gurmantche fled west to Burkina Faso. From those Gurmantche and Kurumba who remained, the Songhay took wives, thus creating affinal ties with the "owners of the land." In this way individual "owners of the land" disappeared; they are remembered today as the Black Spirits of the Songhay pantheon. Offerings are still made to these "Voltaiques" who, like the "owners of the land," control soil fertility and pestilence.[18]

The spirits gave power to the original inhabitants of the Niger River, the Do, enabling them to prosper as fisherman on a swift and dangerous river. When a fisherman seeks the riches of a certain section of the Niger River, he must first ask the local Do's permission, usually accompanied with a small gift. The Do's blessing ensures the fisherman's safety on the river.

The spirits gave to Faran Maka Bote the power to beckon them from their domain in the spirit world. In this way sorkos and zimas have been empowered to protect villages from the vicissitudes of the spirits. The spirits also gave sorkos the power to protect themselves—and others—from witches and other agents of evil.

Most Songhay are not descendants of the "owners of the land," the Do, or Faran Maka Bote. Most Songhay do not "own" the specialized knowledge that gives them power over natural elements. Most Songhay are, in fact, completely powerless in the face of natural forces. Faran Maka Bote staged the first possession dance, the *yene,* so that the powerless, too, might prosper in ancient Songhay. In this way, Faran's possession ceremony, the first yenaandi, was an expression of reverence for the power of the spirits.

The performance of the yenaandi links the spirit to the social worlds, the present and past. In yenaandi, sacrifices are made to appease the spirits. When powerless people make substantial offerings—chickens, goats, grain, and, today, money—they demonstrate their respect for the spirits and their ancestors' practices. In exchange for reverence, the spirits bring rain to Songhay. Rain results in a bountiful millet crop and a prosperous year of health and family growth. If people abandon the ancestral practices, Adamu Jenitongo and Soumana Yacouba told me, they will suffer hard times: drought, famine, and death. At the yenaandi the Tooru remind the Songhay audience of that lesson, raising up their right arms and pointing to the sky. The only path for Songhay to follow, they were saying, is that of the spirits.

A medium possessed by Istanbula, chief of the Hauka.

7

HORRIFIC COMEDY: THE HAUKA

Late one afternoon in December of 1969 a crowd formed near
Chez Jacob, a one-room mudbrick bar in the *zongo* (foreigner)
neighborhood of Tera, a large Songhay town in western Niger. A
violinist played his godji. Two drummers struck their gasis. Having been in Chez Jacob, I left the hot confines of the bar and
joined the crowd. Suddenly, a young man, who had been standing
only a few paces from me, vomited black liquid that stained his
khaki shirt. I thought he was about to die. Like other members of
the audience, I gave the man room to maneuver. He threw himself
to the ground. He threw sand all over his body. He shoved handfuls of sand into his mouth. He stood up and scanned the audience. He stopped and spit sand in my direction. Fixing his gaze
on other people in the audience, he lunged menacingly toward
them. Three men restrained him before he could strike the crowd.
I moved closer and I saw him clearly for the first time. His eyes
bulged. A blood vessel in his forehead throbbed. He groaned. Saliva frothed from his mouth. He broke loose from his restrainers
and came at me. Shaken, I raced to Chez Jacob.

"Is the man crazy?" I asked someone in my inchoate Songhay.
"Oh no," responded another spectator. "He is not a man; he is
one of the Hauka. You must go up and greet him. He will not
harm you."

At first I resisted the man's suggestion, but he insisted. And so
I approached this terrifying Hauka. He thrust his open hand toward mine.

"Sha vas?" he asked in Pidgin French.

"Fine," I answered, still afraid.

"Your mother has no tits."

This provoked great laughter.

"Yes, she does!" I protested.

"Your father has no balls."

This provoked even more laughter from the audience, which
was being entertained at my expense. The man who accompanied
me suggested that I say good-bye to the Hauka, and so I did, having had my first exposure to horrific comedy.

On subsequent research trips I learned that *Hauka* in the Hausa language meant "craziness." I also learned that the Hauka were supposed to be funny as well as terrifying. Although the Hauka undoubtedly terrified their audiences, they occasionally did so while aping the ways of the European. They often wore pith helmets and carried swagger sticks. Sometimes they took the roles of European army generals who spoke to their troops in Pidgin French or Pidgin English. This frivolous burlesque makes impressionable children cringe and seasoned adults laugh.

Colonialism and the Social Context of Hauka

Until the latter part of the nineteenth century, most Songhay had no contact with Europeans.[1] But in the last decade of the nineteenth century, the French military pushed into the hinterlands of West Africa. By the turn of the century, they controlled most of what is today Francophone West Africa. The specter of the French military in Africa must have been staggering to Africans in the Soudan.

> The European must have presented himself to Africans other than those from the coast, who by now knew him well, as an immensely complex and bewildering being. He possessed technological superiority and was fired with missionary zeal that compared only with that of the *mujihaddin*. It was also difficult to assess the extent and nature of his power. He came from overseas. The small pioneer party could be defeated, but those who had sent it?[2]

Thus was born what Ranger has called the "colonial situation": "the effective use of power—military or technological—to extract from . . . Africa what was necessary for the developed economies of the world without creating in . . . Africa itself the foundations of a developed economy."[3]

In Songhay the "colonial situation" undermined the traditional social order. The arrival of the French put into motion waves of sociocultural change that threatened to break forever the links between Songhay and their ancestors. The colonizers put an end to warfare (*guerre intestin*) between the Songhay principalities and other ethnic groups in the Niger River basin. Enforced by the presence of French garrisons, this peace ended the noble-warrior's practice of raiding neighboring groups to replenish the slave labor force.

In 1901 the governor-general of West Africa, William Ponty, abolished slavery in the French Soudan. Although this edict did not bring about the immediate disappearance of slavery, it diminished its social importance. Colonialism brought with it new economic opportunities for the men who had once been *captifs*. With the official abolition of slavery, many former slaves set off to seek their fortunes in distant markets. The extent of the exodus was much greater than the French had anticipated. Colonial officials estimated that some 200,000 captives in the Western Soudan had quit their masters by 1908. In 1911 Governor-General Ponty suggested that 500,000 slaves had liberated themselves. In a report circulated in 1912, French colonial officials estimated that one in every three slaves in the western Soudan had fled from his master.[4]

"Once a domestic slave decided to quit the family that owned him traditionally, the master could not reclaim him."[5] In this way colonialism undermined forever the dynamic interdependence between master and slave. While many nobles and slaves continued their social routines as though nothing had changed (and the pattern persists to this day), the foundation of the precolonial stratified society—slavery—had disappeared. As the old social structure waned, a new one began to emerge.

While the French undermined the old social order through their policies on slavery and their relationships with traditional chiefs (usurping their authorities and appointing them hated tax collectors), they introduced their new subjects to a European universe of meaning. The French policymakers wanted to create new Frenchmen out of colonial populations. The education policy sought to educate a small African elite to help in the governance of the new colonies.

French colonial policy was called "cultural renaissance." As Governor-General Jules Brevie stated, "However pressing may be the need for economic change and development of natural resources, our mission in Africa is to bring about a cultural renaissance, a piece of creative work in human material, an association of the two races which can be brought about only by a free and wholehearted acceptance of the African by the French."[6] Brevie's rhetoric masked the ultimate policy goal: to destroy the cultural foundations of African societies.

In Songhay there was large-scale indirect resistance to French education. Education among the Songhay and other Islamized peoples in French West Africa was not a new phenomenon. Centuries before the coming of the French soldiers, Koranic schools flourished in Songhay. Given the previous educational experience of Songhay, why should any of them resist French education? One reason stemmed from the belief that the way of foreigners, especially Christian foreigners, polluted the mind. A child who went off to school, learned French, and studied European society could never again be a pure Songhay. Such a child would never again have a Songhay "head." The colonialists wanted to enroll in their schools the children of the nobility—a legitimizing tactic. But many Songhay nobles substituted the children of slaves.[7] Consequently, a large percentage of students in French schools were of non-noble origin.

French education, together with the policies on slavery and chiefs, created a climate of irrevocable change. Once revered as links to the ancestors, many chiefs became known and despised as tax collectors. Once the "untouchables" of the precolonial social order, slaves became self-directed free people. Many of them traveled to the edges of their worlds in search of adventure and money. When they returned home, they walked in their villages as free men of wide experience.

Thus there emerged a new educated elite, many of whom were of slave origin. In the later colonial years, they played an increasingly important role as clerks in the local colonial administration. This new elite also engaged actively in the local and national politics that led to independence.

Colonialism brought radical and unsystematic change to Africans living under French rule. In the decay of the old order, there arose not only the beginnings of a new order but also deep despondency. In Songhay and elsewhere in French West Africa, people

> had their old life broken by the shock of European contact: the old order of tribal society, with its cohesion based on unquestioned rule of custom, has been forced into the background; and the native, deracialized by the shattering of everything which has previously guided him, drifts disillusioned and despairing now knowing no hope, and now with the insane joy of the iconoclast aiding the outside forces in rending his life from top to bottom. . . . The future is not clear because the native here a French citizen and there a mere "subject" does not know where he can fit in. Seeing neither a place for himself nor hope for his children, he drifts in reckless despair or gives way to carefree insouciance.[8]

While the quoted remark is overstated and paternalistic, it touches on the well-known idea that when peoples are faced with rapid social change, when they are uprooted from the comforts of centuries-old traditions, they tend to lose themselves in winds of change.[9] But the author failed to realize that people possess a great stock of cultural resources which they can manipulate to cushion blows to their social and cultural vitality.

The onset of colonial rule devastated the economic and social bases of most of the societies of the French Soudan. Songhay was no exception. The first inclination of Songhay was to resist militarily the armies of the French. There was a revolt against the French in 1905–6.[10] This resistance, however, soon proved ineffective and most Songhay reconciled themselves to French military superiority. By 1922 the French had firm control over Songhay country.

Origins of the Hauka

As the French began to consolidate their power in Niger, the Hauka movement emerged. During the course of a social dance for young adults in 1925, the first Hauka took a medium. El Hadj Mohamadou of Filingue, Jean Rouch's informant, described the event:

> It all began during a dance of girls and boys. During the dance, a Soudye woman, Zibo, who was married to a Timbuktu *sharif*, began to be possessed by a spirit. They asked her who it was. It said: "I am Gomno Malia" [Governor of the Red Sea]. The people said that they did not know this spirit. Then others came and took the bodies of some of the young boys. They too spoke their names, and the people did not know them. The spirits said: "We are the Hauka, the guests of Dongo." This occurred at Chikal, very close to Filingue. A few days later, all the boys and girls of Filingue had been possessed by the Hauka.[11]

Appalled at this bizarre turn of events in the ritual life of his town, the Filingue chief, who had enjoyed the support of the French administration, sent word to Niamey, capital of the Niger Territory. He said that the woman Zibo had ruined his community with despicable Hauka. The commandant of Niamey, a Major Crocci-chia, received the message and gave the order that all the Hauka be arrested and brought to Niamey. The Filingue chief presented the sixty participants to the French officials, who brought them to Niamey, where they were kept in prison for three days as punishment for their disruptive behavior. When Croccichia released them, the young people danced and the Hauka came into their bodies. Zibo began to shake from the presence of Gomno Malia. Upon learning this fact, Croccichia ordered his soldiers to bring Zibo to his headquarters. He slapped her and said: "Where are the Hauka?"

He continued to slap Zibo until she said that there was no such thing as the Hauka. The soldiers brought the other Hauka to Croccichia. He and his soldiers slapped them until they too admitted that there were no Hauka. Finally the commandant sent them back to Filingue.

Zibo and her cohorts found no peace there, however. The chief expelled them from the town, and so they traveled to other villages and established new Hauka cults. In this way the Hauka movement spread rapidly. By February 1927 the colonial administration noted that there were Hauka adepts in all the villages of Filingue district. The administration considered the Hauka rivals "of the established order represented by the chieftaincy, the backbone of the administrative system created by the French." [12]

In March of 1927 Gado Namalaya, the old chief of Filingue, died. The French supported the candidacy of Chekou Seyni, one of Gado's sons. Chekou, however, was not unopposed. Manifesting themselves as a political force, the Hauka supported a rival candidate. This action was an intolerable affront to French authority.

Because of its bold defiance of French rule, the Hauka movement grew in size and importance. In uninhabited areas of the countryside, the Hauka founded their own villages and set up their own society, which was overtly anti-French.

The French found in the Hauka "a clear opposition to the traditional chieftaincy. They discovered the presence of an open dissidence, a society the members of which openly defied the social, political and religious order. It is here that we discover the most original aspect of the Hauka movement: their total refusal of the system put into place by the French." [13] The harsh intervention of Major Croccichia, the French commandant of Niamey, had accelerated the diffusion of the Hauka movement. Major Croccichia's brutal treatment of Zibo and her group left such a searing memory that Croccichia was soon deified as a Hauka himself, Korsasi, the wicked major, one of the most violent Hauka. [14]

In the 1930s the Hauka family took form. They also assumed a place in Songhay cosmology through a mythology created for them by zimas. Through their mediums, the Hauka deities aped French colonial society and asserted that Dongo had invited them to Songhay from the Red Sea. The following spirits emerged as early Hauka deities: (1) Istanbula, who lives in Istanbul and is both a pious Muslim and chief of all the Hauka; (2) Gomno, the colonial governor (of the Red Sea); (3) Zeneral Malia, the general of the Red Sea; (4) King Zuzi, the king of judges or the colonial chief justice; (5) Mayaki, the warrior or great soldier; (6) Korsasi, the wicked major who sometimes kills his mediums; (7) Sekter, the secretary or colonial clerk; (8) Kapral Gardi, the corporal of the guard who is Korsasi's assistant and who can break iron with his hands; (9) Babule, the blacksmith; (10) Fadimata Malia, Zeneral Malia's wife, who had her son Cemoko by Kapral Gardi; and (11) Cemoko, the young boy who can pull silver out of the ground.[15]

Many of the mediums of these deities traveled far and wide in the great migrations from Songhay country to the Gold Coast during the colonial period. As they confronted new experiences, new deities manifested themselves in the mediums' bodies. In the Gold Coast the Hauka received two new deities, Kafrankot, the corporal of the coast, and Hanga Beri (big ear), who runs locomotives. Just as the colonial administration had become more complex, so the family of Hauka added new deities, which reflected the expansion of colonial authority. Hauka burlesqued highly placed civil servants: Minis de Ger, or minister of war; simple ministers, or Minis; and Prazidan di la Republik, or president of the French republic. The Hauka also parodied the French colonial army, presenting to audiences colonels, captains, lieutenants, and sergeants, as well as foot soldiers (Bambara Moose, the deity that represented many of the foot soldiers who were either Bambara or Moose in ethnic origin). Local administrative identities were not spared the theatrics of the Hauka. There were Hauka lawyers (Wasiri). The Hauka doctor (Lokotoro) injected people with his syringe. These new Hauka came into being, unbidden, as did the original Filingue group in 1925. During the course of a ceremony, an unknown deity would take a medium. Members of the troupe would ask the deity's name and, upon learning the name, would welcome the new deity to the Hauka family.[16]

The Hauka movement opposed the supremacy of French colonial rule. As a complex, the bizarre and brazen behavior of the Hauka expressed boldly critical statements about the nature of the colonizer and his behavior. The Hauka spoke in a melange of Pidgin French, Pidgin English, and Songhay. Pidgin continues to be a stigmatized linguistic form in both Francophone and Anglophone West Africa, and its use by such identities as Gomno and Korsasi satirized savagely the colonial authorities. Imagine a Songhay medium who aped a colonial administrator. His body was contorted. His eyes bulged. Saliva frothed at this mouth. To add insult to injury, he spoke a mixture of Pidgin French and Songhay. All in all, a terrifying burlesque.

A Hauka Ceremony in Mehanna (1976)

Pinpoints of light flickered in the midnight blue sky over Mehanna. The cool dry air cracked a person's skin and penetrated the body. I labored up a dune behind the village of Mehanna on a December evening in 1976. Sorko Djibo had scheduled a Hauka possession ceremony that evening.

There are only two occasions when Hauka alone are summoned. The first is for the initiation of a novice carrying a Hauka (see chap. 3). The second is when witches have attacked many people in a community. During a witch plague, Hauka take their mediums' bodies and brandish burning bushes above their heads—a warning to witches that the Hauka are after them. Since Mehanna is reputed to have more witches per capita than any other Songhay town, Hauka possession ceremonies are not infrequent.

From a distance I could see two Hauka carrying fiery branches above their heads. One of the two Hauka threw his burning bush to the ground and lit a torch which he held to his bare chest.

"Hurry, Monsieur Paul," said Idrissa Dembo, my compound mate in Mehanna. "Hurry. You must see Zeneral Malia and Lokotoro [the doctor]."

Zeneral Malia was not in uniform, but Lokotoro wore a pith helmet and carried a syringe. As soon as Lokotoro spotted me, he approached to greet me.

"Sha vas?" (How's it going), Lokotoro demanded.

"Ca vas?" (How's it going), I asked.

"Sha vas?"

"Ca vas?"

"Me ne Doctor" (I am called doctor), Lokotoro asserted.

"Ni Doctor?" (You're a doctor?), I wondered.

Laughter interrupted our exchange. Adhering to the context of

Two musicians at a Hauka ceremony in Mehanna (1976).

horrific comedy, I mocked Lokotoro. The audience found my antics hilarious.

"Alahamdu lilaahi. Enchante" (Praise be to God. Enchanted), I said.

"Sha vas?" Lokotoro repeated.

"Ca vas?"

"To Anasara hinka. Tu as conay?" (Okay. There are two Europeans here. Do you know it?)

"Tu as conay?" I echoed.

More laughter. Lokotoro was ridiculing Europeans, and I was appropriately mocking him. We were both being obdurate, playing out the exaggerated roles of two Europeans. The audience greatly appreciated our act.

Djibo Sorko broke into our conversation.

"A ne ni anasara no n'inga manti anasara no." He says that you're a European and that you and he make two Europeans.)

"Wo anasara no? To. Enchante." (This is a European? Okay. Enchanted.)

Laughter erupted. A black man stood before me frothing at the mouth, holding a syringe. He said, however, that he was a white European. I played along with the ridiculous charade, stating that he was indeed a white European. Then I code-switched into French to signify my recognition of his European status and said that I was enchanted to meet him. We had participated in a veritable theater of the absurd that provoked uproarious laughter.

Lokotoro left me, to examine a young girl who had been ill.

"Lokotoro, I've taken my daughter to the Alfaggey [Islamic healers], and the hospital people. The Alfaggey gave her potions and amulets. The hospital people pricked her with needles and gave her pills. In the name of God, Lokotoro, my daughter is still sick."

Lokotoro examined her, blew on her left arm, and injected her with his syringe, which contained a milky fluid.

"She'll get better now, good woman."

Lokotoro returned to me.

"Ah Lokotoro ka." (Ah, the doctor has come), I said.

Djibo Sorko addressed Lokotoro. "Ci wala. Ni ma ci wokom ni ga ba." (Speak now. You must tell [him] what you want.)

Addressing me, Lokotoro said: "To, l'argent." (Okay. [I want] money).

"L'argent?" I asked. "To, a go ka. Ay ma ceece l'argen. Ay ma no Lokotoro se l'argen. Lokotoro, boro hano no." (Okay, it's coming. I need to look for the money. I should give money to the doctor. The doctor is a good person.)

I dug into the pocket of my jeans for a hundred-franc piece and gave it to Lokotoro. He put the coin in his shirt pocket.

"Anasara," Lokotoro said, "sha vas?"

"Ca vas," I responded.

"Mershi." (Thank you [for the contribution].)

In the last sequence Lokotoro addressed me as "Anasara," which signified that we were no longer in the same social category. "Anasara, ca vas?" is a linguistic device that many Songhay use to distance themselves from Europeans. We were suddenly in different social categories; he had objectified me as the generic rich European and asked me for a contribution—a comic slap in my face.

The ludicrous situation of the hulking, frothing figure of Lokotoro burlesquing a European physician and equating himself with the only white person in the audience was also a means of defining Songhay vis-à-vis the European colonizer. The theatrical interaction created and maintained distance between the encroaching European civilization—me, in this instance—and the boundary of Songhay identity.

After completing his grand rounds Lokotoro joined his "brothers" Zeneral Malia and Commandant Bashiru for a discussion about witches in Mehanna. Their conclusions?

"Mehanna people are lazy," Zeneral Malia announced.

"Most Mehanna people are witches," Lokotoro proclaimed.

"Mehanna babies should have wet nurses," Commandant Bashiru suggested. (One becomes a witch by ingesting a witch's breast milk.) "Mehanna must express more reverence for Dongo. If not," Commandant Bashiru continued, "witch sickness will kill many people."

The three Hauka motioned to the musicians, a violinist and a drummer, to play. And they did, faster, faster, and faster until the three dancing Hauka did backflips onto the sand. After five minutes of vigorous massage, Sorko Djibo revived the exhausted mediums.

Hauka at Tillaberi's Yenaandi (1981)

When the Tooru visit the earth, those Hauka who personify French soldiers swoop down to the earth, take the bodies of their mediums, and serve as bodyguards to the spirit world's nobles. In June of 1981 the Tooru held a town meeting at the end of a

A medium possessed by his Hauka.

yenaandi ceremony (see chap. 6). Seated on overturned mortars, the Tooru received people in the Tillaberi audience. Before approaching the Tooru to receive advice, however, the townspeople had to endure the horrific comedy of the Hauka, whose job it was to bring people to the master of the heavens. Commandant Bashiru (CB) and Lieutenant Marseille (LM) provided this escort service.

CB: (Goose-steps from center of dance ground to audience. Stops in front of Young Woman [YW]. Clicks his heels together and salutes YW.) You are a fool, young woman. (Sprays saliva in her face.)

YW: (Recoils.)

CB: (Grabs her hand and yanks her away from audience.)

YW: (Falls to the ground, and speaks as she is dragged.) I don't want to go. I don't want to go.

CB: (Stops. Stands on one foot and looks at the audience.) You are all stupid Songhay. How can you resist? (Looks at YW and smiles.) Come, you daughter of a donkey. (He laughs, audience laughs, and he pulls YW to standing position and takes her to the Tooru.)

(Minutes later)

LM: (Struts toward the crowd and stands on one foot, gazing at the audience for a few moments. Then he struts toward a young man [YM] and salutes him.) In the name of the army, in the name of God, in the name of the spirits in the name of the Tooru . . .

YM: In the name of idiocy? (General laughter.)

LM: (Extends his hand to YM.) You . . . you, the one with the limp penis. Come and seek a solution. (More laughter.)

YM: (Pointing at LM and laughing.) And you with the empty head?

LM: (Grabs YM's arm and shoves him toward the Tooru.)

The audience at a Hauka performance laughs through its fear, because the Hauka are incredibly strong. Besides being able to pick up burning bushes with their bare hands and touch themselves with burning torches, I have seen them knock down thick mudbrick walls with their fists.

Since the Hauka are anything but gentle, when they summon someone to the Tooru's court, people are concerned about bodily injury. These roughhouse tactics, however, are coupled with such outrageously exaggerated military behaviors as goose-stepping and saluting, during which the Hauka hold their hands to their foreheads for as much as two minutes as they froth at the mouth and stare at the people they are saluting. As if following a script, Hauka add to the comedy with typical ritual insults in Songhay. Commandant Bashiru called the young woman the daughter of a donkey, a Songhay ritual insult that normally brings laughter.[17] When Commandant Bashiru said, "You are all stupid Songhay," this too precipitated laughter. Generally, Songhay do not take seriously these kinds of direct insults. Real insults in Songhay are usually indirect statements.

Lieutenant Marseille engaged in the same kind of horrific comedy as Commandant Bashiru. He approached the young man and gave him an exaggerated salute. He mocked the formality of military custom, saying, "In the name of the army . . ." The young man, however, mocked Lieutenant Marseille, saying, "In the name of idiocy?" Most Songhay immensely enjoy this kind of mutual mockery for it corresponds to the verbal duel, a favorite activity of younger people.

At first glance the Hauka movement seems to have represented the era of colonialism; it was a reflection of the confrontation between the French and Songhay society.[18] According to Jean Rouch, the Hauka had much less of a following after independence (1960).[19] While the Hauka were losing their colonial raison d'être, it has been suggested, zimas accelerated the process through which these outlaw spirits were incorporated into the mythology of the spirits.

> So Dongo, the god of thunder, is now considered their [the Hauka] father. And the story is that Bilali, another aspect of Dongo, when he was in Mecca had a lot of sons who came to Africa. They say that Bilali actually sang Hauka songs and did Hauka rituals when he was in Mecca. The Hauka were the *enfants terribles* of Bilali but now they are with us, and we are all together in the same family. And even today in the very remote village the Hauka play an important role.[20]

The Hauka's Force

When a Hauka takes his or her medium's body today, there is ribald comedy and terrifying drama that may be a manifestation of ongoing contact with European "force." There is no longer a separate Hauka movement as there was in 1927, a movement directed against the rule of the European. Opposition to European rule ceased to be the underlying theme for Haukas when France granted independence to the Republic of Niger. But just as today the conceptual residue of being a slave remains among the former slave populations of Songhay, so the psychological yoke of colonialism has remained with many peoples in the Republic of Niger.[21] While Europeans are no longer the political administrators of districts in the Republic of Niger, they still hold many important positions both in the capital city of Niamey and in rural regions of Songhay country. Europeans are technical advisers to various Nigerien ministries. Europeans comprise a large part of the staffs of the national and regional hospitals in the Republic of Niger. Europeans are the technicians responsible for a wide variety of internationally funded development projects. And Europeans still teach in some of Niger's secondary schools and in Niger's university. The "force" of the European continues to be strong in all regions of the Republic of Niger; the need for many Songhay to make sense of this "force" remains equally strong.

Theaters of Songhay Experience

Possession ceremonies are theaters of Songhay experience-in-the-world. When zimas stage possession ceremonies they set into motion an existential reenactment of the Songhay world. The "cries" of the godji and the clack-roll-clacks of the drums are the sounds of the ancestors—seductive sounds that compel the spirits to take the bodies of their mediums. The tam-tam's echoing thumps excite Dongo and his Tooru brothers. The vibrations of the tam-tam, combined with the godji's cries and the gasi's thumps, create the yenaandi context, drawing the Tooru to earth to accept the humble offerings of powerless people. In exchange the Tooru promise life-saving rain and the prospect of a good millet harvest. Such is the drama of life in Songhay. Will there be enough rain in June, in July, in August? Will there be too much rain in September? Will the October sun be hot enough? Will rats and birds decimate the crop before it is harvested? Will there be enough to eat this year? Such are the dramatic themes of yenaandi.

Hauka theatrics have more to do with politics-on-earth than with power-in-the-heavens. Once people in Songhay were masters of their own destinies. Colonialism transformed the social order, creating a new dimension of powerlessness. Before the colonial period people expressed their powerlessness to the spirits; they

Abdoulaye Issifu dancing at a Hauka ceremony in Tillaberi (1987).

asked for supernatural help to combat hunger, disease, and the natural elements. Colonization created a deep social void. Songhay polities lost their autonomy. Beloved chiefs lost the affection and respect of their people when they became tax collectors. Foreign judges adjudicated local disputes, usurping the prerogative of nobles and slaves. Foreign soldiers liberated captives, reducing the labor force and disrupting the established economy. Young children learned the foreigner's language in the foreigner's school. Through their terrifying burlesque the Hauka attempted to make sense of European influences and their impact on life in Songhay, an impact that today is still considerable. And so the powerless ridicule the powerful—an age-old practice that takes on different forms in different parts of the world.[22] But for the Songhay, the "biggest of all . . . problems is the whiteman. Who can understand the white man? What makes him tick? How does he think and why does he think the way he does? Why does he talk so much? Why does he say one thing and do the opposite? Most important of all, how do you deal with him? Obviously, he's here to stay. Sometimes it seems like a hopeless task."[23]

PART THREE: POSSESSION IN A
CHANGING WORLD

8

SEXUAL COMEDY: THE SASALE

It was almost dusk in Tillaberi. The last rays of the sun outlined the dull edges of mudbrick houses against a darkening western sky. A cool eastern wind swept across the dune. Wrapped in thin cotton shawls, people shivered. At the edge of town atop a dune, Adamu Jenitongo's was one of the coldest places in Tillaberi in 1981.

Adamu Jenitongo brought Hausa spirits to Tillaberi that afternoon to help cure a client who had been suffering from paralysis of the left arm. A Hausa spirit had come and told the man to give a jar of honey to the zima. Saying that the ceremony had been a great success, Adamu Jenitongo left the dance ground to enjoy the privacy of his hut. Only part of the crowd had dispersed, however. The musicians played their possession music. Young dancers stomped on the sand of the dance ground.

Suddenly there was movement in the remaining crowd. A young medium was wailing, "wo, wo, wo, wo, woo." She held her head in her hands and meandered about the dance ground as if she had lost her way, a sign that the spirit would soon settle comfortably in the body of its medium, a lanky young woman no more than eighteen years old. Ramu Kong'izo, the Sasale prostitute, had come to visit Tillaberi.

Like the other Sasale, Ramu Kong'izo (lit. Ramu, "daughter of a female slave") is a social iconoclast in the Republic of Niger. Her "brother" and "sister" Sasale, who are prostitutes, gamblers, drunkards, and womanizers, are all abjectly immoral from the vantage of Islam.

And so Ramu Kong'izo (RK) approached the crowd, keeping the palms of her hands on her temples.

> RK: Wo, wo, wo, woo. Yes, I am greeting you. (She undulates her hips as she presses her body against one of the men.) How much [money] will you give?
>
> Man: (Backs away from RK.) Uh, uh, I don't want . . .
>
> RK: (Following the man into the crowd, wagging her finger in his direction.) You do not want? You are a worthless Muslim. You have no penis.
>
> Man: (Leaves the dance ground.)[1]

Just as the emergence of the Hauka spirits can be linked to to the cultural disruption of French colonialism, so the appearance of the Sasale spirits in 1965 can be associated with modernization and the increasing influence of neoconservative Islam in the Republic of Niger. French colonial policy undermined the political autonomy and symbolic importance of chiefs, introduced money into the Songhay economy, and promoted French language and culture to the detriment of Songhay culture. The Hauka brutally satirized the symbols of French supremacy in order to reaffirm and to protect the traditions of Songhay culture. The Sasale mock the practices of a neoconservative Islam that, according to Adamu Jenitongo and his cronies, threatens the very foundation of Songhay society.

"These new marabouts know nothing," Adamu Jenitongo said. "They are spoiling our country. They are ruining our relations with the ancestors."[2]

From the beginning the Sasale did everything a good Muslim should not: they drank alcohol; they cursed; they gambled; they whored; they refused to pray. Sasale, then, represent the antithesis of Islamic behavior in independent Niger.

The Social Context of Sasale

To understand the Sasale movement, one must comprehend how the social structure of contemporary Songhay developed. During the colonial period, the arrival of the French undermined substantially the Songhay social order. The colonizers put an end to warfare between Songhay "principalities" and other ethnic groups in the Niger River basin. Enforced by the French military presence, this peace ended the noble-warriors' practice of raiding neighboring groups to replenish their supply of slaves.

The French also tampered with the structure of Songhay society by creating a new elite through their colonial education policy. Once educated in French language and culture, the new elite, most of whom were Songhay of non-noble origins, clerked in the colonial administration or taught in the primary schools. Some members of this elite were elected to the French Chamber of Deputies and Senate and became, following independence, the first leaders of the Republic of Niger, supplanting the old elite and traditional leadership of the Songhay nobility.

This scenario was played out in the village of Kokoro, the nobles of which trace their descent patrilineally to Askia Mohammed Touré. Their ancestors came to Kokoro, which borders a vast lake in the heart of Songhay, in the early part of the eighteenth-century. From then until the onset of the twentieth-century, these nobles, reputed to be fearless warriors, protected Kokoro from the military challenges of her neighbors. Kokoro first came in contact with the European in 1899, and its leaders, realizing their military plight, cooperated with the French, providing the colonizers with taxes and laborers.

This cooperation did not diminish the prestige of the Kokoro nobles who were descendants of such great Kokoro warriors as Wigindi, Zerma, and Ali. Their cooperation also brought economic prosperity to the region. In the 1930s the French wanted to make Kokoro a major market center. Mounkaila, the Kokoro chief at the time, suggested instead Mehanna, a village of former captives under his jurisdiction. A Niger River village, Mehanna would attract riverain as well as overland commerce. And so in the 1930s Mehanna developed into a bustling three-day (Tuesday–Thursday) market. As Issaka Boulhassane, himself a Kokoro noble and the unofficial historian of his lineage, says, "When the market was bustling, people in the entire region were happy. They said, 'Ba ngawri si, Mehanna ga kano' [Even in the absence of food, Mehanna is sweet]."

Issaka Boulhassane's life, in fact, encapsulates the widespread changes wrought by colonialism and independence. Issaka's father's brother, Mounkaila, was the Kokoro chief during most of the colonial period. Soon after Mounkaila established the Mehanna market, Issaka's father, Boulhassane, moved there and built a compound adjacent to the market plaza. Unlike his other brothers, Boulhassane encouraged his children to study in the schools the French had established in the region. Issaka studied nursing. His brother Djibo became a bureaucrat, and Boreima taught in the primary schools.

Issaka's studies took him to Abidjan and Dakar. He also lived in Paris where he spent many years perfecting his science. But Issaka never forgot the importance of his heritage. On vacations he returned home and talked with his older relatives, the guardians of his tradition. He immersed himself in local lore so that it would not be forgotten.

In 1964 the old Kokoro chief, a patrilineal descendant of Wigindi, founder of Kokoro, died, and the government appointed his successor, a wealthy merchant who was linked to Wigindi matrilineally. The appointment outraged Issaka and his family. Why had the government passed over the true successor—Hamidu Mounkaila—in favor of a merchant? What had happened to tradition?

Boreima Boulhasanne, Issaka's half-brother, and I discussed this problem in 1976. "Things are not the same now," Boreima said. "There is no respect for tradition, for genealogy. Ever since the European times, the merchants have become powerful. You need money to live today. That is why they ruined Kokoro. It's all a question of money. Someday things will be right. Someday, my family will regain its dignity."

"What do you mean, Boreima?" I asked.

"People no longer have great respect for us, the *maigey* [nobles]. They have just as much respect today for wealthy merchants. It all started during the European times, but it has gotten worse now."

During one of his vacations in 1977, Issaka Boulhassane visited Mehanna and stayed with me for one week. I welcomed the company of this worldly man who spoke four languages and who had versed himself in local lore. Then in his late forties, Issaka exuded robust health. He was well over six feet tall, with a baobab neck rooted in a mountainous chest.

Issaka's arrival attracted swarms of relatives and other clients of his family. He gave gifts to his nieces and nephews, his aunts and uncles, his "brothers" and "sisters." And then came the clients who had been in service to his father: smiths, bards, musicians, all of whom received small gifts. And then came the destitute for whom Issaka had reserved a few coins. He looked at me and smiled.

"I never leave Mehanna with money. You know what they say?"

"What?" I asked.

"If a noble is penniless, he will give you the shirt off his back."

For lunch and dinner the compound was filled with cronies who ate fine food—millet paste covered in oily peanut and tomato sauces. They washed down these delicacies with river water. Despite my reserves of boiled and filtered water, Issaka, a state nurse with more than twenty years of experience, opted to drink river water. His disregard of his own professional preachings soon resulted in nausea and dysentery. I offered him clean water once again.

I'll drink the same water as my brothers." Issaka said.

I soon understood the reason for Issaka's insistence on drinking river water. One afternoon just before the two o'clock prayer, a local noble, one of Issaka's cousins, came into the compound.

"Is the Anasara [European] there?"

"The Anasara?" I asked, perplexed. "I'm right here. I'm the Anasara."

"No, no. Not you," said the noble, a bit flustered. "I'm looking for Issaka."

"He went to the mosque."

Times had indeed changed. This man, Issaka, the nephew of a renowned Kokoro chief, had been called an Anasara.

I asked Issaka about that incident when he returned from prayer. He told me that when people learn the European's language and live in the European's country, they, for many people, become Europeans. "It works the same way as the Songhay proverb, Boro kom goro maiga windo ra, inga no maiga no [The person who lives in the noble's compound becomes a noble]."[3]

Issaka's Alienation in Contemporary Songhay

Issaka's alienation stems from a number of sources. Colonial policies on taxation and economic development reinforced the merchants in Songhay at the expense of the nobles, allowing wealthy "commercants" to establish local networks of economic clients, much as the nobles had networks of politico-economic clients a generation earlier. In this way merchants gained control of local economies in Songhay; nobles, still rooted to a past in which "money never fixed anything," lost prestige. Nobles like Issaka, who left Songhay to educate themselves, also lost prestige from the local perspective; they had become "Europeans."

Independence has exacerbated these alienating tensions. The gulf separating the Songhay noble and the former slave on the one hand, and the non-Songhay merchant and the member of the educated elite on the other hand, has widened greatly. The merchants have increased their control over the flow of money. They have expanded their economic influence from local to regional markets. The wealthier merchants have become patrons of large networks of economic clients and have incorporated much of the old noble style. They carry canes. They dress in white robes. They speak to others through intermediaries—the symbolic image of a Songhay chief. The elite, for their part, live increasingly in urban areas from which vantage they help to direct the local, regional, and national affairs of the Republic of Niger. They see themselves as government officials whose first allegiance is not to their ethnic group but to the state.[4]

This social divergence has created a climate of social competition in contemporary Songhay, which sets the old noble families against the merchants (government officials play a minor administrative role in the competition, but their actions benefit considerably the merchants). This competition does not affect political authority; it concerns, rather, social influence in Songhay.

In contemporary Songhay the nobles (patrilineal descendants of Askia Mohammed) want to preserve their influence and reassert their prestige. Through a variety of symbolic manipulations (arrangements of fields and neighborhoods, management of space at community celebrations, and praise-poetry, which lauds the kings of Songhay and the noble-warriors of the past) they attempt to manage their public image to legitimate the old social order. This old view of the Songhay world is reinforced by a fundamental belief in social inequality which is ascribed at birth.[5] Issaka Boulhassane "played" the traditional noble during his Mehanna visit: he gave away his hard-earned money, and he drank river water with the cronies of his network.

In the barter economy of precolonial Songhay, the slaves and artisans were clients to noble patrons, providing the nobles with grain and services. The nobles provided them with military protection and redistributed grain, cows, and horses. In the money economy of the modern era, a noble must pay his client in cash. In sum, the nobles must compete with the men who control cash—merchants—for loyal clients. Educated younger former slaves have joined the ranks of the urban elite. Uneducated younger men from former slave families have joined the client networks of merchants. Older uneducated men in this category, however, continue in the client networks of nobles.

Songhay is still marked by ethnic diversity. Since precolonial times the Songhay have coexisted with the Fulan, Tuareg, Gurmantche, and Moose. These "strangers" today play little or no sociopolitical role in local-level Songhay social life. Zerma and Hausa merchants who migrated to Songhay during the colonial period, however, have become highly visible social actors in the competition for social prestige—especially the middle-aged and younger merchants.[6]

In independent Niger one must add the government agent to the social mixture of Songhay. Although government agents are the ultimate political authority in Niger today, they are not directly engaged in the local competition for social prestige. First, government agents are generally more concerned about competition in the wider bureaucracy. Second, many government agents posted in Songhay are educated Hausa from eastern Niger who do not speak Songhay. Third, government agents are isolated socially from the communities they serve.

The social, political, and cultural distance between the government agents and the Songhay peasants among whom they live is perhaps the most important dynamic of social life in Songhay today. As in the case of Issaka Boulhassane, Songhay often refer to government agents as Anasarey (pl.), "Europeans," even if the functionaries are themselves Songhay. This linguistic practice reflects the further erosion of local power, authority, and autonomy. The new "Europeans" want to develop Niger. The Songhay peasants want to be left alone. From the perspective of the Songhay peasant, the transformation of Niger from a colony to an independent country has had few positive economic repercussions. As a result of government policies, the Songhay peasant is part of a world market in which rates of inflation and currency fluctuations make it increasingly difficult for him to feed his family.

The Songhay in the Republic of Niger

Songhay-speaking peoples constitute roughly 40 percent of the population of the Republic of Niger. Like the other ethnic groups in Niger (Hausa, Fulan, Kanuri), Songhay has remained a distinct social grouping. Consciousness of one's ethnic identity very often supercedes consciousness of national identity. The persistence of what some call "tribalism" is one of Niger's major problems as it attempts to forge a nation-state from ethnic elements that have long histories of mutual enmity.[7]

There are many socioeconomic problems facing Songhay in the Republic of Niger. These include chronic agricultural underproduction, migration, and uncontrolled urbanization. The problems are compounded by their interrelatedness. The need for money forces young Songhay men to leave the countryside for the city where they might exchange their labor for wages. In many Songhay villages one is hard-pressed to find young men in residence. During the nonplanting season (November–May) many young men travel to Niamey; others go to Togo, Nigeria, and the Ivory Coast. This flood of young men from the countryside has brought on rapid and uncontrolled urbanization. Since many of these young men never return home, the rural labor force has been depleted. As cities such as Niamey have grown exponentially, the amount of millet grown in the countryside has dwindled. Shortages in millet, in turn, increase the price of this Sahelian staple. The high price of grain stiffens the resolve of young men to leave their village in search of wage labor. Songhay in remote rural areas today would not be able to remain there if not for the money sent home by their departed sons.[8] Add to this cycle the ecological horrors of chronic drought and the economic picture in Niger is complete—a picture in which the importance of village life has diminished.[9]

The government has attempted to solve the problems of underproduction, migration, urbanization, and ethnic enmity. The late President Seyni Kountché's government, which took power in 1974, recognized that if Niger is to become a viable nation-state, there must emerge a radically new social order. The government seems to understand that

> modernization carries with it a conception of a relatively autonomous individual with a considerable capacity for adaptation to new situations and for innovation. Such an individual has a relatively high degree of self-consciousness and requires a family structure in which his independence and personal dignity will be recognized and where he can relate to others not so much in terms of authority and obedience as in terms of companionship and emotional participation. Such an individual also requires a society in which he feels like a full, participating member, whose goals he shares and can meaningfully contribute to.[10]

To achieve these social goals the government of Niger has promoted a set of social policies based on the tenets of scripturalist Islam, for the Koran contains many statements about the dignity of the individual and about the high status of women in the kinship network.

> The reassertion of the basic message of the Qu'ran in the face of the overgrown garden of magic in late medieval Islam has had a profoundly modernizing consequence. Awakening membership in the universal community of Islam has often been the first mode of consciousness to break through stagnant localisms. . . . Anticolonialist and nationalist impulses as well as all kinds of social reform efforts have originated at this source. There can be no clearer tribute to the universalistic, progressive and indeed, revolutionary potential of Qu'ranic religion.[11]

Following this prescription, the government began in 1978 to appeal to the population not as Songhay, Hausa, or Fulan, but as citizen-believers in the Islamic community of Umma. In a speech made in February 1981, the late President Kountché said that Umma "gives us the wherewithal to follow the straight road. . . . All Muslims, despite their variation in color and language, are one community. They follow the same path and are of one culture." [12] Planners have also argued that if there is moral purity in a Niger united through Islam, the citizen-believers will be mobilized to meet the twin goals of agricultural and industrial self-sufficiency in a climate of national harmony. Government publications abound with references to the desirability of Islamic purity.

The writers of these publications, all members of the educated elite, exhort their fellow believers to practice their religion in all its purity. Pure religious practice, in behavioral terms, means that people should recite their prayers five times daily, give to the poor, and refrain from drinking alcohol. In these publications prostitutes are treated with special vehemence. "Some of our sisters have thrown themselves into delinquency. They are called prostitutes. In our Society of Developement [reference to the proposed new social order] each Nigerien woman would be a responsible, vigilant, and conscientious person." [13] Another writer focuses his comments on illegitimate birth. "A woman who gave birth to a bastard was given away as a slave in some African societies. Some young women have abortions to maintain their youth or to continue their studies. To avoid pregnancy one must avoid carnal relations." [14]

Songhay today are not only confronted with the continuing erosion of their social autonomy but also with the intentions of the government—the educated elite—to make them model citizens in an Islamic nation-state. Although almost all Songhay people are putatively Muslims, some continue to resist those elements of Islam that threaten themes central to Songhay identity and consciousness.

The Sasale Movement
Enter the Sasale movement. The term *sasale* originally denoted a group of slaves who were notorious for their dancing. When they danced for chiefs,

> they took off their clothing, sang sexual songs and danced sexual dances. And the spectators paid them to stop. You see the

idea: It's a kind of strip-tease, only you pay them not to go on! Well, when the Sasale possess boys and girls they do the same thing, they start to take off their clothes and start to make love when they are possessed. It was considered shameful, it was forbidden by the Niger police, and they were put in jail.[15]

The Sasale flaunt the immorality that the government abhors: permissive sexuality, foul language, womanizing, gambling, laziness, and prostitution. The first Sasale deities appeared in the mid-1960s and the movement continues to grow in reaction to more than fifteen years of the government of Niger's socioeconomic policies.[16]

The first Sasale to appear was Alibiyo (Black Ali). He was

a young and very handsome man who had been a propagandist for the RDA, the Rassemblement Democratique Africain, a political party in the fight for independence. In '61 the minstrels, guitar players, fiddle players—the griot—composed a very famous song called "Alibiyo." The Niger Army was looking for some traditional tunes to play and chose "Alibiyo." When Alibiyo appeared three years later he said, "You are calling me all the time, even the army is calling me. Well, here I am, I'm Alibiyo, the playboy," and that was the beginning.[17]

Of Alibiyo it is said that he is a treacherous playboy. He will betray the best of his friends. He will grab and have intercourse with any woman who pleases him.

Many Sasale deities, however, are women—the visitations of recently deceased prostitutes and other free spirits who are, from the vantage of Koranic Islam, social deviates. (Prostitutes are among the most independent women in Niger. Having earned considerable sums of money as young women, many prostitutes invest their savings in legitimate businesses and become prosperous entrepreneurs in the larger Songhay towns.) Some of the female Sasale are (1) Ramu Kong'izo, or Ramu, the daughter of a female slave, who was a famous prostitute;[18] (2) Bell'izo, or the daughter of a Bella, a former slave to the Tuareg; she is the chief of the Sasale and especially foul-mouthed; (3) Kadidja Cendaaj'izo, or Kadidja from Cendaaji, who approaches male strangers in a possession audience and attempts to thrust her hands into their trousers and grab their penises; and (4) Fadimata Idrissa, or Fadimata, daughter of Idrissa, who attempts to grab the testicles of men in a possession audience.[19]

Sasale Ceremonies

Zimas use the same means to bring Sasale to earth—music, dance, and sacred texts—as they use for the other spirit "families" in the Songhay pantheon. There are some differences, however. Chanted by the ritual musicians, Sasale songs are far more scatological and sexual than those sung for other spirits. When calling for the Sasale, musicians sing the following verses:

1. Nya ngoko. (Fuck your mother.)
2. Nya dufe. (Your mother's cunt.)
3. Duf'izey kulu bene. (All clitorises are above [with God].)
4. Fulan benda, a ga wey ngoko. (A Fulan's penis fucks women.)
5. Benda, benda, a si ngoko weybora kala jina, jina nga hari kogo. (A penis, penis, it will only fuck women again and again [but] its water [sperm] is dried up.)
6. Duf'izey kosu, a ga labduru ga dang tonka. (Into the clitoris and cunt, she will pour porridge with hot pepper.) [20]

These insults are designed to compel the Sasale to take their mediums' bodies, and when they do, they begin their own barrage of insults. They insult the musicians. They insult the sorko. They insult members of the audience. At one possession ceremony in 1981, Ramu Kong'izo picked me out in the crowd of more than a hundred onlookers. She announced five times to the audience that "this European [me] had brains of dried semen." [21]

Sasale songs are not sung until the very end of prearranged possession ceremonies. When the majority of the audience goes home at dusk, the musicians sometimes play their ribald Sasale songs. Sometimes the Sasale successfully take their mediums.

Just as the older possession participants disassociated themselves from the Hauka in 1925, so older zima, like Adamu Jenitongo, have distanced themselves from the Sasale. When Sasale songs are played today, the audience consists mostly of teenagers and young adults—the group that seems to be entertained by the Sasale's sexual and scatological antics. When the singers chant, for example, "A Fulan's penis fucks women," a woman dancer takes a long piece of cloth and twists it into a phallic shape. She places the "penis" between her legs and twirls it as she dances.

Sasale "Morality"

The Sasale movement celebrates people in Songhay society who have violated the moral code of Islam. Opposition to the moral preeminence of Islam is expressed through ritually framed sexual perversion. Jean Rouch has called the Sasale movement a new religion:

> This new religion is . . . absolutely underground because the government is against sex. I began a film about it, but they [the government] asked me not to show it because, of course, the people were, well, they were not making love in front of the camera, but all the dances, all the songs were about sex: "Look at my clitoris," "Oh, your testicles are wonderful," and so on. . . . These religions are a kind of *inconscient collectif.* The people can't explain what they're doing, they can only show what they're thinking of, and it means that during these years from the 20's to Independence [the Hauka movement] they were thinking about power, military, administrative and bureaucratic power, and now they are thinking of sex.[22]

It is too simple to say that the Sasale represent what Victor Turner would have called the antistructure of Songhay social life in independent Niger.[23] True, Sasale deities are the antithesis of the neoconservative Islam that the government has promoted as a solution to its problems. But why are many Songhay thinking about sex today? The answer may lie deep in the history of possession in Songhay.

Possession in Songhay seemingly emerged in reaction to the Askiad, imperial Islam, and the dissolution of the lineage as a unit of social governance. As an aesthetic form, possession ceremonies stretched with Songhay sociocultural experience. Eventually the Hauka movement emerged at a time when colonialism had undermined the precolonial social order. In both the imperial and colonial cases, new deities came into existence in response to profoundly stressing social change and reflected, often with mockery, the influential Other. By contrast, the Sasale might be seen as a parody of the Songhay themselves. Despite government propaganda, which most Songhay peasants cannot read, sexual promiscuity is commonplace—at least in the villages where I have lived. Recently divorced women in their late teens and early twenties rent their bodies to eager customers. These may be young men too poor to pay a brideprice, recently divorced men in need of sexual gratification, or married men seeking sexual variety. But sex in Songhay social life is a private affair; public discussion of sex is shameful.

And yet the Sasale play with sex, inverting longstanding attitudes about sexual expectations. By flaunting sexual excess in the wake of the prudish government policy, the Sasale register perhaps a widely shared social protest. In addition, the government's neoconservative Islam, according to people like Adamu Jenitongo and Soumana Yacouba, is a more serious cultural challenge than the threats of the past, for it may ultimately undermine the Songhay concept of the self-in-the world by severing age-old ties to the ancestors. The Sasale's shameful public display of sex is a way of saying to the government: "Look what you are doing to us. This is what you have forced us to become."

On another level the Sasale may represent a warning to their Songhay audiences: "This is what is left of Songhay. We must restore our ties to the ancestors." Ultimately, the sexual license and social perversion of Sasale are an expression of personal freedom in a social climate where the individual Songhay has lost her or his sociocultural autonomy. The Sasale movement is cultural resistance par excellence.

A Spiritual Encounter

High, thin cirrus clouds stretched across the deep blue sky. The air was mild and dry in Niamey that January 1980. I had just returned to Niger's capital from three months of fieldwork, mostly in the Songhay villages of Mehanna and Tillaberi.

Two days before I was to leave Niger, Jean Rouch, the irrepressible French anthropologist and filmmaker, asked if I would meet him that afternoon. I gladly accepted the invitation, not knowing what to expect from Rouch, who had studied the Songhay for more than forty years.

Rouch called for me in his battered Peugeot. I squeezed in and we drove off. He refused to tell me where we were going. We crossed the John F. Kennedy Bridge to the west bank of the Niger River. We turned onto a dusty sand road. To our left was a motley assortment of houses. Some were small square mudbrick structures; others were sprawling *banco amélioré,* which is mudbrick covered with a smooth surface of cement. To our right was the majestic Niger with its many islands. In the background, Niamey's Plateau neighborhood (originally the European quarter) shimmered in the afternoon heat. We drove on, passing men working in their riverfront gardens.

Our destination turned out to be the site of a possession ceremony.

"Look." Rouch pointed his finger in the direction of a small canopy. "They have been dancing since last night, and this is the Prophet Mohammed's birthday, no less."

Rouch supplied more background on the possession troupe. He pointed to a large white villa well within earshot of the dance ground. The villa, Rouch told me, belonged to the president of the Islamic University of Niamey.

"My God!" I blurted. "How could they!" How bold it was for this possession troupe to stage their ceremonies on the doorstep of the president of the Islamic University—on the Prophet Mohammed's birthday.

But there was more, for during the previous night the sorko, musicians, and zima had insulted loudly the deities that they wanted to bring to the social world. And so throughout that night the air was filled with obscenities which the president of the Islamic University must have heard. But there was still more. The musicians had insulted the president of the Islamic University, suggesting that he have sexual intercourse with his mother.

"Why insult the president of the Islamic University?" I asked the zima of the troupe.

"Because he is ruining our country. People are hungry. There is not enough rain. They are the ones who are ruining everything."

9

TWO MOUTHS, TWO HEARTS

In times of suffering Songhay often use the idiomatic expression "mey hinka, bina hinka" (two mouths, two hearts). When a person speaks with two mouths, she or he speaks with duplicity, the sign of deceitfulness. When a person feels with two hearts, she or he is insincere, the mark of hypocrisy.

Many Songhay believe that mey hinka, bina hinka is the cause of widespread misfortune in Songhay communities. When there is mey hinka, bina hinka, there are social catastrophies. The rains stop falling. The millet dries and dies in the fields. Deadly epidemics sweep the land. Cholera kills old people. Meningitis kills young people. People starve to death. But drought and famine also unravel the social fabric of Songhay; they force people to leave ancestral villages, which are depleted of food and will and filled with disease and duplicity. In Songhay, mendacity kills.

The Famine of 1984

In Songhay, 1984 was a year of mey hinka, bina hinka, a year of duplicity. The rains failed. At first there were hopeful signs that in 1984 Songhay farmers would produce a bumper crop. In May the sky "cried," saturating parched Songhay fields. With the expectation of a fine harvest, Songhay farmers sowed their fields. But the rains did not return. The May millet emerged from the sandy fields only to shrivel and die under the relentless Sahelian sun. Each day farmers sat in their fields watching the cloudless sky. If new rains did not come soon, the planting season would be a failure, bringing famine during the upcoming year.

In Tillaberi, the *sous-préfet* (regional administrator) was beside himself. Through his various irrigation projects, he had attempted to ensure the local food supply against the uncertainties of climate. If the rains failed, according to the logic of European and Nigerien development plans, one could always rely on the rice produced in the irrigated fields that bordered the Niger River. But the drought was so pervasive in 1984 that the unforeseen had occurred: the great Niger was drying up, having been reduced to a series of disconnected, stagnant pools. No rice. No fish. Hunger.

In early June of 1984 the sous-préfet in Tillaberi called a meeting of the local Islamic clerics: "For the next month, I would like you to organize the community to pray for rain. Do what you must. Recite the *alfatia* [prayer for protection]. Ask Allah to save us from peril."

The local clerics responded with an energetic campaign. Supplementing their normal routine of daily prayers with the alfatia, the community prayed fervently for one month. Clouds gathered in the east. The wind gusted, kicking up dust that "closed off" the sun. The sky groaned. But the rains did not come to Tillaberi.

In early July of 1984 the sous-préfet summoned Adamu Jenitongo to his office. "Baba, I am desparate. Do what is necessary to bring us rain."

In early July Adamu Jenitongo prepared a special ritual to bring rain.

"The yenaandi did not work for us. There was too much dissension. Mey hinka, bina hinka."

And so he gathered the possession troupe and proposed that they perform sacrifices in the bush on July 5, a Thursday. The sous-préfet supplied animals for sacrifice and trucks to transport the troupe to the bush.

In the shimmering heat of midday the troupe left town for an ant hill located at a crossroads. Adamu Jenitongo planted his forked stick (korom genji) into the ant hill and sacrificed one black goat, one black chicken, one red chicken, and one speckled chicken.

"Our work is not yet finished," Adamu Jenitongo announced to the group. "We must go on to Sadyara's home."

They marched on to the second bush altar, a large hole in a deep laterite gully that cut into the earth just below a barren brown mesa about six kilometers east of Tillaberi. In the hole lived Sadyara, the powerful two-headed snake that cries like a sheep. Carrying his violin, Daouda Godji entered the gully. The cries of the violin pierced the humid afternoon air. Moru and Halidu, the drummers, followed Daouda into the gully. They struck their instruments rhythmically. The cries, clacks, and rolls shot into air. Adamu Jenitongo sang incantations to the spirits. And then Nya Beri took the body of her medium, a fat woman whose loose flesh glistened in the midafternoon sunlight. Bellowing and moaning, Nya Beri threw the body of her medium against the rocks of the gully. She was furious.

"The people of Tillaberi," Nya Beri proclaimed, "are not on the path of the spirits. They walk with two hearts and two mouths. I am tired of people who do not believe in the path of the past."

The gully suddenly shook. Sadyara was coming. Sadyara was coming. "Bah. Bah. Bah."

"Run, run, everyone! Run!" Daouda Godji screamed. "Run to safety!" They believed that the serpent would kill anyone who got too close.

Adamu Jenitongo and his troupe ran from the gully to safety. From a hundred meters away, they waited for Sadyara to rise from his hole, ascend to the heavens, and transform himself into a thick band of black storm clouds. Nothing happened.

Dejectedly, the troupe climbed into the sous-préfet's trucks and returned to Tillaberi.

"What can we do to bring rain?" Daouda Godji asked.

"We must work," Adamu Jenitongo answered. "We must show the spirits that we are reverent, that we speak with *mey fo, bina fo* [one mouth and one heart]."

The next day, Friday, July 6, dark gray storm clouds gathered in the north, in the west, and in the south. It drizzled a bit, dappling the parched millet fields. Farmers would have to wait yet another day to plant their millet. Mey hinka, bina hinka.

Dissension in Tillaberi

Adamu Jenitongo said in 1984: "People say one thing and do another. People profess their beliefs, but they are not true to their beliefs. This is destroying our country. Look at the fields: dry, dead, lifeless. Where is the rain? We are killing ourselves. If there is to be rain, a community must be united: one mouth, one heart." [1]

For years Tillaberi had been a village of dangerous dissension. The year before the rains had been late, and the sous-préfet had asked Adamu Jenitongo to make sacrifices to the spirits. During one ceremony Istanbula, the chief of the Hauka, shook himself into his medium's body. Istanbula has two great talents: reading a person's mind and uncovering sorcery. Saliva frothing from his quivering mouth, he wagged his finger toward the mountain east of Tillaberi. "It is there," he said. "It is there."

"What is there?" asked Adamu Jenitongo.

Istanbula stomped both feet on the group and shook his head. Large drops of saliva fell from his mouth to the sand.

"What is there?" asked Adamu Jenitongo.

Istanbula took the zima's hand and led him to the ritual canopy. "Zima. Ziimma."

"Yes."

"We must go. You, me, and Djingarey must go to fine some bad medicine."

"Bad medicine?"

Djingarey, the soldier who was also a sorko, had come to the zima's compound in his battered Deux Chevaux Citroen. "Bad medicine? What bad medicine?"

"In the name of Bonji [Bon Dieu]," Istanbula bellowed.

Dingarey took Istanbula's hand and led him to the Deux Chevaux. Adamu Jenitongo ducked into the back seat. Djingarey plopped Istanbula in the front seat, then rolled back the Deux Chevaux's canvas top and started the engine.

They sputtered off to the east toward the scrubby mesa. Djingarey deftly drove his car around ruts and through deep sand as Istanbula, standing as though he were at the helm of a Niger River dugout, waved his finger toward the east. "Bad medicine!" he screamed in three languages (Pidgin English, Pidgin French, and Songhay).

They came to a fork in the road.

"What way do we go?" Djingarey asked the Hauka.

Istanbula moaned three times and directed them to the left, a path that took them onto a rust-colored volcanic plain strewn with thousands of small blackened rocks and pebbles. They drove slowly, for there were many thorn branches on the road.

"Yes! Yes! There it is," Istanbula said breathily. Despite his agitation—foam was oozing from his mouth—he managed to direct Djingarey and Adamu Jenitongo to a five-foot termite hill. "Look. In the name of Bongi. Look."

Djingarey stopped the Deux Chevaux. The trio got out and examined the termite hill. It was about four feet thick at the base, tapering to one foot at its summit.

"I see nothing here, Baba," Djingarey said to Adamu Jenitongo.

"Neither do I," said the zima.

Istanbula ran his hands over the termite hill. He stopped at a point facing west and poked a small hole in it with his forefinger. Djingarey took out his knife and dug out more dirt, revealing the outline of a cylindrical object.

"Do you see, Baba?"

He scraped around the object until he was able to pull it out; it was an antelope horn. Djingarey knocked it gently against the termite hill to loosen the dirt caked inside. Small pieces of folded paper fell to the ground. Djingarey retrieved a few and examined them.

"It's full of Arabic writing," he said. "Full of Arabic."

"Gris-gris [amulets]" Adamu Jenitongo said. "Gris-gris to block Dongo's path [the path of the rain storm]."

Adamu Jenitongo had seen this kind of sorcery before. For whatever reason, an Islamic cleric steals into the bush with an antelope horn filled with charms. He recites his Arabic incantations over the horn and buries it someplace. When the rain, which follows Dongo's path—comes upon the gris-gris, it dissipates altogether or it bifurcates, falling to the north and south of a village. "This treachery [called *figiri*, in Songhay] destroys a community," said Adamu Jenitongo, shaking his head. "We must take this to the sous-préfet," Djingarey suggested.

They drove back to Tillaberi to present their evidence to the sous-préfet.

Djingarey spoke in French: "We have found some Islamic sorcery that is destroying the community, Monsieur le Sous-préfet."

"Let's see."

Djingarey presented the antelope horn and the Islamic writings.

"Where did you find this?"

Djingarey described the expedition.

Switching into Songhay, the sous-préfet, a large fleshy man with filmy eyes, asked Adamu Jenitongo: "What kind of medicine is this, Baba?"

"It prevents the rain from coming to Tillaberi, Commando [the term used by Songhay to denote a sous-préfet]."

The sous-préfet used his office intercom to buzz one of his aides, who materialized in the doorway.

"Find the Imam and tell him to come here at once."

The sous-préfet asked Djingarey and Adamu Jenitongo to wait in the reception room until the Imam arrived.

Twenty-minutes later, the Imam arrived, dressed elaborately in a blue boubou with thick gold embroidery. They all entered the sous-préfet's office.

The sous-préfet gave the gris-gris to the Imam.

"Iman, what do you make of this?" the sous-préfet asked.

"They are very, very bad, these writings. They prevent the rain from coming to Tillaberi."

The muzzim's tower in Mehanna.

"What!" exclaimed the sous-préfet, now convinced of the veracity of Adamu Jenitongo's interpretation. "How could anyone . . ." Controlling his rage, he turned to Adamu Jenitongo. "Baba, do you know how to break this curse on our town?"

"Yes, Commando, I do."

"Then do it."

Djingarey drove Adamu Jenitongo to the base of a gao tree (*Acacia albida*) that stood at a crossroads just to the east of Tillaberi. There Adamu Jenitongo built a fire. Reciting an incantation, the genji how (that which harmonizes the forces of the bush), he threw the gris-gris and the antelope horn into the flames. "The curse is broken," he said.

"We thank God," Djingarey said.

Adamu Jenitongo shook his head. "Why do the Islamic clerics hate us? We have done nothing to them. We recite their prayers. We pay homage to Allah. In return, they mock us. They curse the spirits. They reject our ancestors. And you see the result, Djingarey. Look at our land. Look at the people who die. The evil marabouts are ruining our country with their two hearts and two mouths."

This episode was but another chapter in the book of Tillaberi dissension. The year before a similar discovery was made in a village on the left bank of the Niger opposite Tillaberi.

That year Istanbula led Djingarey and Adamu Jenitongo to Sakoire, ten kilometers north of Tillaberi on the Niger's right bank. But Istanbula pointed west, toward the left bank. They hired a dugout. The boatman glided them through rice fields and around islands until they approached the left bank. A golden dune rose abruptly from the river's edge.

Istanbula pointed to the village atop the dune. They got out of the dugout, ascended the dune, struggling upward through deep sands toward the village. Adamu Jenitongo and Djingarey hurried to follow Istanbula, who goose-stepped through the village.

"In the name of Bonji, I am close. In the name of Bonji," Istanbula cried, as he walked.

Istanbula's search ended at the very edge of the village, where he drew a circle in the sand. "There, there it is, in the name of Bonji."

By this time the villagers crowded around the trio. "What is this about?" a village elder asked Djingarey, who was in uniform.

"Bad medicine," Djingarey said bluntly.

"Dig," Istanbula said, pointing at the circle. "Dig."

Djingarey ordered the villagers to dig a hole. They brought shovels and went to work. Rocks made the task a difficult one.

The villagers complained.

"There is nothing here."

"This is a waste of time."

"Can we stop now?"

"How can you listen to this devil?"

They dug down one meter, two; Djingarey frowned at Istambula. "Is there anything there?"

Istambula moaned and pointed at the spot. "Dig. Dig," he said.

And so they dug for hours, reaching two meters, three meters. Night approached and they had yet to find anything. Ducks flew overhead seeking their nocturnal roosts. Fulan shepherds led cows into the village from their day's grazing in the bush.

"Hey! Hey!" one of the men shouted. "Hey, hey!" He had uncovered the rim of a clay pot.

"Dig carefully. We don't want to break the pot," Djingarey said.

A short time later they freed the pot and discovered in it pieces of paper covered with Arabic writing.

The next day the sous-préfet ordered Adamu Jenitongo to break the curse.

And so the rains failed in Tillaberi in 1984. Members of the possession troupe blamed the marabouts. Had they not spoiled the community with their sorcery? Did they not incessantly insult the zimas, the mediums, the sorkos and their musicians, calling them devil worshipers? The marabouts blamed the drought on blasphemy.

"As long as there is a possession troupe in Tillaberi," one of the fundamentalist clerics told me in 1984, "there will be no rain. Allah will not allow it."

The young millet shoots shriveled and died in the sun. Without the necessary diet of fresh green grasses, cows lost their milk. Ravaged by hunger, entire herds dropped dead, their rotting carcasses littering the dry riverbed that separates the older and newer neighborhoods in Tillaberi. Without the cleansing rain, the dusty air infected children with meningitis. The Niger's waters carried cholera. Weakened by the heat and hunger, hundreds of people died in Tillaberi.

"Tillaberi people have not yet understood," said Adamu Jenitongo. "We will try to bring rain, but if there are two mouths and two hearts, what can be done?"

An Offering to Nya Beri

A filmy haze covered Tillaberi on the morning of July 10, a Tuesday. Djingarey and Adamu Jenitongo had decided to stage a ceremony at Nya Beri's altar, a smooth piece of grayish granite jutting fifty centimeters out of a sandy millet field. Shaped like a shallow bowl, the stone was a meter in diameter.[2]

The troupe converged on the site at midday; the Tooru spirits like the midday heat. The musicians set up three meters to the west of the altar and began to play Tooru music. Imitating the practice of farmers when they bury sanctified nails to protect their crops, Moussa Zima, Adamu Jenitongo's nephew, put four nails in the center of the stone's crater, and at its east a vial of Bint al Sudan, Dongo's perfume. Another zima gave a red cock to Adamu Jenitongo, who waved it in the air and spoke inaudibly to the spirits. The zima invited the other mediums to do the same.

"Speak to the spirits from your hearts, from your hearts," he told them.

Each medium held that red cock over the altar and spoke to the spirits from her or his heart.

"The spirits must know we respect their way," Moussa Zima stated. "We must swear to them our allegiance."

The time of sacrifice had arrived. A Hauka medium, Soumana Yacouba, furrowed four canals from the altar in the four cardinal directions. Moussa Zima secured the squirming, squawking cock, stretching its neck over the altar. Another zima slit its throat. Blood spurted into the granite bowl of the altar. The zima sacrificed a speckled chicken in the same manner. In the background, thumping, clacking music echoed in the fiery midday air. The Hauka mediums walked counterclockwise in a circle just to the east of the altar. Suddenly, Istanbula plunged into Soumana's body. He cried. He hyperventilated. He frothed at the mouth. He thumped his chest and strutted toward the altar. In a mixture of English, Arabic, and Songhay he spoke of his long journey from beyond the Red Sea.

"I am tired. I feel thirst," he announced.

Eyeing the pooled blood on the altar, Istanbula sprang toward the stone and lapped it, catlike.

Blood dripping from his lips, he addressed the group.

"There is filth in Tillaberi," he said. "Much filth. There must be more sacrifices. My brothers from Malia [the Red Sea] will not come unless we see the proper respect."

He crouched over the altar once again and muttered to it in an

Nya Beri's altar.

unrecognizable language. Moussa Zima gave him an egg. He whispered and walked around the altar.

Istanbula's performance brought Lokotoro, the doctor, who slid into the body of an old man who had come to the ceremony dressed in a pith helmet and a white smock. Blue crosses had been stitched over the smock's pockets. Commandant Selma joined Lokotoro and Istanbula minutes later.

"I have come to warn Tillaberi," he announced in a mixture of Songhay and Tamasheq (the Tuareg language). "There is much dissension and treachery here. We bring only death and disease to people who betray one another, people who show us no respect."

The trio gathered to discuss what Tillaberi might do to bring rain.

"They must sacrifice a bull at Sadyara's hole," Lokotoro suggested.

"That's not enough," Istanbula said. "They must sacrifice chickens, goats, and sheep. We need blood to satisfy our thirst."

The musicians now played Dongo's music, which reverberated in the birdlike body of sixty-year-old Djami. She shuddered. Her left hand quivered. The left side of her faced twitched. A tear rolled down her left cheek. Her body stiffened. And then a low-pitched scream exploded from her frail body. Dongo, the thunder deity, hopped along the sand and greeted the violinists and the drummers. He greeted members of the audience officiously, inspecting the blood on the altar. Meanwhile, Djingarey sang praise-songs in a plump young woman's ear. Soon thereafter Cirey, deity of lightning, threw her body onto the sand. Cirey's high scream sliced through the air.

Cirey addressed the group: "If the community demonstrates one heart and one mouth, the rain will come tomorrow."

"There is no respect in Tillaberi," Dongo said. "But today was good. Tomorrow there will be rain."

There were many ceremonies and sacrifices during May and June of 1984. Would this one bring rain? Weary of their efforts, the Tillaberi mediums doubted the words of Dongo and Cirey.

"We've heard this before, and nothing has happened," one medium complained.

"I wondered whether Dongo and Cirey truly came to Tillaberi today," another medium opined.

That evening, the beginning of the next lunar calendar day,

stars flickered in an inky sky. Shooting stars streaked to their vanishing points. No clouds. No rain. The next morning the rim of the eastern sky glowed bright orange. The first rays of the sun knifed through the heavy dawn air, beginning another cloudless day. By midday the intense heat was promising another day without rain. Late morning brought oven winds from the east. By midday a few fleecy cumulus clouds had gathered in the eastern sky. By late afternoon the winds stiffened and changed directions. Dark gray rain clouds built to the east. In the dim dusk light the sky was a bank of thick brown fog. Dongo's voice thundered in the distance. In Adamu Jenitongo's compound we were watching the eastern sky. The west wind dried the sweat on the back of my neck.

"Baba," I asked Adamu Jenitongo, "won't that wind blow the rain away?"

"Wait," said Adamu Jenitongo.

Dongo roared again. Was he coming closer? People skygazed. No one talked. Like me, they spoke silently to the sky from their hearts.

Suddenly the wind changed direction. Coming from the east now, the wind swept upon Tillaberi a giant wave of reddish brown dust which hid the sun. Dongo's voice came closer and closer. The first large drops of rain splattered on the parched ground, hitting one by one, randomly. Then the full force of the storm hit Tillaberi in windswept sheets. The bone-dry compound quickly filled with water. The sky groaned. The daub roof of Moussa's house sprang a leak. Mud streamed into the house, splashing on the table and soiling pages of field notes and rolls of toilet paper.

We stood outside to let the fading storm caress us with a drizzle. We heard a deep grunt, faint at first and then getting louder. Lieutenant Marseille, in the mud-caked body of a bare-breasted woman, ran into the compound. He had taken his medium more than two kilometers to greet the old zima.

"My father," Lieutenant Marseille said, referring to Dongo, "is mean today. He is quite mean. Beware. Be careful. Pay homage to him." Marseille greeted people in the zima's compound. "We do know how to bring rain, do we not?" He pointed to the sky. "There is but one road to follow," Lieutenant Marseille proclaimed. "There must be one mouth and one heart in the community." The spirit belly flopped into the mud, and Adamu Jenitongo helped a coughing Bibata, the medium, to her feet.

"Thank you for your work," he told her.

Saying nothing, she covered her muddy chest with a piece of cloth and left for home.

The next morning confident Tillaberi farmers marched to their fields to plant millet for the second time that year. Adamu Jenitongo and sons went to their millet fields which were close to Nya Beri's altar, a trip of three kilometers. While his sons hoed the fields, Adamu Jenitongo and I planted the millet seeds. The rain had soaked into the sandy loam.

"These seeds will sprout," Adamu Jenitongo said. "May God bring us more rain."

"Inshallah," I said. I did not doubt that the seeds would sprout. But when they emerged from the earth, would new rains ensure their survival under the hot sun?

A Failed Yenaandi

The rain-stopping dissension in Tillaberi ran very deep. Not only was there the conflict between the marabouts and the possession troupe, purist Muslims and non-Muslims, but there was dangerous dissension in the Tillaberi possession troupe itself.

By all accounts the 1984 yenaandi had been disasterous. Although more than fifteen spirits had taken the bodies of their mediums, the zimas had insulted them, having sacrificed only two chickens in their honor.

"Much blood must be spilled at the yenaandi," Adamu Jenitongo said. "But at this one the zimas did not know what they were doing."

In the 1977 and 1981 yenaandis the requisite four chickens and one black goat had been sacrificed. In 1977 and 1981 the zimas had etched a crossroad in the sand and burned on it a mixture of millet seeds and dried grass; Dongo had stomped out the fire. In 1984 the zimas had omitted this part of the ceremony. In 1977 and 1981 the spirits had drunk the special Tooru porridge from the ritual vase. In 1984 the zimas had not prepared the Tooru porridge.

"No wonder," complained Adamu Jenitongo, "that the rains have come very late this year. No wonder there will be much hunger this year."

The flawed performance in 1984 resulted from the feuding of two factions in the Tillaberi possession troupe. Led by Issifu Zima and Gusabu, the majority of the mediums and the young zimas comprised the first faction, which directed its antipathies against Adamu Jenitongo, the leader of the minority faction.

"Tillaberi people don't like me anymore," Adamu Jenitongo told me in 1984. "They don't come here anymore. When we do have ceremonies here, they tell people not to come."

The Tillaberi zimas were jealous of Adamu Jenitongo, the most knowledgeable zima in the region. Until 1984, most possession ceremonies were staged in Adamu Jenitongo's compound, for which the old zima received a small fee. His fame as a healer brought him scores of clients, who paid handsomely to be cured of spirit sickness. But money alone did not motivate Adamu Jenitongo's work.

"Let's wait to see if the treatment works," he told his clients, "and then we shall see about payment."

Gusabu and Issifu wanted a greater share of the possession pie. Competing with Adamu Jenitongo, they staged ceremonies in Gusabu's river-front compound, a location more convenient than Adamu Jenitongo's bush-front site.

"Yes, they [Gusabu and Issifu] invited me to their ceremonies. I walked all that way for nothing. They didn't feed me. They didn't even give me water. My sons said: 'Baba, why walk two kilometers only to be insulted by people who don't know their work.' And so I remain here in peace and tranquillity. I am too old for such noise."

In 1984 Issifu and Gusabu succeeded in diverting clients from Adamu Jenitongo. They received high fees for their services, despite a record of uneven results. In years past Gusabu had been accused of stealing money from the possession troupe kitty.

Adamu Jenitongo could not be more of a contrast to Issifu Zima. Far from flamboyant, he dressed in filthy robes and ate simple foods. He refused to charge high fees for his services. Clients paid what they could: money, chickens, goats, clothing. Ceremonies like initiation required great amounts of money, but he distributed the proceeds equitably to the troupe: mediums, musicians, sorkos, lesser zimas. A deadly serious man, he did not tolerate "the frivolous" Sasale possession in his compound. In his tastes, he was plain; in his action, he was powerful. In a rapidly changing town, Adamu Jenitongo was a vestige of the past.

Adamu Jenitongo had a very small following in Tillaberi in 1984, mostly members of the possession troupe. His income and pride, however, were supplemented by clients from towns other than Tillaberi. Some of these clients traveled from Mali and Burkina Faso to see the *cimi koy,* the possessor of the truth.

"Why don't you leave Tillaberi?" I often asked him.

"Because," he said, "it is not my path. The cowry shells indicate that I must remain. That is my fate. I will remain and teach my heritage to my sons."

The Tillaberi sous-préfet recognized Adamu Jenitongo's preeminence in 1984. Had he not asked him to organize ceremonies to bring rain? Had he not asked him to break Islamic curses preventing rain? But the confidence of the sous-préfet did not diminish the dissension in the Tillaberi possession troupe.

"They don't care about spirits. They don't care about the community or its people. They are looking for money, and that is all," Adamu Jenitongo told me. "Zimas who walk their paths in search of money alone will not grow old."

Commandant Bashiru's Advice

Adamu Jenitongo looked up at the cloudless sky and shook his head. Days had passed without new rains. Like most storms in the Sahel, the rain that had followed the sacrifice at Nya Beri's altar had been widely scattered. The rains had soaked Adamu Jenitongo's field but had scarcely touched the fields of many Tillaberi farmers.

One morning Commandant Bashiru, a Hauka, thrust himself into the body of Daouda Godji. Besides giving advice to Adamu Jenitongo's niece, he reaffirmed what the spirits had been saying.

"There is dissension in the possession troupe. With dissension, there are many problems and much suffering."

"What are we to do?" Adamu Jenitongo asked.

"Make an offering to your *hampi* [ritual vase]," Commandant Bashiru directed.

Adamu Jenitongo quickly prepared his offering. He placed his ritual vase in the spirit hut and filled it with water drawn from a whirlpool in the Niger River. Such water, the zima explained, is Harakoy's medicine. He added three measures of the following pulverized plants to the water in the vase: *kabu beri, kabu kayna, zem turi,* and *yaggi.*[3] He then scooped a shallow trench around the base of the vase and lined it with millet seeds, which he covered with sand.

"There must be unity in the community," he said to the vase.

Putting his index finger on the rim of the vase, he recited in-

Spirit divination in Adamu Jenitongo's compound.

cantations: the genji how, which harmonizes the forces of the bush; and praise-poems that paid homage to the spirits. Then he covered the vase with a woven lid. "In four days, the Tillaberi mediums will come and drink this water," he said.

A Tillakaina Ceremony

The next day Moussa Zima sent word that he had organized a ceremony for that afternoon. Moussa Zima lived in Tillakaina, a small village two kilometers north of Tillaberi, but this ceremony would be staged under a sacred *garbey* tree (*Balanites aegyptica*) midway between a sacred mountain and Tillakaina.

Because of his blood ties to Moussa Zima, Adamu Jenitongo decided to attend the ceremony. We left the compound at mid-afternoon and walked north across a copper-colored, rock-strewn plain where nothing grew. We climbed up a small rocky hill and down another and saw in the distance a gathering of about fifty people. The musicians had positioned the drums under the garbey tree, facing north toward the sacred mountain, a jagged outcropping of gray and black rock which dominated Tillaberi and Tillakaina.

Adamu Jenitongo pointed to the summit of the mountain.

"On top of the mountain, there is an altar on which Tillakaina people make sacrifices to the mountain genie."

"Did they make a sacrifice this year?" I asked.

"I don't think so," he answered.

"Why not?"

"The dissension in Tillakaina is worse than that in Tillaberi. Too many witches in Tillakaina. Too many witches."

Meanwhile, Moussa Zima had sprinkled some Bint al Sudan perfume on the three drums and into the cavity of the monochord violin. He bowed to the sacred mountain and sprinkled more perfume over the dance ground. A ritual vase containing an infusion had been placed south of the garbey tree.

"All mediums," Moussa Zima announced, "must drink from the hampi."

The mediums drank.

The music did not begin until midafternoon.

"The tooru won't come now," Adamu Jenitongo told me. "It's too late. They like to come at midday, not midafternoon. They know nothing here," he muttered.

The musicians played nonetheless, and one hour passed without possession. The music set the Tooru and Hauka mediums dancing and walking, shivering with prepossession tremors. The Hauka mediums formed a circle and marched counterclockwise. Djingarey Sorko's son stood in the center of the circle, shaking Dongo's hatchet. The hatchet's "ping" brought no results. After two hours of effort, Capral Gardi suddenly threw his medium to the ground and then, just as quickly, left the social world. The grunts of Capral Gardi prompted Lieutenant Marseille to take his medium. Marseille dove onto the sand and brought himself to military attention—on one foot. Saluting the audience, he goose-stepped to Dongo's medium and spat in her ear. But Dongo was far away. He lunged toward Mahamane Surgu's medium and spat in her ear. Surgu thrashed his medium's large body. Perhaps the ceremony would be a success after all?

"Maybe Moussa Nyori and Cirey will follow Surgu," Adamu Jenitongo told me.

Moussa Nyori and Cirey did not come, however. Soon Surgu left his medium's body. The musicians played on; Djingarey Sorko recited praise-poetry. Disgusted with the results of dissension, Adamu Jenitongo returned to his compound. I accompanied him.

We were told later that night that General Malia, a Hauka, took his medium's body just before sunset. He warned the group of the great hunger and death that was coming.

"You must divide into two groups," General Malia told the audience, "and go to the distant mountain where Sadyara lives. There, you must dance and make sacrifices. This will bring rain, health, and happiness."

Djingarey Sorko said he would talk to the sous-préfet.

Three days later, Adamu Jenitongo uncovered the ritual vase he had prepared. It stank of fermented ginger and garlic, two of the ingredients of yaggi. Moru, his son, lifted the heavy vase, revealing the millet sprouts that had germinated beneath its base. The pattern indicated the prognosis for the October harvest, and it was not good for Tillaberi. On the north and the west sides, thick bunches of millet had sprouted.

Adamu Jenitongo pointed to the thick fringes. "That is the Kurmey region [west of Tillaberi]. They will have a good harvest. They have strong millet medicine there."

In the rest of the space the millet had sprouted sparsely or not at all. Adamu Jenitongo stroked his white beard. "This will be a very difficult year for all of us here."

He sent word to the Tillaberi mediums to come and drink the water from the offering to protect them from the coming danger.

Only three mediums showed up.

The sous-préfet refused to sponsor a second expedition to Sadyara's mountain hole.

The millet turned brown and died in the fields. The rains did not fall until the end of July—too late to plant the millet crop. "Dissension," Adamu Jenitongo said, "is a deadly enemy."

Dissension in Mehanna

In 1984 the rains failed in Mehanna. Millet harvests had been bad in 1982 and 1983, but most people in Mehanna had plenty of rice to eat. In 1984 the river shrank and there was no rice, only meningitis and cholera. Many people died in Mehanna that summer. Many more would die that fall.

There was dissension in Mehanna. The chief had not arranged a yenaandi in ten years. No sacrifice had been performed to the genie that lived behind Mehanna. Muslim clerics blamed one another for the drought. The chief blamed the Muslim clerics.The chief and the Muslim clerics condemned members of the moribund possession troupe. "Your devil worship has brought us this catastrophe," the chief proclaimed at a town meeting.

Townspeople blamed the government officials for the drought. The government officials cursed the townspeople. Food ran out. Sons stole food from fathers. Fathers stole food from sons. Starving Fulan, who consider their cows as members of their lineages, sold to butchers their dying cattle for as little as $2. Hungry Tuaregs sold their personal treasures, ornate leather pouches, and silver jewelry at rural markets.

Dissension in Wanzerbe

In 1984 the rains failed in Wanzerbe, a village some hundred kilometers west of the Niger. A yenaandi had been staged. In a separate ceremony people had sacrificed animals on the mountain called Surgumey. Though well performed, the rituals had not brought rain. Meningitis and cholera had affected Wanzerbe too. Reduced to eating gruel made from stumps of the previous year's millet stalks, many Wanzerbe people succumbed to disease. Even those people who had beans to eat were not assured of good health. Those who lacked food cast spells on their more fortunate brothers and sisters. In 1984 Wanzerbe was a mean place. One could feel the spiteful treachery in the air.

In Wanzerbe it rained on May 1, 1984, and the farmers joyfully planted millet in their fields. Soon the millet emerged from the sandy fields. But a second rain did not fall until July 30. The early millet had long since died, and it was too late in the rainy season to plant again. But the farmers had no choice. I watched them drag out of town the morning after the rain to plant another crop. They knew full well that their efforts were futile. A few families packed up their possessions and left Wanzerbe for the capital city—three hundred kilometers away.

Theories on Drought

What had caused the drought? Meteorologists blamed it on an upper atmosphere high-pressure system that had stalled over Libya. The high pressure prevented the northward surge of the moisture-laden intertropical front. Cynics took this meteorological evidence and blamed the drought on Gadafy, Niger's hostile neighbor.

"I wouldn't put it past Gadafy to do something to stall that high-pressure system over his country. It's just like him to bring pain and suffering to the peoples of Niger," one Nigerien government official told me.

The most common explanation I heard, however, was that the ancestors and spirits had had their fill of neglect and duplicity— mey hinka, bina hinka.

"The spirits are teaching us a lesson," another Nigerien official told me. "I hope we've learned."

Fatouma Seyni, Dongo's medium in Mehanna, spoke of 1984–85, a time of famine in Niger.

> The people suffered greatly. Many children died, and the chief finally understood what had to be done. In mid-May he organized a sacrifice to the genie of Mehanna's dune. United, we marched up the dune to sacrifice a bull to the genie. Djibo Sorko cut the bull's throat and the blood flowed toward the village, a sign that the genie had accepted the offering. One week later the chief organized a rain dance. In the name of God, as soon at the drummers beat their gourds, the rain began to fall. They played, the spirits took the bodies of mediums, and the rain fell and fell and fell. What a glorious day![4]

In 1985 the rains continued to fall abundantly until mid-September, allowing the millet to ripen in the hot sun. The October harvest was so good that the price for a hundred-kilo sack of millet plummeted from 25,000 CFA (roughly $80) in June to 3,000 CFA (roughly $10) in November. The level of the Niger was appreciably higher, which was good news for the December–January rice harvest.

"People understand now," Fatouma told me in December of 1985.

"What do they understand?"

"They understand that we must maintain respect for our ancestors. That means we must respect the spirits. If we do not, we will be ruined."

In 1984 people in Mehanna had scorned Fatouma Seyni. She was, after all, a devotee of the local possession troupe. In her compound, she kept Dongo's goat, a black male with a bell around its neck. She was also a diviner who made regular offerings to the spirits. In 1984 no one had time to talk to her; no one would help her in her moments of desperation. Suddenly in 1985, people showered her with gifts.

"It is strange to be alone one year and in demand the next," she said.

"Does the insincerity bother you?" I asked.

"No, I know whom I can trust. I only hope that the people remain behind the spirits. Perhaps they have learned their lesson."

In Tillaberi, 1984–85 had been a difficult year. There had been precious little millet there, but the rice harvest, meager though it was, provided enough grain for most Tillaberi people. And yet village dissension had again prevented the staging of a proper rain dance in May of 1985.

Despite the dissension, problems within the possession troupe abated somewhat. The sous-préfet warned Gusabu and Issifu Zima about treating patients. Two of Gusabu's patients died. One of Issifu's almost died. Gusabu herself was also quite sick during 1985.

"One doesn't insult a man like Adamu Jenitongo and remain healthy," Daouda Godji told me.

Issifu too almost died of a mysterious illness that he contracted in the village of Sangara.

"Issifu at least has grown up," says Moussa Adamu, the zima's son; "he now knows that the path of a zima is a dangerous one. You must walk carefully on that path."

In 1985 many possession dances were staged in Adamu Jenitongo's compound. Local people returned to his compound for his effective cures. The new police chief and the Hausa and Songhay soldiers in Tillaberi frequently visited the old zima in the evenings. When prisoners escaped, the police asked for his help.

Where is the prisoner hiding? Did he escape to the north? the east? the west? Adamu Jenitongo's divinations usually directed the police to their escaped prisoner's hideouts.

What brought this turn of events? Scientists put forward new meteorological explanations. The Muslim clerics credited their fervent prayers. The zimas spoke about a new harmony in the social and spirit worlds. In public contexts officials in Niamey insisted on the scientific explanations of drought. In private contexts the same officials might cite the fervency of Islamic prayer. But beneath these surface explanations lay a centuries' deep belief in the spirits and the ancestors.

"Possession is in our blood," one Nigerien official, a good friend of mine, told me. "All of us are touched by it in one way or another. Maybe our mother is a medium. Maybe our father was a musician. Maybe we ourselves were initiated many years ago. Soldiers are mediums. Government ministers are mediums. Professors and researchers are mediums. That is our experience."

Adamu Jenitongo encouraging his mediums at a Genji Bi ceremony in Tillaberi (1987).

EPILOGUE: FUSION OF THE WORLDS

In June of 1987 I returned to Adamu Jenitongo's compound in Tillaberi. In honor of my visit the zima staged a one-day possession ceremony on June 20, a Saturday.

"Paul, we are going to look for the Genji Bi (the Black Spirits). They will do good work for you."

"What do you need, Baba?"

"We need two black chickens, kola, tobacco, condiments, and rice. We must feed our musicians, mediums, and guests, must we not?"

"By all means."

By the morning of June 20, the zima had purchased food, condiments, kola, and sacrificial animals. The previous day he had spread the word about the upcoming Genji Bi ceremony.

"Saturday is a good day for the ceremony. The spirits like Saturday, and people don't work today."

"Work?" I asked. "Do you mean that the civil servants are going to come to a Genji Bi ceremony?"

"Yes, of course," Adamu Jenitongo responded.

The hour of the ceremony arrived. Although the rains had been good in 1985 and 1986, they were late in 1987. As of June 20, not one drop had fallen in Tillaberi, and although the heavy air suggested that rain was close to Tillaberi, the cloudless heat-blanched sky promised another day of drought.

The musicians played Genji Bi rhythms for more than two hours without result.

"Baba," I said to Adamu Jenitongo, who was sitting next to me on a straw mat in the shade of his younger son's house, "the spirits are being difficult today."

"They *are* difficult today," he observed.

He then stood up and walked across the compound to his wife's house. The Genji Bi music droned on, but no one danced. Soon thereafter Adamu Jenitongo emerged from Jemma's house. He walked to the center of the dance ground and tied a sash of white cotton cloth around his waist.

The din of the crowd died. Several mediums rushed to the dance ground and prostrated themselves on the ground in two

205

parallel lines. Adamu Jenitongo stood stiffly at the head of a path bordered by prone bodies. Suddenly he screamed and threw off his shirt. He knelt on the ground and threw dirt over his head and then rolled up the legs of his trousers. His older son, Moussa, and I fetched the costume and ritual objects of Baganbeize, the Genji Bi that had entered Adamu Jenitongo's body. We dressed him in a blue-and-white-striped tunic and a matching pair of short pants. We gave him an antelope horn. Fully dressed, he marched over to the site of the compound's cooking fire and washed his face with warm ashes.

Moru, the zima's younger son, presented Baganbeize with an overturned mortar.

"Sit Baganbeize. Sit and rest."

Baganbeize sat down and summoned people in the audience to present themselves. He told one woman to sacrifice a white chicken on the upcoming Thursday.

"Why should I do this?" she asked the spirit.

"It will bring peace and harmony to your troubled compound," Baganbeize answered. "If you don't do it, sickness will visit your people."

Baganbeize told me to buy a black chicken. "You must kill it, cook it, and give away the cooked meat. Do you understand?" Banganbeize asked me.

"I do."

He nodded. "Do this and your work will rise to the heavens."

Baganbeize summoned a short balding man whose high fore-head gleamed in the midafternoon light.

"You have been stuck. You walk forward but don't go anywhere, my son."

"That's correct," the man said.

"You must sacrifice a brown goat. But this is only the beginning. You sacrifice a brown goat, and you sacrifice to me, Baganbeize."

"Yes, Baganbeize. I'll do it."

"Do you understand? Do you see me?"

"Yes Baganbeize."

The man seemed familiar to me. When he retreated into the crowd I followed him.

"Don't I know you?" I asked.

He squinted at me for several seconds and then asked in French, "Did you not live in Mehanna?"

"Yes," I said, now able to place the man, "and you were the agricultural agent there."

"Right."

"You are the man with the doctorate in agricultural science."

"You've got a good memory."

"Are you in Tillaberi?"

"No, I'm in Tillakaina."

"Have you procured your university post?"

He frowned. "I've been trying for eight years without success."

I understood his reasons for attending the ceremony.

He excused himself.

I returned to the ritual canopy and sat next to Daouda Godji, who played more Genji Bi music.

Other spirits came that day:

—Alpha Duwokoy, who vomited black ink on his medium's beautiful white damask boubou and spoke to me in Arabic, French, and Songhay. "I'm not one of these disgusting lowly spirits. I'm from the heavens, a messenger from God. I'm Alpha Duwokoy. Fahemti Larabia?" (Do you understand Arabic?)

"Ma fahemsh" (I don't understand), I answered.

"European," he said to me. "You must buy a white chicken. You must kill it, and then you must give away the meat."

"I'll do it. I'll do it."

"Do you understand?" He used Moussa's shoulder to support himself.

"I understand."

"Did he understand?" he asked Moussa.

"He did."

Then Alpha Duwokoy grabbed my arm and arched his back. Duwokoy groaned and grunted. Holding on to Moussa and me, Duwokoy's medium's body stiffened.

"Easy now," Moussa said to him. "Easy."

Duwokoy's medium's body convulsed.

"Let him go," Moussa said.

We released him.

—Moss'izey chased away Alpha Duwokoy. Moss'izey ripped off his shirt and rolled up the legs of his trousers. He washed himself with sand and marched over to the fire where he heaped on a plate a mountain of hot ash. He marched back to the ritual canopy and greeted people. Moss'izey yanked Moru from his drummer's seat and demanded his blue-and-white-striped trousers. Moru stripped in front of 150 people, gave Moss'izey his trousers, and ran to his house for another pair.

"European," Moss'izey bellowed, looking at me with blazing eyes. "I am Moss'izey. I'm a captive. I know no shame." With that proclamation, Moss'izey took his plate of hot ash and poured it on my head.

—Malla, the Hauka, goose-stepped from the audience to the ritual canopy. He greeted Daouda Godji. He greeted the drummers, Halidu and Moru. He wrenched me from my seat next to the violinist. Holding onto my arm, he used me to support his weight as he greeted other people in the audience.

By plucking people from the audience, he soon gathered about him a small entourage. One of the Hauka mediums put a pith helmet on his head.

"European," Malla said to me.

"Yes."

"Bring me 505 francs and a vial of perfume."

"Yes."

Malla waved the pith helmet in the air and put it on my head. "Bring me the money and perfume. Now!"

I went to my borrowed house, found the perfume and money, and returned to Malla, who counted the money and blew on the perfume, a bottle of Bint al Sudan.

"Take this perfume and put it in your pocket when you're in a car that's running or an airplane that's flying."

"Very good. Wonderful," I chanted. "Praise be to God."

"I have more work for you," Malla continued. "Buy one box of sugar. From the box take three cubes and put them in your pocket. Give the rest of it away to children. When the airplane that takes you home leaves the ground, throw the three sugar cubes behind you. "Do you follow me?"

"Yes."

"Do this," Malla insisted, "and your work will rise to the heavens."

Fusion of the Worlds

In France, a group of scholars, inspired in part by Aristotle's writings on trance in *The Politics,* has focused on possession as a form of cultural theater. Put forward by such writers as André

Schaeffner, Michel Leiris, and Gilbert Rouget, this hypothesis on possession is a highly attractive one.[1] The Tillaberi possession troupe is organized like a repertory company. The impresario is the zima, who is also a stage director and provides the scripts of possession performances. Mediums are actors, chorus dancers, and stagehands. Music, as Rouget reminds us, is an integral part of possession. In Songhay, musicians such as Daouda Godji and Moru Adamu produce the sound waves that, like a gentle zephyr, carry the spirits to the social world. But sound in Songhay is a dimension grander than music; the sound contours of the sorko's ancient words direct the spirits into the bodies of their mediums.

In possession, the sounds of the Songhay possession ceremonies *are* the voices of the ancestors. These distant voices are heard in the godji's cries, the gasi's clacks, the sorko's words, and the spirits' screams—all of which Faran Maka Bote witnessed at the first possession ceremony.

Taking the theatrical metaphor to its logical end suggests that in Songhay, possession troupes produce plays full of historical, sociological, and cultural themes. No matter their form, these plays articulate unexpressable themes of Songhay cultural tradition, themes that must be provoked and evoked, themes that cannot be described only in laws, theories, or hypotheses lying dead on a printed page.

The metaphor of theater, however, provides only a framework—a stage—for the apprehension of possession in Songhay. To reduce possession to a theatricalization of cultural history, cultural resistance, or cultural texts is, to paraphrase Merleau-Ponty, to manipulate things and give up living in them.[2]

My long and intense participation in the Tillaberi troupe has plunged me deeply into the human dimension of possession. To grasp possession in Songhay we need to explore what Maurice Merleau-Ponty called the texture of inner space in which "quality, light, color, and depth . . . are there before us only because they awaken an echo in our body and because the body welcomes them."[3] The inner space of Songhay possession consists of two domains which are inexorably linked: the human and the imageric.

The human domain of possession considers the lives, problems, and thoughts of priests, mediums, praise-singers, and musicians. To apprehend the inner space of Songhay possession, one needs to sense the pain of prepossession sickness, to appreciate the financial burdens of initiation, to realize the dangers of walking the zima's, sorko's, or musician's path, to comprehend the human costs of dissension in Songhay. My personal association with members of the Tillaberi troupe moved me to probe in the first part of this book the emotive, human story of Songhay possession.

Knowing the stories of individual members of the possession troupe, the people who stage the ceremonies, creates for us a path leading into a Songhay domain of images that defy categorization and operational thinking. It is a space in which boundaries are blurred, in which the distinction among cultural things is fuzzy, in which people produce evocative "picture puzzles" that turn life inside out, making the ordinary unthinkable and the unthinkable ordinary.[4]

In his monumental *Eye and Mind,* Merleau-Ponty wrote of the world of images: "The eye sees the world, sees what inadequacies [*manqués*] keep the world from being a painting, sees what keeps a painting from being itself, sees—on the palette—the colors awaited by the painting that answers to all these inadequacies just as it sees the paintings of others as other answers to other inadequacies."[5]

In Songhay, possession creates a fusion of the worlds, which is "a deliberate attack on reality but for transformation of life."[6] A black man playing the role of Malla, a white man, puts a pith helmet on the head of a white man playing the role of an anthropologist. Moss'izey and Baganbeize wash with sand and ash. Hauka spirits drink blood, handle fire, and eat poisonous plants. Sasale spirits speak scatologically, tear off their clothes, and engage in mock sexual intercourse. But this attack on everyday reality is for the betterment of the community; the spirits solve the problems and sooth the pain of the living.

Possession in Songhay is a creative act, an aesthetic reaction to the inadequacies of the world. As Merleau-Ponty wrote, "It is by lending his body to the world that the artist changes the world into paintings."[7] It is by lending her body to the world that the spirit medium renders meaningful a harsh Sahelian world filled with dissension, drought, famine, and death.

As we have seen, possession in Songhay is a microcosm of Songhay culture. This ethnography of Songhay possession has obliged us to consider such diverse topics as agriculture, climate, kinship, marriage, ecology, social change, colonization, magic and sorcery, myth, history, and poetics. But possession is more than a domain of philosophical reflection and academic exegesis; it is also an arena of human passion in which individuals of diverse social standing are thrown together. In Tillaberi, frustration, despair, loss, and fear impel illiterate market women and educated civil servants to attend possession ceremonies. And there in the shadow of Adamu Jenitongo's ritual canopy, these same market women and civil servants confront other market women and civil servants whose bodies have been invaded by their spirits—veritably, the fusion of the worlds.

An Evolved Initiation

On June 21, 1987, a Sunday, a civil servant from Niamey visited Adamu Jenitongo's compound. His hairline had retreated from his forehead and his belly had advanced under his expansive cotton suit.

"Baba. I've come to talk to you about my brother."

"Oh, the one who needs to be initiated."

"Yes, him."

"Baba, we can't wait any longer. He has suffered terribly."

"It will have to be a seven-day festival."

"When do you want us to start, then?"

"Very soon, because he begins a course of study on July 1. My brother has lived in France and is now a scientist. He cannot continue to suffer, but he also cannot report late to his 'training.'"

"Good," Adamu Jenitongo said, "we will stage the initiation on Wednesday night" (which is Tuesday night, June 23, following the solar calendar).

The initiate's family arrived from Niamey during the afternoon of June 23—three men, including the initiate, two women, including the initiate's mother, a teenage girl, and a teenage boy. The men were dressed in Western business attire—black permanant press dress slacks, black socks, black dress shoes, and white short-sleeved dress shirts. The youngest woman and the teenage girl wore Niamey haute couture—pink dresses with ruffled lace shoulders and hair pieces of red and black rope woven into checkerboard. The boy wore faded blue jeans and a T-shirt that read "Atlantic City, N.J." He wore Reeboks.

The family did not mingle with the other people in Adamu Jenitongo's compound. The men sat by themselves under the ritual canopy. I sat there too—the only place to escape the burning sun.

They struck up a conversation with me in French.

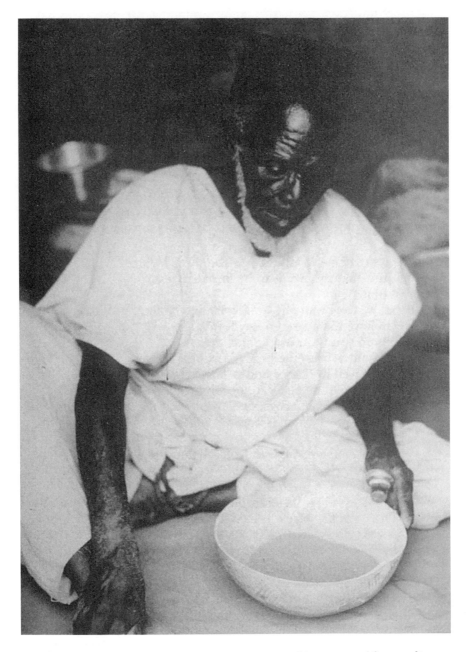

Adamu Jenitongo reciting an incantation to protect his compound from malicious spirits.

"What are you doing here?" ventured Mounkaila, the initiate's older brother.

"I'm visiting Baba. I visit him every year."

"I hear that you're a writer and an anthropologist. They say you've written a book," Mounkaila remarked.

"That's true. It's about Adamu Jenitongo."

"How long is it?" the initiate asked.

"About 240 pages."

The three men laughed.

"That's pretty long," the initiate said.

"It took me five years."

We lapsed into silence. I rekindled the conversation.

"And you?" I turned to the initiate. "I hear you're an agronomist."

"That's right. I'm doing agro, I should complete my professional training this summer."

"Wonderful."

The men left.

The entire family returned to the zima's compound just before dusk to go over last-minute details with Adamu Jenitongo. Suddenly, the initiate snorted and snarled. He jumped up. Arms flailing, he punched wildly at the air. Then he marched around us in a circle, smiling, shaking his head, and mumbling to himself. Just as suddenly, the spirit left him.

"That happens all the time at any time," Mounkaila explained to Adamu Jenitongo. "He has suffered like this for two years."

"His suffering will soon be over," Adamu Jenitongo said.

Stars twinkled in the inky sky. A cool breeze from the west swept through Tillaberi. Ready to begin the ceremony, we filed out of Adamu Jenitongo's compound, headed for a crossroads in the bush on which there is a large ant hill. On arrival, Adamu Jenitongo thrust his forked stick into the ant hill, and Moru, his younger son, encircled the space with a mixture of millet, sorghum, corn, sugar, sesame, hard candy, and *kusu maasa* (the crust of grains cooked in pots), all the rich produce of human labor.

Halidu Gasi gathered brush and lit a fire.

Dressed in black robes, Adamu Jenitongo stood with another zima in the center of the circle, flashes of firelight silhouetting their shadowy forms.

"Where is he?" Adamu Jenitongo asked.

Still dressed in his black trousers and white shirt, the initiate stood and walked stiffy into the circle.

"Young man," Adamu Jenitongo said. "Tonight we start a long journey. The end of this path is but the beginning of another. Do you understand?"

"I do."

"Do you agree to join us."

"I do."

"Do you agree?"

"I do."

"Do you agree?" he repeated.

"I agree."

"So be it."

Daouda Godji played Tooru music, and the boy's possessing spirit entered his body. He growled, dropped to his knees, and crawled in the darkness toward Daouda, who was seated near the crackling fire.

The Tooru invaded their mediums. Cirey streaked through the darkness. Moussa Nyori, the hunter, strutted toward Daouda Godji. Those Hauka who protect the Tooru rose in the bodies of their mediums. Shrieks, screams, grunts, and snarls echoed in the night air.

Meanwhile, Halidu asked the spirit in the initiate's body to identify itself.

"There are four spirits, but I will not tell you who they are," the spirit chuckled.

Halidu went through the list of spirits.

"Are you Za Beri? Are you Dongo? Are you Mahamane Surgu?" The godji cried.

The initiate's older brother, Mounkaila, lost control of his legs, which wildly kicked sand in the air; his Hauka was about to rise. Fulan Benya, a Hausa spirit, rose in the body of the initiate's other brother. Then Fulan, another Hausa spirit, took the initiate's sister. A visiting Sasale spoke of the penises, foreskins, vaginas, and clitorises, and offered herself to the men.

After three hours Halidu had determined that the initiate carried four spirits: Dongo, deity of thunder; Nya Beri, mother of the Cold Spirits and a clarivoyant; Fulan, a Hausa spirit who is the harbinger of good will; and Funfun'ize, the incessant talker who steals from the Hauka.

For seven days we regaled these four spirits. Adamu Jenitongo performed sacrifices—four chickens and two goats. And on several occasions the spirits took the expensively clad bodies of most of the initiate's family.

At noon on the seventh day, the newly initiated medium prepared to leave for his training session in agronomy. He smiled warmly, quite a contrast to the sullen expression he wore on his arrival, and thanked Adamu Jenitongo for his good work.

"Now you can move forward on your path, my son," Adamu Jenitongo told him.

"When you come here to the 'owner of truth's' compound," Daouda Godji added, "you always leave in peace and health."

Mounkaila bade me good-bye.

"It was a good initiation wasn't it Monsieur Paul?"

"Yes, it was."

"Next year, my sister Sofia will be initiated," he said.

"She has spirits?"

"Yes. The spirits are in front of us. They are behind us. They are above and below us." he said solemnly. "The spirits are nothing without us, and we are nothing without the spirits. That is the way it has been here. That is the way it shall be in the future."

NOTES

Prologue
1. Merleau-Ponty 1964, 159.

Chapter 1. Looking for Serci
1. The coming of the European represents the surface of Songhay historical consciousness. Despite the fact that Songhay history can be recounted as a series of foreign invasions both military and cultural, the "Songhay does not feel lost in a foreign history, for he is one of its indispensable chains" (Rouch 1953, 143, 144).

2. From an interview conducted in Tillaberi on December 26, 1985. See also Rouch 1960, 56; Hama 1973; 1986, 40; and Olivier de Sardan 1982, 37–38.

3. See Rouch 1953, 152; Hama 1968, 90.

4. See Rouch 1953.

5. B. Hama 1968, 92.

6. Kati 1913, es-Saadi 1900, and Hama 1968 suggest that Aliaman Za came from Yemen. Citing linguistic and archeaological evidence, Rouch 1953 suggests that Za was a Lemta Berber who migrated to the Niger River bend (near Gao, republic of Mali) from the Gharmantes in southern Libya.

7. Es-Saadi 1900.

8. See Boulnois and Hama 1953. Rouch 1953 and 1960, and Olivier de Sardan 1982 suggest that Za Beri is the representation of Sonni Ali Ber.

9. Konare Ba 1977.

10. See Stoller 1978; Olivier de Sardan 1982, 1984.

11. Ibid.

12. See Olivier de Sardan 1984; Stoller 1978, 1981.

13. See Stoller 1984a.

14. See Stoller 1981.

15. Ibid.

16. See Stoller, in press; Olivier de Sardan 1982.

17. Rouch 1960 and Olivier de Sardan 1982.

18. Olivier de Sardan 1982; Stoller, in press.

Chapter 2. Zimas from Tillaberi
1. This statement is based on interviews conducted in Tillaberi on July 5, 1984, and December 23, 1985. Accounts of the French invasion of Niger are numerous. Kimba 1981, Kanya-Forstner 1969, Crowder 1968, and records and reports in the Archives d'A.O.F./Paris (Afrique III, dossiers 26 and 38 bis) all suggest an early military resistance to the French army. The infamous Voulet-Chanoine mission, which massacred hundreds of Songhay along its bloody path,

constituted some of the earliest contacts between the French military and Songhay-speaking peoples. In 1905, Songhay-speaking people staged a revolt in San-
sane-Haussa, a small town on the east bank of the Niger River, some sixty
kilometers north of Niamey.

2. There are two general accounts of the death of Sonni Ali Ber (also known
as Si) in the literature. In Songhay myths and oral accounts, Askia Mohammed
Touré murdered him publicly during a festival. There are no records of this
event, however. Adam Konaré Ba (1977) suggests that Ali Ber drowned in 1492
as he returned to Gao from a military campaign. His death may have been acci-
dental or may have been the result of death sorcery. Konaré Ba mentions that the
Timbuctu kadis, the Islamic enemies of Ali Ber, had been praying (and preparing
amulets) for the emperor's death. Lansiné Kaba (1984) writes of Sonni Ali Ber's
death and the historical forces that lead to Askia Mohammed's overthrow of Si
Baru, Sonni Ali Ber's heir.

Sonni Ali Ber's legacy lies in his considerable ability as a soldier and a sorcerer. He led an army that brought much territory and many peoples under
Songhay control. His knowledge and practice of sorcery legitimized his rule. He
was the most renowned sorcerer of his day, a legacy he left to his descendants
who are called sohanci. After the overthrow of the Sonnis—the lineage of Ali
Ber—his descendants practiced military sorcerey, a sohanci speciality, at the be-
quest of local nobles, descendants of Askia Mohammed Touré. Jenitongo, Adamu
Jenitongo's father, worked for a variety of Songhay nobles in the territory of the
Zerma east of the Niger River in the Republic of Niger.

3. Adamu Jenitongo is a guunu, the most powerful subgroup of sohanci. If a
man is a guunu, his ancestor married a witch (cerkaw), a genealogical fact that
gives him great power. Adamu Jenitongo's grandfather, Seyni Sohanci, married
Dawmo, a witch living in Jesse. After he neutralized her power, Seyni fathered
five children, one of whom was Adamu Jenitongo's father.

There is, however, some disagreement about what constitutes a guunu. Rouch
and Boubou Hama say that the guunu is a man whose mother alone is a sohanci,
and that his specialization is circumcision and female initiation (gosi). Adamu
Jenitongo's genealogy makes the Rouch-Hama hypothesis somewhat question-
able. It is because of his great power that the guunu is entrusted with the most
sacred Songhay ceremonies, the circumcision. In fact, guunu are so powerful
that other sohanci are powerless in their presence.

4. Based on interviews in Tillaberi on January 8, 1983, and July 5, 1984.

5. From sessions with Sorko Djibo Mounmouni of Mehanna, December 1979.

6. These statements are taken from recorded interviews with Adamu Jenitongo in Tillaberi, July 5, 1984, December 23, 1985, January 14, 1983, and from
informal talks during fieldwork in 1981, 1979–80, and 1977.

7. From an interview with Daouda Godji of Tillaberi, June 17, 1981.

8. See Rouch 1960; Olivier de Sardan 1982.

9. Observed and recorded during a possession ceremony at Djamona in January 1977.

10. See Monfouga-Nicholas 1972.

11. See Rouch 1960; Olivier de Sardan 1982.

12. Recorded from sessions with Sorko Djibo Mounmouni of Mehanna, March 1977.

13. Recorded during an interview with Daouda Godji, June 17, 1981.

14. The most graphic example of this is in Rouch's incomparable film, *Les maitres fous* (1957).

15. These statements are taken from recorded interviews with Adamu Jenitongo in Tillaberi, January 14, 1983, July 5, 1984, December 23, 1985, and from informal talks during fieldwork in 1981, 1979–80, and 1977. More detailed information on the onset of Songhay possession is available in Rouch 1960, 1978, and in a number of Jean Rouch's films (*Les maitres fous, Tourou et bitti,* and *Horendi*), all of which are distributed by the Comité des Films Ethnographiques, Musée de l'Homme, Paris.

16. This cosmology is derived from two sources: Adamu Jenitongo in interviews in 1985, 1984, and 1983; and Alfaggah Abdoulaye Cisse in an interview in Mehanna conducted on February 21, 1977.

17. The theory of the double and its relation to Songhay witchcraft is based on interviews with Adamu Jenitongo in 1985, 1984, and 1983 and with Sorko Djibo Mounmouni in Mehanna in 1979, 1981, and 1982. The theory is further explicated in Rouch 1960, Hama 1968, Boulnois and Hama 1953, and Stoller 1984b. Songhay shares affinity with other cases reported in the literature. As in E. E. Evans-Pritchard's Zande work, witchcraft is an ascribed category in Songhay. If individuals ingest their mother's breast milk and their mother is a witch, then they too become witches. Similar to the Zande, Songhay witches possess a witchcraft substance; in the Songhay case, it is a magical egg. For further elaboration on Songhay witchcraft, see Stoller and Olkes 1987.

18. Like many social categories among the Songhay, *zima* is broadly defined. Some zimas are sohancis; others are sorkos. There are roughly equal numbers of male and female zimas. But healing is a secondary function among the zimas. The major responsibility of the zima, rather, is the role as impresario of the possession troupe. The zimas who garner the greatest respect in Niger, in my view, are those who lead successful—money-making—troupes. Such was the source of Howa Koda's reputation in Ayoru. Although some zimas are known for their sorcery, the greatest sorcerers in Songhay are sohancis and sorkos.

Chapter 3. Gusabu's Mediums

1. Large households of seventy-five or more people exist only in more rural areas of Songhay, having disappeared from commercial centers north of Niamey (Tillaberi, Sakoire, Mehanna, Ayoru). In the Garuol of extreme western Niger, however (Wanzerbe, Yatakala, Bellekoire, Dolbel), the large household is the typical pattern. In Wanzerbe, for example, there are some compounds with more than thirty houses and more than a hundred occupants.

2. This pattern of social stratification was typical of the great Sahelian empires (Ghana, Mali, Songhay, and Kanem-Bornu). Olivier de Sardan, among others, has written (1969, 1975, 1976, 1982, 1984) extensively about slavery and social organization in nineteenth-century Songhay. See also Stoller 1978, 1981.

3. See Stoller 1977, 1981.

NOTES

4. Fatouma Seyni, interview in Mehanna, December 27, 1985.

5. For further information on various theoretical approaches to spirit possession see Lewis 1971, Harris 1957, Mischel and Mischel 1958, Freed and Freed 1964, Bourguignon 1976 (functionalist); Monfouga-Nicholas 1972, Pidoux 1955, Roheim 1967, Zempleni 1966 and 1968 (psychoanalytic); Kehoe and Giletti 1981, Gell 1980 (biological); Balandier 1966, Ackerman and Lee 1981, Lambek 1980 and 1981 (communication model); Leiris [1958] 1980, Schaeffner 1965; Rouget 1980 (theatrical model).

6. Interview conducted in Mehanna, January 4, 1986.

7. Ibid.

8. Ibid.

9. Initiation ceremonies are no longer elaborate. In the past the initiation of a Tooru medium took seven years to complete. In most troupes today the Tooru initiation, like that of Genji Kwaari or Genji Bi, lasts seven days. In Tillaberi, however, Tooru initiations are taken quite seriously. In 1982–83 I observed the finale of a seven-year Tooru initiation cycle, at the end of which the medium received her Tooru ring. Among the lesser spirits (Hauka and Hargay), initiation ceremonies may last only two or three days. There are a number of possible explanations. Initiations have become quite expensive. The novice's family must pay for the zimas, sorkos, musicians, mediums, food, kola nuts, and sacrificial animals. The longer the ceremony, the greater the expense. More important, perhaps, is the contemporary impatience with detailed and tiresome ritual (see Olivier de Sardin 1982, 148). The color white here represents Islamic purity, according to Adamu Jenitongo and Djibo Mounmouni (Mehanna). In some initiations there are no protectors.

10. These comments are derived from long observation and from conversations with Adamu Jenitongo, Djibo Mounmouni, and Amadu Zima (Mehanna).

11. See Gleason (1982) for a cogent analysis of the relationship between movement and Zarma-Songhay cosmology.

12. Ibid. The importance of dance—movement—should not be underestimated, for it is an expression of reverence, in movement and in meaning, for the spirits. See Hanna 1979 for cross-cultural examples.

13. The *fimbi* corresponds in many ways to Gell's (1980) hypthothesis about the onset of possession. Gell correctly asserts that just prior to possession, most mediums either spin, sway, or shake their heads. This motion, in turn, disturbs the inner ear. Inner ear disturbance may contribute to the onset of the possessed state.

14. Based on interviews in Tillaberi, July 5, 1984, and December 23, 1986.

15. Based on interviews with Adamu Jenitongo, Djibo Mounmouni, and Amadu Zima as well as personal communication from Jean Rouch.

16. This progression denotes the progress of the initiation cycle. As the ceremony unfolds, danger to the novice is reduced.

17. See Olivier de Sardan 1982.

18. Ibid. See also Fuglestad 1975 and Stoller 1984a. From most accounts and observations, one can suggest that the more recent the spirit family, the less

elaborate the initiation ceremony. The similar relationship between spirit age and behavior is also evident. The most ancient spirits (the Tooru) behave in a markedly constrained manner—the code of the Songhay noble. They speak little if at all. They employ intermediaries. They carry themselves with dignity, walking slowly and stiffly, holding their heads high. More recent spirits, by contrast, behave in a highly unconstrained manner. They speak directly to the audience, often insulting them (Hauka, Doguwa, Sasale).

19. This is an example, in English translation, of Adamu Jenitongo's genji how:

> In the name of God, Koosh.
> In the name of God, Koosh.
> I speak to N'Debbi.
> I speak to the seven heavens.
> I speak to the seven hells.
> I speak to the east.
> I speak to the west.
> I speak to the north.
> I speak to the south.
> My words must travel until, until, until
> They are known and understood.
> N'Debbi was before human beings.
> He gave the path to Soumana.
> Soumana gave it to Nyandu.
> Nyandu gave it to Mata.
> Mata gave it to me.
> What they have given me is better than good.
> My path is beyond theirs.
> N'Debbi gave us seven hatchets and seven picks.
> He came and gave us speech,
> And he took it back.
> He showed us the rock.
> He made the princes strong.
> Now the angels will not see.
> Bullets will not see.
> All is protected by the force of the heavens.

20. The exaggerated goose step mocks the ritual movements of the French military.

21. Dusk marks the end of most possession ceremonies among the Songhay. The only exceptions are Hargay ceremonies which are often held at night.

22. Interview with Fatouma Seyni in Mehanna, January 3, 1986.

Chapter 4. Praise-Singers from the River

1. From an interview with Djibo Mounmouni on June 29, 1981.
2. See Rouch 1960, 57–58.

3. This is the text of Kalia and Sanhori, sorkos of Niamey and Gube respectively, published in Rouch 1960, 58–59. There are minor variations in other texts of *Faran and Zinkibaru,* but all of the texts I have seen include the major themes of Kalia and Sanhori's version.

4. This text is from Oumarou Godje, cited in Rouch 1960, 65.

5. Rouch makes this comment in *La religion et la magie songhay.* Adamu Jenitongo and Djibo Mounmouni agree with this assertion.

6. Discussion with Abdou Kano in Mehanna, December 29, 1985.

7. The notion of the magical word has long been associated with cosmogony. Mythmakers and scholars alike have grappled with the preeminence of the word. As Tambiah (1968) suggests, Freud (1913) was speculating in *Totem and Taboo* that the deed preceded the word. Linguistic philosophers, by contrast, have suggested that the word is deed. The elegant arguments of Austin (1962) and Searle (1968) on performative utterances certainly lend some credence to this position. Taking the anthropological perspective, Tambiah reminds us of Goethe's view of the chicken-and-egg question concerning the word and the deed. In *Faust* the protagonists progress "from word, to thought, then to the notion of power, and [end] with deed" (1968, 175). However, none of these philosophical ruminations solves the problem Tambiah raises: when an informant is asked why a particular ritual or magic rite is effective, he or she invariably answers, "The power is in the words."

Malinowski, among others, paid considerable attention to the relationship between words and magic. He was convinced, in fact, that for the Trobriander the very essence of magic was the spell: "Each rite is the production of force and the conveyance of it, directly or indirectly, to a certain given object, which, as the native believes, is affected by this force" (1935, 215). Malinowski's notion of force was not of some external energy of supernatural origin; rather, it was an outgrowth of his pragmatic view of language, in which the force of an utterance stems from the reproduction of its consequences, a force that Austin (1962) calls "perlocutionary" (see Tambiah 1968, 185).

Although Malinowski's contextual ethnographic theory of the language of magic was a major contribution, Tambiah refines Malinowski's view by conjoining word and deed. He writes that language "ingeniously conjoins the expressive and metaphoric properties of language with the operational and empirical properties of technical activity. It is this which gives magical operations a 'realistic' coloring and allows them to achieve their expressiveness through verbal substitution and transfer combined with an instrumental technique that imitates practical action" (1968, 202). In essence, he attempts to explain the power of words through a description of their sociolinguistic mechanics. Such an analysis is fine, but it presents us with little more than a cursory look at the force of words.

Perhaps one reason for Tambiah's reluctance to enter the existential space of magical words is that he views magic and the word from the vantage of what Foucault (1975) calls the classical *episteme:* words are objectified, becoming neutral objects that represent things and/or functions. As a consequence, Tambiah does not take into consideration how differing modes of communication might correspond to differing interpretations of the (magical) word. Ong (1967, 113) writes:

> cultures which do not reduce words to space but know them only as aural-oral phenomena, in actuality or in the imagination, naturally regard words as more powerful than do literature cultures. Words *are* powerful. Being powered projections, spoken words themselves have an aura of power. Words in the aural-oral culture are inseparable from action for they are always sound.
>
> In aural-aural cultures it is thus eminently credible that words can be used to achieve an effect such as weapons or tools can achieve. Saying evil things of another is thought to bring him direct physical harm. This attitude toward words in more or less illiterate societies is an anthropological commonplace, but the connection of the attitude with the nature of sound and the absence of writing has not until recently begun to grow clear.

Throughout Africa, and elsewhere in the world, the sounds of words are believed to carry very special powers. The Jelgobe Fulani of Burkina Faso "do not find it necessary to imbue their words with emotion when speaking of painful things. To name pain and suffering in a neutral tone is to master them because words do not escape thoughtlessly but are spoken consciously" (Riesman 1977, 148). Indeed, the everyday speech of the Jelgobe has a power of its own. Among the Dinka it is the spoken invocation "which is said to affect and weaken its object, whether a sacrificial victim or a human enemy" (Lienhardt 1961, 236). In the Bocage of western France,

> witchcraft is spoken words but these spoken words are power, not knowledge or information.
>
> To talk in witchcraft is never to inform. Or if information is given it is so that the person who is to kill [the unwitcher] will know where to aim his blows. Informing an ethnographer, that is, someone who has no intention of using this information, is literally unthinkable. For a single word [and only a word] can tie or untie a fate, and whoever puts himself in a position to utter it is formidable.
>
> ... In short, there is no neutral position with spoken words: in witchcraft, words wage war. (Favret-Saada 1980, 9–10)

Words, then, are seen as a kind of energy by many peoples in the world, an energy that should be apprehended in and of itself rather than only as a representation of something. For the Tiv of Nigeria the sound of words combined with music—song—"is energy, a power, a life force" (Keil 1979, 257). Similarly, sound is the foundation of deep-seated Songhay cultural experience.

8. This is referenced in the myth of Faran and Zinkibaru cited in chapter 4.
9. See Irvine 1980.
10. Ibid., 6.
11. This comment by Sorko Djibo Mounmouni of Mehanna was made in May

of 1977. Sorko Djibo's comments, like those of Jeanne Favret-Saada's Bocagiens, challenge fundamental assumptions of anthropological fieldwork. How much time must one commit to learning praise-poetry? Should one become a sorko in order to learn his praise-poetry? Is it possible—or desirable?—to maintain a discrete distance from one's informants? Many of these questions are evoked in Stoller and Olkes's *In Sorcery's Shadow* (1987).

12. This version of "Tooru Ce" is from Sorko Djibo Mounmouni of Mehanna and was recorded in June of 1981. See also Stoller and Olkes 1987.

Chapter 5. Cries of the Violin, Rhythms of the Drum

1. Zuckerkandl 1958 suggests that the majesty of vision in the epistemology of Western thought stems from our traditional stress on the observation of material things within a field of vision. From Aristotle on we have been conditioned to see colored illuminated things, not colors or light. We feel hard or smooth things, not hardness or smoothness. "In seeing, touching, tasting, we reach through the sensation to an object, to a thing. Tone is the only sensation not that of a thing" (1958, 70). The gaze of Western thought has seemingly ignored the dimension of sound. For Zukerkandl, sound can be organized into melodies, rhythms, meters, and, most of all, into forces. The meaning of a sound "lies not in what it points to, but in the pointing itself" (p. 68). He considers the sounds of music as dynamic symbols: "We hear forces in them as the believer sees the divine in the [religious] symbol" (p. 69). Indeed, Zukerkandl's musical view of the universe presents for us an entry into the world of intangibles: "Because music exists, the tangible and the visible cannot be the whole of the given world, something we encounter, something to which we respond" (p. 71). With our ears finely tuned to the existential nature of sound, we can better appreciate the intangible and can cross thresholds into the deep recesses of a people's experience. Feld (1982, 3) demonstrates this very point. In his monograph on Kaluli sound as a cultural system, he shows "how an analysis of modes and codes of sound communication leads to an understanding of the ethos and quality of life in Kaluli society. By analyzing the form and performance of weeping, poetics, and song in relation to their origin myth and the bird world they metamorphize, Kaluli sound expressions are revealed as embodiments of deeply felt sentiments." For the Songhay, sound is a foundation of cultural experience.

2. See Surugue 1972, 29.

3. Adamu Jenitongo, interview in Tillaberi, December 28, 1982.

4. Ibid.

5. See Surugue 1972, 20–21.

6. The assertion that the spirits can easily kill a person who displeases them is based on my own observations as well as the commentary of Adamu Jenitongo, Djibo Mounmouni, Zakaribaba Mounmouni, and Amadu Zima. One case I observed involved a soldier who defied Dongo at a public possession ceremony. Dongo drew a line in the sand, promising death to anyone who crossed it. The soldier, a big, burly man, laughed at Dongo who was in the body of a tiny woman. "This is all play acting," he said boastfully. "I'll cross the line so everyone can see that the spirits amount to nothing at all." As soon as the soldier crossed

Dongo's "line of death," he collapsed. He was rushed to the nearest hospital where he died.

7. The information on color symbolism comes from discussions with Mounmouni Koda, Djibo Mounmouni, and Amadu Zima (Mehanna), and Amadu Jenitongo and Daouda Godji (Tillaberi).

8. Surugue 1972: 23–25.

9. Adamu Jenitongo, interview in Tillaberi, December 28, 1982. See also Stoller 1984b.

10. Adamu Jenitongo, December 28, 1982.

11. Stoller 1984b.

12. Ibid.

Chapter 6. Rain Dance

1. See Sidikou 1974.

2. Interview with Soumana Yacouba in Tillaberi, December 29, 1985.

3. Ibid.

4. Ibid.

5. Ibid.

6. See Sidikou 1974.

7. Ibid.

8. Interview with Soumana Yacouba in Tilliberi, December 29, 1985.

9. Interviews with Adamu Jenitongo in Tillaberi, July 15–17, 1984.

10. Jean Rouch, personal communication, January 16, 1987.

11. There are two special days on the possession troupe's weekly calendar: Sunday (*Alhadi*), the first day, on which many of the lesser (non-Tooru) spirits take their mediums; and Thursday (Alkamisa, the fifth day), the day of Tooru possession. Over the years I have asked Adamu Jenitongo about five-day weeks in precolonial Songhay. He has never given me a direct answer, indicating only that Thursday was *han beri*, which translates to "a big day" or "a holiday." Elsewhere in the Sahel there were five-day weeks in precolonial times, which may explain why the most sacred spirit day is a Thursday. Thursday is also the day when Adamu Jenitongo performs various sohanci sacrifices, including one to his family's altar. Like the nobles of the spirit world, sacrificial altars are called *tooru* in Songhay.

12. Rouch writes of the gesture language in *La religion et la magie songhay* (1960). There is also some explication of spirit gestures in Rouch's film, *Les maitres fous* (1958). Adamu Jenitongo and Djibo Mounmouni instructed me in spirit gesture language in 1977, 1979, and 1981.

13. I have on several occasions observed Tooru dieties furrow the earth at the onset of possession during rain dance ceremonies. My initial theory about this furrowing was that it represented a kind of sympathetic magic. If the Tooru deities furrow the earth, then the Songhay farmer's furrowing and planting will be that much more successful. The furrowing seemed to represent, in gesture, the goals of the rain ceremony: a planting season blessed with rain and a bountiful millet harvest. But this idea must remain simply a theory. None of my teachers has responded to my questions on this subject. Perhaps they do not want me

NOTES

to know more about the furrowing. Perhaps they simply consider my question irrelevant. They simply say that the Tooru like to furrow the earth.

14. Rouch (1960) writes of the ritual vase as the material representation of the world. In my observations, the ritual vase is the centerpiece of the rain dance ceremony; it is the vessel from which the Tooru take their nourishment—the community's offerings—during their visit to the social world.

15. Interviews with Adamu Jenitongo in Tillaberi, June 16, 1977, June 25, 1981, and December 28, 1982.

16. After observing Faran Baru Koda make his X mark in the sand, I asked Adamu Jenitongo about its significance. He told me that it represented the genji how. He did not explain, however, how the X corresponded symbolically to a text that "harmonizes the bush."

17. According to Adamu Jenitongo and to Amadu Zima (Mehanna), the nail offerings, part of Kurumba farming magic, can also protect millet fields. Although the Kurumba people today live in Burkina Faso, they once lived in the western regions of Niger. In Songhay, Kurumba are called Kurmey, which is also the name of the Kokoro region west of Mehanna. Elders suggest that millet harvests are always better in the Kurmey than elsewhere in Songhay country. Hama (1968) writes of so-called magic grains of millet that ensure bountiful harvests. Rouch (1960, 278) suggests that the Kurmey have always attempted to steal the millet stalk's "double." This act would enable them to control vital millet harvests. These secrets are owned by the Kurmey—descendants of the first inhabitants of the land. The center of Kurmey culture today is Aribinda in Burkina Faso. Both Adamu Jenitongo and Amadu Zima studied with Kurumba masters and brought back with them millet magic in which the nail offering is paramount. See also Olivier de Sardan 1982, 271.

18. See Rouch 1960.

Chapter 7. Horrific Comedy

1. See Olivier de Sardan 1969, 1976, 1984; Kimba 1981; Stoller 1978, 1981.
2. Crowder 1968, 74.
3. Ranger 1975, 1.
4. Roberts and Klein 1980, 393.
5. Crowder 1967, 184.
6. Mumforde and Orde-Brown 1935, 96.
7. Interview with Seybu Harouna in Mehanna, February 22, 1977.
8. Roberts 1963, 312–13.
9. See Kiev 1972 for an exposition on the psychological consequences of rapid, irrevocable change and stress. He writes that great sociocultural displacement "is experienced by the educated yet still semi-primitive marginal African, who has become a member of a partially urbanized and Westernized society. Having renounced his old culture, yet so far having failed to assimilate the new, he is particularly prone to malignant anxiety" (p. 9).
10. See Kanya-Forstner 1969; Kimba 1981.
11. Rouch 1960, 73.
12. Fugelstad 1975, 205.

13. Ibid.

14. There are numerous versions of the incident involving Major Croccichia. This version presents a reasonably accurate view of the birth of Korsasi, the wicked major.

15. Rouch 1960, 74–75.

16. See Rouch 1960; Stoller 1984a.

17. There are three kinds of Songhay insults: ritual, situational-personal, and personal-formal. In Songhay, the setting for ritual insults is always public. The participants know one another and are generally adolescents. The interactional pattern of Songhay ritual insults resembles "sounding" as it is practiced by black Americans. In Songhay, ritual insults are generally offensive statements that are not taken seriously. Although ritual insults are not injurious, situational conditions can shift, tranforming a ritual into a personal insult. By contrast, situational-personal insults are usually nonoffensive statements that, given the right conditions, become misunderstandings or personal insults. Finally, there are the rare formal-personal insults which elders use publicly to correct inappropriate behavior. See Stoller 1977.

18. See Rouch 1953, 1960; Gado 1980; Stoller 1984a.

19. Rouch 1978.

20. Ibid., 1009.

21. See Olivier de Sardan 1969, 1976, 1984; Memmi 1962. Olivier de Sardan (1984, 201) writes:

> Elles sont indéniables. De chacun on dira encore aujourd'hui "c'est un captif" ou "c'est un noble." Le mariage d'un captif avec une fille noble susciterait, y compris au sein de la bourgeoisie urbaine et occidentalisée, un grand scandale familial et social. L'interdit matrimonial joue partout. Les stéréotypes sont toujours en vigeur: les defauts de caractére de l'un seront imputés à son statut servile, les comportements positifs de l'autre à son ascendance aristocratique; par contre les faits contraires aux prejugés habituels ne seront pas relevés, ne même perçus, par la conscience collective et le sens commun. On conçoit que, dan les villages, la discrimination idéologique soit encore vivace, dans la mesure où l'ancienne aristocratie est toujours en place, intermédiare du pouvoir administratif et politique, alliée de la bourgeoisie d'état, installée en position de force dans les nouveaux rapports fonciers. Mais pourquoi en ville, où les rapports de classes, tant au niveau économique que politique, s'édifient selon d'autres critères et traversent largement les anciennes categories de maitres et de captifs, pêut-on observer de tells survivances dans les mentalités et les esprits.

22. For discussion of cultural resistance see Bastide's monumental *The African Religions of Brazil* (1978). See also Thompson 1974 (examples and analysis of British cultural resistance); July 1970, Oliver and Fage 1962, Ajaye and Crowder 1972, Shack and Skinner 1979; Demott 1982, Drewall 1974, Beier 1964, Cole 1981, and Ottenberg 1975 (examples of African resistance to African and European strangers).

NOTES

23. See Basso 1979, 3. Basso's book, *Portraits of the Whiteman: Linguistic Play and Cultural Symbols among the Western Apache,* is a sensitive exposition on the role of burlesque—caricatures of the white man—among the western Apache in the United States.

Chapter 8. Sexual Comedy

1. This ceremony occurred on June 23, 1981, in Tillaberi.

2. Interview with Adamu Jenitongo in Tillaberi, December 28, 1985.

3. Interview with Issaka Boulhassane, January 2, 1986.

4. Stoller 1978, 1980, 1981.

5. Stoller 1981, 770.

6. Ibid.

7. Stoller 1978.

8. See Stoller (in press, 15) on the contemporary problems facing the government of Niger. See also the World Bank 1981 for the statistical measures from which Stoller drew his conclusions on contemporary socioeconomic problems in Niger, and U.S. Congress, Office of Technology Assessment 1986.

9. See Sidikou 1974 for an analysis of population migration to western Niger. See Franke and Chasin 1981 for a comprehensive analysis of the Sahelian drought (1968–74). In general, Franke and Chasin focus on ecological practices as primary causes of the Sahelian famine in 1968–74. They do not rule out, however, the impact of national and international policy on the problem of famine in the Sahel. Sahelian governments reinforce a growing division between themselves, the privileged elite, and the peasants, subsistence farmers and pastoralists. The internalization of the Sahelian economy has created the context in which Sahelian governments emphasize cash cropping over the production of staple crops. (See Wallerstein 1984 for an overview of the world economy.) Unlike many writers on famine, Franke and Chasin recommend development alternatives. In place of capital-intensive large-scale development projects, they favor localized, small-scale experiments. These have worked in the past and, according to Franke and Chasin, should work in the future. "With the participation and decision-making by producers instead of elite bureaucratic domination, with local needs overruling overseas corporate or political interests, the creative powers, the knowledge, the experience, and the hard-working habits of the Sahel's farmers and herders could be integrated with advances in modern science and technology in a genuine development of the region" (Franke and Chasin 1981, 236–37).

10. Bellah 1970, 159.

11. Ibid., 160.

12. *La Voix du Sahel* 2051: 4–5. All translations from French are by the author unless otherwise noted.

13. Ibid., 2125: 2.

14. *Sahel Hebdo* 269: 8.

15. Rouch 1978, 1010.

16. Ibid.

17. Ibid.

18. Daouda Godji, interview in Tillaberi, June 21, 1981.

19. Ibid.

20. Ibid.

21. This incident occurred during a possession ceremony in Tillaberi, June 25, 1981.

22. Rouch 1978, 1010.

23. See Victor Turner (1969, vii) for an analysis of the symbolism of anti-structure. Turner's orientation stems at least indirectly from Gluckman's *Custom and Conflict in Africa*.

> The antistructural liminality provided in the cores of ritual and aesthetic forms represents the reflexivity of the social process, wherein society becomes at once subject and direct object: it represents also its subjective mood, where suppositions, desires, hypotheses, possibilities, and so forth, all become legitimate. We have been too prone to think, in static terms, that cultural superstructures are passive mirrors, mere reflections of substructural productive modes and relations or of the political processes that enforce the dominance of the productively privileged. If we were as dialectical as we claim to be, we would see that it is more a matter of existential bending back upon ourselves: the same plural subject is the active superstructure that assesses the substructural and structural modalities we *also* are. Our concreteness, our substantiality is with us in our reflexivity, even in the ludic play domain of certain of our liminal moments: play is more serious than we, the inheritors of Western Puritanism, have thought.

Chapter 9. Two Mouths, Two Hearts

1. Adamu Jenitongo, interviews in Tillaberi July 5, 1984, and December 23, 1985.

2. In the bush near Songhay villages there are various spirit altars. These are generally secret places. Despite the fact that I first lived in Tillaberi in 1970, I did not see Nya Beri's altar until the summer of 1984. Had there been no drought in 1984, I would still not know of it.

3. *Kabe beri* (*Mitragyna inermis*) and *kabu kayna* (unidentified) are considered Tooru food. *Zem turi* (lit., "the blacksmith's wood or tree," also unidentified) is also linked to the spirit world. *Yaggi* is a mixture of ginger powder and red pepper and is used as a meat spice. Generally, yaggi can be purchased in any market. A special yaggi, however, is an aphrodisiac. Men purchase special yaggi from an herbalist—usually a sorko or a sohanci. Since yaggi is quite aromatic, specialists believe that it attracts the spirits; hence it is used in some ablutions and sacrificial offerings.

4. Interview with Fatouma Seyni in Mehanna, January 3, 1986.

Epilogue

1. The theatrical premise is mentioned by Rouget 1980, Gibbal 1982, Leiris [1958], 1980, and Schaeffner 1965. Leiris and Schaeffner were members of the

famous Dakar-Djibouti (1931–33) mission organized by Marcel Griaule. In the second half of *Afrique fantome* Leiris discusses the Zar cult from, among other things, a theatrical perspective. This analysis is extended and refined in Leiris's specific work on Zar ([1958] 1980). Both Rouget and Schaeffner focus on possession as a precursor of theater in ancient Greek society. Gibbal probes some theatrical aspects of possession in contemporary Mali, focusing on the Jin Don cult of the Bambara.

2. Merleau-Ponty 1964, 159.

3. Ibid., 164.

4. Wolin 1982, 125.

5. Merleau-Ponty 1964, 165.

6. René Magritte, L'Invention Collective, 1940, cited in Schneede 1982, 131.

7. Merleau Ponty 1964, 162.

GLOSSARY

Alfatia: the Islamic prayer for protection.

Anasara: European; from the Arabic, *insara,* i.e., Christian.

Atakurma: the first people, were either small and thin or short and fat.

Baata: a sorcerer's sacrificial container.

Bakillo: a miser.

Banniya: a captive, who could be bought or sold.

Bia: the human double.

Borcin: a free man.

Bori: the Hausa spirit possession cult.

Cerkaw: a witch.

Cerkawtarey: the act of witchcraft.

Daarendi: the rite of sacrifice that occurs on the sixth day of the seven-day initiation of a spirit medium.

Desi: a catfish found in the Niger River which is also the sorko's totem. Sorkos cannot eat the desi's flesh.

Do: the original inhabitants of the Niger River valley; masters of water.

Don borey: the people of the past.

Dugu nya: an unidentified plant associated with sorkos.

Duwa: the black ink vomited by Hauka spirits. It is also used by Muslim clerics to make inscriptions for amulets.

Figiri: a curse that prevents rain from coming to a village.

Fimbi: to shake (lit.); the term also corresponds to one of three possession dance forms.

Fombo: Dongo's brother.

Fonda tilas: the necessary path (lit.); the term is used to express one's condolences at funerals.

Fulan: a cattle-herding pastoral people who are neighbors of the Songhay.

Gabibi: black skin (lit.); the term refers to the original farming populations of Songhay.

Gani: to dance (lit.); the term also corresponds to one of the three possession dance forms.

Garbey: Balinites aegytica.

Gasi: the gourd drum used for possession ceremonies.

231

Genji: the bush (lit.); the term is also used to denote the spirits.

Genji Bi Hori: a ceremony held to protect Songhay fields from pestilence.

Genji how: to attach or tie up the bush (lit.); this is the most important incantation in a sorcerer's repertoire—its aim is to harmonize the forces of the bush.

Gind'ize gina: the first incantation (lit.); this text was known only to Songhay kings, who revealed it to their successors just before their deaths.

Godji: the monochord violin.

Gosi: female initiation; the ceremony is no longer practiced in Songhay.

Gow: hunters.

Gunda Beri; big belly (lit.), as well as the name for the great Sahelian famine of 1911–14.

Gunda Ce: a riverfront neighborhood in Tillaberi.

Gurmantche: an agricultural people who are neighbors of the Songhay.

Guunu: the name of special sohancis who perform circumcisions. It is said that the guunu's fathers are descendants of Sonni Ali Ber and that their mothers are witches. This geneaology makes them alone powerful enough to perform rites of manhood.

Hampi: a ritual vase used during possession ceremonies.

Hannandi: a rite of purification performed during the third day of the seven-day initiation of spirit mediums.

Holle: crazy (lit.), as well as a general term for spirits.

Holle hori: possession ceremony.

Horso: the offspring of captives, who cannot be bought or sold.

Kabu beri: a plant used in possession ceremonies.

Kabu kayna: an unidentified plant used in possession ceremonies.

Kadi: an Islamic judge.

Kurmey: a fertile region west of the Niger River famous for its copious millet harvests; also the Songhay term for the Kurumba.

Kurumba: an agricultural people who once inhabited Songhay.

Laabu koy: masters of the earth.

Lolo: an iron staff which is held by the oldest member of sohanci families.

Lombo Kumbenya: Dongo's brother.

Maiga; maigey (pl.): nobles who are descendants of Askia Mohammed Touré, king of the Songhay (1493–1528).

Moose: an agricultural people who once lived in Songhay; today they are the most populous ethnic group in Burkina Faso.

Munakufa: the devil of dischord.

N'Debbi: the intermediary with the High God. Incantations are recited to N'debbi who relays the message to the High God.

Nyaize: maternal consanguineal kin.

Sah nya: an unidentified plant associated with sorkos.

Sambeli: to shoot the magic arrow; this technique is used by Songhay sorcerers to maim or kill their victims.

Sherif: from the Arabic, a direct descendant of the Prophet Mohammed.

Si: the title taken by the descendants of Ali Kolon, a Songhay king who reigned in the twelfth century.

Si Hamey: descendants of Sonni Ali Ber, king of the Songhay in 1463–91.

Sodje: soldier.

Sohanci: a clan of sorcerers who are patrilineal descendants of Sonni Ali Ber, king of the Songhay in 1463–91.

Sorko: descendants of Faran Maka Bote, they are praise-singers to the Songhay spirits.

Sorko benya: the sorko's slave; a non-sorko who is "pointed out" as having the capacities to learn the knowledge of the sorko.

Tooru: a sacrificial altar; also the spirits that control the natural forces of the universe: water, clouds, lightning, and thunder.

Tooru Ce: the principal praise-poem in a sorko's repertoire.

Tuareg: desert nomads who are neighbors of the Songhay.

Tumbalaagi: baggy draw-string trousers.

Tunaandi: the act of lifting up (lit.); the term refers to the moment when a spirit invades the body of its medium.

Windi: a family compound; it also refers to one of the three possession dance forms.

Yaggi: a condiment used during some possession rites.

Yenaandi: the rain ceremony.

Yene: cool (lit.); this term also refers to the first possession ceremony.

Za: the title of the kings of the first Songhay dynasty.

Zima: the priest or priestess of the Songhay possession troup.

Zoa: the founder of the town, Sangara; a great hunter and sorcerer.

Zongo: the section of a village or town set off for recently arrived foreigners.

REFERENCES

Ackerman, S. E., and Raymond L. Lee. 1981. Communication and cognitive pluralism in a spirit possession event in Malaysia. *American Ethnologist* 8(4): 787–800.

Ajaye, J. F., and M. Crowder. 1972. *History of West Africa.* Vol. 1. New York: Columbia University Press.

Aristotle. 1970. *La politique.* Paris: Vrin.

Austin, J. L. 1962. *How to do things with words.* London: Oxford University Press.

Balandier, Georges. 1966. *Ambiguous Africa.* London: Chatto and Windus.

Basso, Keith. 1979. *Portraits of the whiteman: Linguistic play and cultural symbols among the western Apache.* New York: Cambridge University Press.

Bastide, Roger. 1978. *The African religions of Brazil.* Baltimore: Johns Hopkins University Press.

Beier, Ulli. 1964. The Agbigido masquerades. *Nigeria Magazine* 82: 188–200.

Bellah, Robert. 1970. *Beyond belief: Essays on religion in a post-traditonal world.* New York: Harper and Row.

Boulnois, J., and B. Hama. 1953. *L'empire de Gao: Histoire, coutumes, et magie des songhai.* Paris: Maisonneuve.

Bourguignon, Erica. 1976. *Possession.* San Francisco: Chandler and Sharp.

Cole, Herbert. 1981. *Mbari: Art and life among the Owerri Igbo.* Bloomington: Indiana University Press.

Crowder, Michael. 1967. *Senegal: A study of French assimilationist policy.* London: Cambridge University Press.

———. 1968. *West Africa under colonial rule.* Evanston, Ill.: Northwestern University Press.

Demott, Barbara. 1982. *Dogon masks: A structural study of form and meaning.* Ann Arbor: University of Michigan Press.

Drewal, H. 1974. Gelede masquerades: Imagery and motif. *African Arts* 7: 8–20.

es-Saadi, Mohammed. 1900. *Tarikh es-Soudan.* Trans. O. Houdas. Paris: Leroux.

Favret-Saada, Jeanne. 1980. *Deadly words: Witchcraft in the Bocage.* London: Cambridge University Press.

Feld, Steven. 1982. *Sound and sentiment: Birds, weeping, poetics, and song in Kaluli expression.* Philadelphia: University of Pennsylvania Press.

Foucault, Michel. 1975. *The birth of the clinic.* New York: Random House.

———. 1980. *The order of things.* New York: Random House.

Franke, Richard, and Barbara Chasin. 1981. *Seeds of famine.* Totowa, N.J.: Rowman and Allanheld.

Freed, Stanley, and Ruth Freed. 1964. Possession dance as illness in a north Indian village. *Ethnology* 3: 152–171.

REFERENCES

Freud, Sigmund. 1913. *Totem and taboo.* London: Hogarth Press.

Fugelstad, Finn. 1975. Les Hauka: Une interpretation historique. *Cahiers d'Etudes Africaines* 58: 203–16.

Gado, Boube. 1980. *Le Zermatarey: Contribution à l'histoire des populations d'entre Niger et Dollo Mawri.* Etudes Nigeriennes No. 45. Niamey: Université de Niamey.

Gell, Alfred. 1980. The gods at play: Vertigo and possession in Muria religion. *Man,* n.s., 15: 219–49.

Gibbal, Jean-Marie. 1982. *Tambours d'eau.* Paris: Le Sycamore.

Gleason, Judith. 1982. Out of water, onto the ground and into the cosmos: An analysis of the three phases of sacred initiatory dance among the Zarma (Songhay) of Niger. In *Spring: An annual of archetypal psychology and Jungian thought,* 3–12. Dallas, Tex.: Spring Publications.

Gluckman, Max. 1955. *Custom and conflict in Africa.* London: Oxford University Press.

Hama, Boubou. 1968. *Histoire des songhay.* Paris: Présence Africaine.

———. 1973. *Kotia.* Paris: Présence Africaine.

Hanna, Judith. 1979. *To dance is human.* Austin: University of Texas Press.

Harris, Grace. 1957. Possession "hysteria" in a Kenyan tribe. *American Anthropologist* 59: 1046–66.

Irvine, Judith. 1980. Address as magic and rhetoric: Praise-naming in West Africa. Paper presented at the seventy-ninth Annual Meeting of the American Anthropological Association, Washington, D.C.

July, Robert. 1970. *A history of the African people.* New York: Scribners.

Kaba, Lansiné. 1984. The pen, the sword, and the crown: Islam and revolution in Songhay reconsidered, 1464–1493. *Journal of African History* 25: 241–56.

Kanya-Forstner, A. N. 1969. *The conquest of the western Soudan.* London: Cambridge University Press.

Kati Mahmoud. 1913. *Tarikh al-Fattach.* Trans. M. Delafosse. Paris: Maisonneuve.

Kehoe, Alice B., and Dody H. Giletti. 1981. Women's preponderance in possession cults: The calcium-deficiency hypothesis extended. *American Anthropologist* 83(3): 549–62.

Keil, Charles. 1979. *Tiv song.* Chicago: University of Chicago Press.

Kiev, Ari. 1972. *Transcultural psychiatry.* New York: Free Press.

Kimba, Idrissa. 1981. *Guerres et sociétés.* Études Nigeriennes No. 46. Niamey: Université de Niamey.

Konaré Ba, Adam. 1977. *Sonni Ali Ber.* Études Nigeriennes No. 40. Niamey: Université de Niamey.

Lambek, Michael. 1980. Possession as a system of communication among the Malagasy speakers of Mayotte. *American Ethnologist* 7(2): 318–32.

———. 1981. *Human spirits: A cultural account of trance in Mayotte.* New York: Cambridge University Press.

Leiris, Michel. [1958] 1980. *La possession et ses aspects theatraux chez les ethiopiens de Gondar.* Reprint. Paris: Le Sycamore.

————. 1984. *Afrique fantôme*. Paris: Gallimard.

Lewis, I. M. 1971. *Ecstatic religion: An anthropological study of spirit possession and shamanism*. Harmonsworth, England: Penguin Books.

Lienhart, Godfrey. 1961. *Divinity and experience*. Oxford: Oxford University Press.

Malinowski, Bronislaw. 1935. *The coral gardens and their magic*. Vol 2. London: Allen and Unwin.

Memmi, Albert. 1962. *The colonizer and the colonized*. Boston: Beacon Press.

Merleau-Ponty, Maurice. 1964. *Eye and mind*. In *The primacy of perception*. Trans. C. Dallery. Evanston, Ill: Northwestern University Press.

Mischel, Walter, and Frances Mischel. 1958. Psychological aspects of spirit possession. *American Anthropologist* 60: 249–60.

Monfouga-Nicholas, Jacqueline. 1972. *Ambivalence et culte de possession*. Paris: Éditions Anthropos.

Mumforde, W., and G. St. John Orde-Brown. 1935. *Africans learn to be French*. London: Evans Brothers.

Oliver, R., and F. Fage. 1962. *A short history of West Africa*. London: Oxford University Press.

Olivier de Sardan, Jean-Pierre. 1969. *Les voleurs d'hommes*. Études Nigeriennes No. 25. Niamey: Université de Niamey.

————. 1975. Captifs ruraux et esclaves imperiaux du Songhai. In C. Meillassoux, ed., *Esclavage en Afrique précoloniale*, 99–135. Paris: Maspero.

————. 1976. *Quand nos Pères étaient captifs*. Paris: Nubia.

————. 1982. *Concepts et conceptions Songhay-Zarma*. Paris: Nubia.

————. 1984. *Sociétés Songay-Zarma*. Paris: Karthala.

Ong, Walter. 1967. *The presence of the word*. New Haven: Yale University Press.

Ottenberg, Simon. 1975. *The masked rituals of Afikpo Igbo*. Seattle: University of Washington Press.

Pidoux, Ch. 1955. Les états de possession rituelle chez les melano-africains. *Evolution Psychiatrique*, Fasc. II.

Ranger, T. O. 1975. *Dance and society in East Africa: The Beni Ngoma*. Berkeley: University of California Press.

Riesman, Paul. 1977. *Freedom in Fulani social life*. Chicago: University of Chicago Press.

Roberts, Richard, and Martin Klein. 1980. The Bamana slave exodus in 1905 and the decline of slavery in the western Soudan. *Journal of African History* 21(3): 375–95.

Roberts, Steven. 1963. *The history of French colonial policy, 1870–1925*. London: Archon Books.

Roheim, Geza. 1967. *Psychanalyse et anthropologie*. Paris: Gallimard.

Rouch, Jean. 1953. *Contribution à l'histoire des Songhay*. Memoires No. 29. Dakar: Institut Français d'Afrique Noire.

————. 1960. *La religion et la magie Songhay*. Paris: P.U.F.

————. 1978. Jean Rouch talks about his films to John Marshall and Jown W. Adams. *American Anthropologist* 80: 1005–22.

Rouget, Gilbert. 1980. *La musique et la trance*. Paris: Gallimard.

REFERENCES

Schaeffner, André. 1965. Rituel et pré-theatre. In *Histoire des spectacles,* 21–54. Paris: Gallimard.

Schneede, Uwe. 1982. *René Magritte: Life and work.* New York: Barrons.

Searle, John. 1968. *Speech acts.* London: Cambridge University Press.

Shack, William, and Elliot P. Skinner, eds. 1979. *Strangers in African societies.* Berkeley: University of California Press.

Sidikou, Arouna Hamidou. 1974. *Sedentarité et mobilité entre Niger et Zagret.* Etudes Nigeriennes No. 34. Niamey: Université de Niamey.

Stoller, Paul A. 1977. Ritual and personal insults in Songrai Sonni. *Anthropology* 2(1): 33–38.

———. 1978. The dynamics of Bankwano: Communication and political legitimacy among the Songhay (Republic of Niger). Ph.D. dissertation, Department of Anthropology, University of Texas at Austin.

———. 1980. The negotiation of Songhay space: Phenomenology in the heart of darkness. *American Ethnologist* 7: 419–31.

———. 1981. Social interaction and the management of Songhay sociopolitical change. *Africa* 51(3): 419–31.

———. 1984a. Horrific comedy: Cultural resistance and Songhay possession dance. *Ethos* 11: 165–87.

———. 1984b. Sound in Songhay cultural experience. *American Ethnologist* 11(3): 559–70.

———. In press. Stressing social change and Songhay possession. In C. Ward., ed., *Altered states of consciousness and mental health: A cross-cultural perspective.* Newbury Park, Calif.: Sage.

Stoller, Paul A., and Cheryl Olkes. 1987. *In sorcery's shadow: A memoir of apprenticeship among the Songhay of Niger.* Chicago: University of Chicago Press.

Surugue. Bernard. 1972. *Contribution à l'étude de la musique sacrée Zarma-Songhay.* Etudes Nigeriennes No. 30. Niamey: Université de Niamey.

Tambiah, Stanley J. 1968. The magical power of words. *Man,* n.s., 3: 175–203.

Thompson, E. P. 1974. Patrician society, pleb culture. *Journal of Social History* 7(4): 582–604.

Turner, Victor. 1969. *The ritual process.* Ithaca, N.Y.: Cornell University Press.

U.S. Congress, Office of Technology Assessment. 1986. *Continuing the commitment: Agricultural development in the Sahel.* Washington D.C.: U.S. Government Printing Office.

Wallerstein, Emanuel. 1984. *The politics of the world economy.* New York: Cambridge University Press.

Wolin, Richard. 1982. *Walter Benjamin: An aesthetic of redemption.* New York: Columbia University Press.

World Bank. 1981. *Accelerated development in sub-Saharan Africa.* Washington, D.C.: International Bank for Reconstruction and Development.

Zempleni, Andras. 1966. La dimension thérapeutique du culte des Rab Ndop, Tuuru et Samp: Rites de possession chez les Lebou et les Wolof. *Psychopathologie Africaine* 2(3): 1–144.

———. 1968. *L'interprétation et la therápie: Traditionelle du désordre mental chez les Wolof et les Lebou (Senegal)*. Paris: Institut d'Ethnologie.

Zukerkandl, Victor. 1958. *Sound and symbol: Music and the external world.* Trans. Willard R. Trask. Princeton: Princeton University Press.

INDEX